MARCO POLO

VENICE

www.marco-polo.com

Do You Feel Like . . .

... crafts, culinary specialties, exploring the sights on the water, no matter if in the Centro Storico or in the lagoon, gardens or unusual textiles? Discover Venice just the way you like.

SPRIZZ & SHADE
- **Fashionable drink**
  Venice is the home of the fashionable drink made with Aperol/Campari with white wine or prosecco and an Austrian spray of soda water, e.g. in the Bar all'Angolo, San Marco 3464, Campo Santo Stefano, tel. 04 15 22 07 10.
- ◄ **A glass of wine**
  Wine comes »in the shade«, a 100-ml glass called an »ombra«, and is served with cicheti, small snacks.
  page 116

HANDICRAFT
- **Masks** ►
  Pantalone, Columbina, Arlecchino – since the Venetians revived the carnival in 1979 this traditional craft is flourishing again. Hands off the cheap fakes!
  page 129
- **Glassmaking & lace**
  In the lagoon each one of the 118 islands has its purpose. Murano is famous for its glass work, Burano for its lace work. Here true as well: quality has its price – hands off the cheap fakes!
  page 127, 128

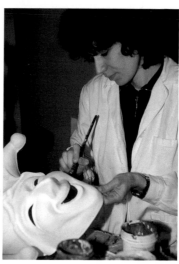

BOAT RIDES

- **Pure romance**
  Gondolas don't cost any more
  than taxis, but are more romantic.
- **By water bus**
  A city tour on a water bus is part
  of every visit to Venice. The trip
  leaves enough time to admire the
  palaces and churches.
- **Excursion into the lagoon**
  An excursion into the lagoon, a
  labyrinth between sea and land.
- **Rowing**
  How about a course in rowing or
  in Venetian rowing, »Voga alla
  veneta«?

GARDENS

- **Green is rare ..**
  ... in Venice. Here are some tips for
  secret gardens and places to stroll.

FABRICS

- ◄ **Fortuny & Co**
  Titian and Veronese dressed their
  ladies in precious silk brocade.
  Luxurious fabrics are still woven in
  and around Venice – for fashion,
  wall covering and furniture.

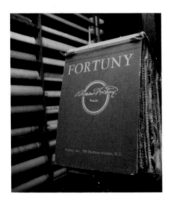

FISH FROM THE LAGOON

- **Cucina di pesce** ►
  Sarde in soar, bigoli pasta with
  sardine paste followed by moleche
  or San Pietro (shrimp or John
  Dory). For cucina de pesce
  Venetian style it is best to get ideas
  in the Pescheria, the Rialto fish
  market.

BACKGROUND

ENJOY VENICE

TOURS

Café Florian on St Mark's Square

Bird's eye view of Venice

SIGHTS FROM A TO Z

PRICE CATEGORIES
Restaurants
(a menu as Primo and Secondo
without a drink)
€€€€ = over €50
€€€ = €40 – €50
€€ = €25 – €40
€ = up to e25
Hotels (double room)
€€€€ = over €170€
€€€ = €140 – €170
€€ = €100 – €140
€ = up to €100

Note
Billable service telephone
numbers are marked with an
asterisk: *0180....

PRACTICAL INFORMATION

»Main road«
Canal Grande

BACKGROUND

The enchanting city in the water relates a history of more than 1500 years: from its foundation to its rise to be queen of the seas, from its fall to the present – one of the most beautiful cities in the world.

Facts

Population · Politics · Economy

From the air Venice looks like a fish, and the Ponte della Libertà, the liberty bridge, which was built in 1846, is like the fishing line. In fact, Venice »swims« at the northern end of the Adriatic Sea, just 4km/2.5mi from the mainland and 2km/1.2mi from the open sea in the Lagoon of Venice.

POPULATION AND CITY DISTRICTS

The city of Venice has around 271,000 residents. Of these about 59,300 (1951 it was still 174,800) live in the Centro Storico, 29,800 on the islands and 181,700 on the mainland.

The Centro Storico, the old city, has been divided into »city sixths«, Venetian **Sestieri**, since the 12th century. Their names are San Marco, Castello, Cannaregio, Santa Croce, San Polo and Dorsoduro; the latter includes the islands Giudecca and San Giorgio.

Six (plus one) sestieri

There are supposed to be Venetians who have never seen St Mark's Square. The Venetians' true point of reference is their Sestiere. Only a few generations ago, after all, the individual Sestieri still engaged in skirmishes on the bridges. Until today the Sestieri are more than just administrative units; each has its own flair and keeps its own identity. Moreover they are indispensable for getting around Venice. Some street names occur six times in Venice, once in each Sestiere.

San Marco, the heart of the city, is the most fashionable Sestiere but also the most visited by tourists. Along with the cathedral of St Mark and the Doge's Palace Venetian nobility had their apartments here, which were called casinos, where they kept their wealth and held gambling parties. The expensive cafés around St Mark's Square, luxury hotels, posh boutiques, art galleries and museums characterize this quarter of the city.

Dorsoduro is no less noble, but quieter; the quarter where the Accademia, the Guggenheim Museum and the Dogana da Mar are located The quiet, narrow streets along canals are popular among wealthy foreigners. Galleries, artists' studios and a few more up-scale ristoranti make up the picture. The university towards the west make for a younger clientele; in summer nights students like to meet on the Campo S. Margherita with its pizzerias and on Zattere with its ice cream shops.

Venice has more than 400 bridges. One of the best known ones is the Bridge of Sighs (Ponte dei Sospiri, top of the picture).

Lively, labyrinthine, full of small shops, boutiques, enotecas, that's **S. Polo**. From the Rialto market one of the chronically clogged »pedestrian highways« runs towards the Frari church through the charming and smallest Sestiere. The Sestiere **S. Croce** near the railway station is quieter. Here there are many art historical discoveries to be made and secluded campi (squares) to be explored.

The Sestiere **Cannaregio** in the north with the ghetto and the low houses along straight, long canals is the most traditional part of Venice. In the evenings fishermen, tradesmen, stonemasons and grave diggers still meet here in out of the way osterias; the poverty of the once metropolitan Venice is still noticeable here. The student night life has been concentrated here recently.

Castello with the arsenal, the biennale gardens and the broad shopping street Via Garibaldi is almost a city of its own. It was once the quarter of the shipyard workers (arsenalotti) and is still caharacterized by social housing. There are even a few streets here where bicycles can be ridden!

The »seventh Sestiere« is the elongated **island Giudecca**, which was once famous for its gardens and which belongs to the Sestiere Dorsoduro. Today a mixture of industrial buildings, post-war apartments, harbour bars and luxury spots like the Hilton Hotel in the Molino Stucky make up the quarter.

POLITICS AND ADMINISTRATION

Venice was the first republic of the Middle Ages, a great constitutional achievement of the 11th and 12th centuries. It existed until its conquest by Napoleon in 1797. Today, Venice is the capital of the

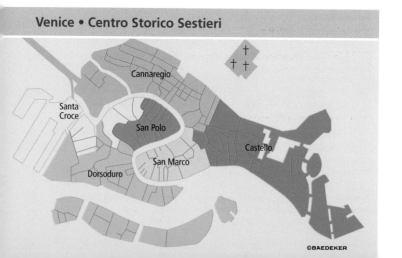

Venice • Centro Storico Sestieri

Cannaregio

Santa Croce

San Polo

Castello

San Marco

Dorsoduro

©BAEDEKER

province by the same name which includes a total of 43 communal districts, as well as being the capital of the northern Italian region of Veneto. Like all major Italian cities, it is administered by a mayor (sindaco) and a magistracy (giunta municipale) who are newly elected every five years. The seat of local government is the Ca' Farsetti near the Rialto bridge.

ECONOMY

The main source of employment in the island city is **tourism**. After Rome, Venice is the most visited city in Italy: every year, approximately 7 million overnight guests and more than 8 million day visitors come here. Most businesses in the inner city live from tourism. This also explains the high density of craft workshops and souvenir stores by comparison to the population, producing glass art, lace, textiles, handmade paper and especially masks. Many Venetians also work in the **public sector**. Furthermore, Venice is Italy's third largest **port** (after Genoa and Trieste). The port is on the mainland in Marghera, the location of a huge petrochemical conglomerate, Italy's **chemical centre** with 45,000 workers. Aside from the giant chemical plants, the largest **heating power plant** in Italy and the largest **crude oil depots** on the Mediterranean are here and in Fusina. Every day, about 25,000 residents of the insular part of Venice travel to the mainland to work, while 20,000 commuters, 5,000 of them from the surrounding islands, come to the historic centre to work or study. The university Ca' Foscari and the architectural college (IUAV) have 26,000 registered students.

> **MARCO ⊕ POLO INSIGHT**
>
> **?** *Did you know?*
>
> More than 22 million people visit Venice every year. More than 80% of them spend less than eight hours and under €15 in the city. 90% of them, mainly cruise ship passengers, visit only the Piazza San Marco and the cathedral. So it is not surprising that the authorities would like to limit the number of day trippers.

TRANSPORT

Venice's international airport Marco Polo lies on the mainland, at the north edge of the lagoon at Tessera. The large cruise ships and the car ferries – from here, there are connections to many Adriatic ports and to Greece – leave from the Stazione Marittima (Tronchetto); Zattere and Riva degli Schiavoni are popular ports for cruise ships. Since 1846, the island has been connected to the mainland by a railroad

Facts and Figures

Location
Venice is located in a lagoon on the northern end of the Adriatic Sea, 4km/2.4mi from the mainland and 2km/1.2mi from the open sea

Area:
415 sq km/160 sq mi

Population:
Comune di Venezia: 271,000
Centro Storico: **59,300**,
remaining islands **29,800**,
mainland **191,700**

Population density:
653 per sq km/980 per sq mi

12° 02'
east longitude

Munich

307km/
191mi

Venice

41° 2
north latitud

651km/404mi

245mi

394km/
245mi

Rome

Sardinia

▶ **Foundation**

In the 5th century mainland Venetians fled to the inaccessible lagoon for protection against invading Germanic peoples. In the 9th cent. The islands around the Rialto became the core of the new Venice

▶ **Coat of arms**

▶ **Seat of the administration**

Ca' Farsetti on the Canal Grande, near Rialto Bridge

▶ **Economy**

Tourism is the most important employer: The Comune di Venezia hosts 7 mil. guests every year, who stay and average of 2.15 days. It has about 400 hotels with about 25,000 beds as well as about 12,000 beds in private homes. Add to that an additional 8 million day guests. Other important employers are administration, industry and port.

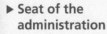

The Centro Storico, the old city, is divided into sixths (sestieri).

A: San Polo D: Castello
B: Dorsoduro E: Cannaregio
C: San Marco F: Santa Croce

Climate

Venice enjoys a moderate Mediterranean climate. The winters are cool, sometimes cold and foggy; the summers are sunny and hot, but without the typical Mediterranean dry time.

Population growth

1600	**160,000**
1900	**189,000**
1950	**317,000**
2000	**271,000**
2010	**271,000**

Average temperatures

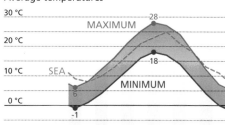

30 °C
MAXIMUM
28
20 °C
18
10 °C SEA
MINIMUM
0 °C
-1

J F M A M J J A S O N D

Precipitation

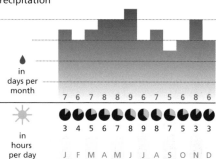

in days per month

| 7 | 6 | 7 | 8 | 8 | 9 | 6 | 7 | 5 | 6 | 8 | 6 |

in hours per day

| 3 | 4 | 5 | 6 | 7 | 8 | 9 | 8 | 7 | 5 | 3 | 3 |

J F M A M J J A S O N D

Flooding/Acqua Alta

The water rises above the critical mark of 110cm (44in) more and more often.

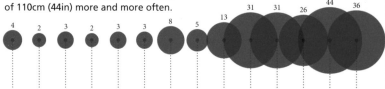

| 4 | 2 | 3 | 2 | 3 | 3 | 8 | 5 | 13 | 31 | 31 | 26 | 44 | 36 |

1870-79 1880-89 1890-99 1900-09 1910-19 1920-29 1930-39 1940-49 1950-59 1960-69 1970-79 1980-89 1990-99 2000-09

The phases of a flood
in cm above normal level

140
130 — Emergency, 90% of the city is affected
120 — 50 % of the city is affected
110 — 14 % of the city is affected
100 — 5 % of the Centro Storico
90   is affected
80 — until 80cm normal high tide: no flooding

Why is Venice sinking?
Sea level is rising

Sandy Underground

The city sank a total of 23cm (9in) in the past 100 years.

Welcome to Every Day Life!

Statistically every resident of Venice is »visited« by 366 tourists every year. This can upset daily life. So Venetians tend to withdraw. Social contact thus is not possible without an effort and compassion for the concerns and mentality of the residents of the laguna.

FACTORY TOUR
FONDERIA VALESE

The Valese Foundry was established in 1913 and it supplies hotels, antique restorers and museums. It shows the traditional methods of making bronze its workshop upon appointment. A fascinating look at Venetian tradecraft.

Cannaregio, Madonna dell'Orto
3535, tel. 0 41 72 02 34

ANGLICAN
SERVICES

On Sundays and Festivals, at 10.30 am, Anglican Services are held in St George's Anglican Church. The church is in the former warehouse of the Venezia-Murano Glass and Mosaic Company and was dedicated in 1892. Of course baptised Christians of all denomination are welcome.

Campo San Vio, Dorsoduro
Vaporetto 1 or 2 to Accademia
www.stgeorgesvenice.com
tel. 0 41 09 90 019

COOKING COURSE

Shopping in the Rialto market, followed by Cucina veneziana in the family palazzo – with wines from the Veneto. Courses with Enrica Rocca, who also teaches in London and Tokyo, start at €180. Courses are in Italian or English.
www.enricarocca.com

VENICE OF THE VENETIANS

The tour guides recommended on page 132 offer a variety of walks on special themes, including tours on the subject of everyday life in the city on the laguna both past and present, in the »giardini segreti«, »hidden« gardens, as well as culinary tours. Other topics:
www.veneziasi.it

FISHING IN THE LAGOON

Guided tours with fishermen through the lagoon and its pools for raising oysters and shrimps are organised by Hotel Rigel on the Lido.
www.hotelrigel.it

bridge. In 1933, the »freedom bridge« (Ponte della Libertà), was opened for motor traffic. Of course, cars have to be parked no further than at the Tronchetto parking site or in the parking garages at Piazzale Roma at the end of the road bridge. From here, progress is only possible on foot or by boat.

Water travel in Venice The 118 islands (the number varies according to the sources) which form Venice are very close together and built up to their very outer edges, but the waterways between the islands were kept clear. This resulted in a network of more than 170 canals. Boats are therefore the most important mode of transport. In addition to the canals, Venice has about 3,000 »streets«. There is only one so-called **strada**, Strada Nova, which was built through the labyrinth of Cannaregio at the end of the 19th century, and two known as **vie**, Via 22 Marzo in the Sestiere of San Marco and Via Garibaldi in Castello. All others are called either **calle** (plural calli; from Latin callis for path, narrow alley) – the second name of many calli is a reminder of the guilds which once resided here, such as the Calle dei Lavadori (washers), dei Saoneri (soap makers), dei Spezieri (spice dealers) or dei Boteri (barrel makers) – or **ramo** (branch), **ruga** (groove), **salizzada** (from selciato meaning paved, the name for the first paved streets in the city), **rio terrà** (filled-in canal), **fondamenta** or **riva** (shore road); **sottoportego** is a narrow passage which even leads under houses in some cases. There is also only one **piazza**, namely that of San Marco. The adjacent smaller squares are called Piazzetta (in front of the Doge's Palace) and Piazzetta dei Leoncini (next to St Mark's Basilica). All other squares in the city are called **campo** (meaning field, plural campi) or, if they are very small, campiello. Corte (plural corti) is a term for a closed inner courtyard. 400 bridges (**ponte**, plural ponti) hold the city together and lead the twisted alleys and streets over the canals, three of them across the Grand Canal: the wooden Ponte del'Accademia, the famous Rialto bridge and the Ponte dei Scalzi at the railway station. In 2008 the Ponte della Costituzione, which was built by the Spanish architect Santiago Calatrava between the railway station and Piazzale Roma, was opened after endless quarrels about the technical difficulties, because it is useless and because the building costs rose from €3.5 mil. to 14 mil. The bridge is optically very attractive but also very slippery, which has earned it the nickname Ponte dei Caduti (bridge of the fallen). The first structural damage is

? MARCO POLO INSIGHT

Did you know?

The houses within a sestiere are continuously numbered (only the island of Giudecca has its own numbering). For instance, Castello ends with the record number 6828, while Cannaregio ends at 6426 – a system which goes back to Napoleon and is practically incomprehensible to non-Venetians.

also visible. It was made accessible to the handicapped in 2011 after strong public protests.

THE LAGOON OF VENICE

Flat land and water as far as the eye can see, many islands and islets of which twelve are inhabited today, innumerable small banks of sand or slick (barene) some of which are only visible at ebb (velme): this is the Laguna Veneta, **Italy's second-largest wet biotope** after the Po delta, in which Venice lies like a pearl. This landlocked lake in the shape of a half-moon is about 40km/25mi long and no more than 15km/9mi

? *Did you know?*

MARCO POLO INSIGHT

Almost 20,000 of Venice's buildings, including churches and bridgeheads, »swim« on a sunken forest that is standing on its head, so to speak. Whole forests in the Carnic Alps were cut down for Venice.

wide. The laguna viva, the »living« lagoon, reaches as far as salt water at high tide. Salt water rarely penetrates the laguna morta, which accounts for nearly half of the lagoon. The water in the canals near the port has a depth of 15–20m/50–65ft, but otherwise only 50cm/20in on average, and is more or less brackish, depending on the tides. The lagoon, in which fresh water and sea water mix, provides excellent living conditions for plants, water birds and fish. The south is occupied particularly by valli da pesca (fish ponds) where fish, mussels (cozze) and hard-shell clams (vongole) are farmed (recognizable by the nets and ropes stretched between poles). By contrast the north has remained an almost unspoiled world of islands and is a protected nature reserve.

This unique landscape was created in prehistoric times when the rivers that flow into the Mediterranean here – particularly the Brenta, Sile and Piave – deposited the masses of sand and stone which they had carried down from the Alps. The changing watercourses, ebb and flow of the tide, storms and the constant sea surf formed this material into sand banks (litorali or barre) and coastal strips (lidi) about 20km/12mi in front of the actual coastline. The lagoons disappeared where humans did not intervene (e.g. at Ravenna). Since increasing silting damaged the shipping, commerce and also the defence of Venice, the lagoon residents began to redirect the large rivers as early as the 14th century. Today, the lagoon has only three large through-flows (bocche): the 900m/2950ft-wide Bocca di Lido, the 470m/ 1540ft-wide Bocca di Malamocco and the nearly 500m/1640ft-wide Bocca di Chioggia.

Origin

Is Venice Sinking?

From an urban perspective, the ancient queen of the seas, now over a thousand years old, is up to her neck in water. More and more residents are turning their backs on their city, for it is sinking into the lagoon while sea levels rise.

Venice was created in the early Middle Ages and has remained almost unchanged. However, there have been dramatic changes in the **population**. In 1951, approximately 174,000 people lived in the lagoon city. Today, there are only just 60,000. Of these, more than 33% are over the age of 65. And the exodus continues.

Population Decline

Every year, about 2,000 Venetians leave the city centre. Most remain within the Comune di Venezia, but move to the mainland, to Mestre (in 1926, Venice and Mestre merged), Marghera or another area of the city. Young people, in particular, move away. There are numerous reasons, among others the **high rents** in apartments that are often uncomfortable, lacking heating and bathrooms, and the **high investments** needed to maintain apartments or houses. In 2011 the tradtional old bookseller Fantoni closed because the rent was tripled. **Mass tourism** with more than 22 million visitors annually has enormous effects on the city infrastructure. Grocery stores, kindergartens and schools are displaced by souvenir stores, restaurants, hotels or recently bed & breakfasts. Prices in cafes, bars and restaurants are much higher than normal. The city also offers little to young people in general – there is limited **nightlife**, and trips to the mainland require a car, which costs a lot in parking fees. Venice is also inconvenient. All goods must be brought from the mainland, loaded onto boats and transported on foot and by hand cart. Due to the many bridges, shoppers and mothers pushing their children need to be fit. In the inner city, **employment opportunities are very limited**, and the exodus has caused the loss of many jobs. Today, about 25,000 commuters go to work in Mestre or the surrounding area.

The City Sinks

Venice's buildings stand on larch piles. Every year, these piles sink a little deeper under this weight **into the muddy lagoon bed**. This also happened in past centuries. Venetians reacted by building one floor on top of another, up to six layers. However, the situation worsened dramatically when, after 1930, ground water was taken in greater quantities, particularly for the emerging industry on the mainland in Mestre and Marghera, and the three entrances into the lagoon were enlarged to a depth of 12m/40ft so that the oil tankers could reach the refineries. In consequence the ground sank even more rapidly. Since 1908, it has dropped by 12cm/5in (more than in

the two preceding centuries). Ground water removal was finally stopped at the end of the 1970s, and the situation became a little less critical.

Floods

In the same time period, sea levels rose by 12cm/5in. Acqua alta, flooding, is the name of the danger, which is mainly concentrated in the period between September and March. Conditions become critical at a level of 80cm/32in above normal sea level, when visitors to the atrium of St Mark's Basilica (63cm/25in above sea level) and on St Mark's Square get wet feet. Between 1923 and 1932, flood waters higher than 110cm/44in occurred only every few years. From 1943 to 1952, flooding occurred once annually, and from 1993 to 2002, five times annually. Since the flood catastrophe of 1966, with levels of 194cm/6ft 4in, the acqua alta has exceeded the one-metre mark (3ft 4in) more than 220 times. If the forecast global warming and the associated rise in sea levels occurs, this would mean acqua alta on one day in three within 50 years! But extremely low tides are also damaging. Too little fresh sea water in the lagoon means **insufficient oxygen**, which acutely threatens the marine life, mussel farming and fishing. Very low water levels are also dangerous to the city, since the thousands of larch piles on which Venice is built start to rot having contact with oxygen.

Environmental Pollution

The pier of San Marco is currently being raised, the edges of the Piazzetta lifted, and all foundations renewed. The magic formula against rising sea levels goes by the name of MOSE (▶p.29). However, critics object that this is only fighting the symptoms. For the toxic industry of Marghera, which has been pouring thousands of tons of highly poisonous wastes such as chlorine or nitrogen solutions, cyanide and heavy metals directly into the lagoon, continues to operate. And even though a recycling system is meanwhile being built, the effluents of the hundreds of thousands of residents still flow unfiltered into the lagoon. This and the exhaust gases from the 1,500 factory chimneys of Marghera continue to eat away at the piles and the brickwork of the buildings. They are probably also responsible for the fact that the province of Venice has a 50% higher rate of cancer than the world average.

What's New in the Lagoon

For over a decade work has been proceeding intensively on city planning policies, not only for the historic centre, but also for the twin city of Venice-Mestre. Numerous projects have been planned or already completed, all with the goal of making Venice more attractive to the people who live here. With city subsidies and low-cost loans, young Venetians and small entrepreneurs are being encouraged to stay in or even return to the old city. **San Giuliano**, the island between Venice and Mestre, is currently undergoing major change. Where sulphuric acid and fertilizer used to be produced there is now the technology and science park VEnice GAteway (www.vegapark.ve.it) with about 200 businesses; on the coast where industrial and other waste was stored for decades a 74ha/182ac sports and recreational park has been built (www.parchidimestre. it). Since 2006 traffic crosses the

The constant movement of the water eats through any and all walls

Since St Mark's Square is rather low, it is especially prone to flooding

harbour basin of Marghera on a cable-stayed bridge (A. Novarin). In Dorsoduro, the new headquarters of the architectural institute IUAV (by Enric Miralles) was created in the Magazzini Frigoriferi. The neighbouring old freight port is purely a passenger terminal today (Ugo Camerino and others). On **Giudecca** Island the former Junghans property was converted into a stylish residential quarter. **An enlargement of the cemetery island of San Michele** in monumental architectural forms is being carried out by David Chipperfield. A complete restoration of the Arsenale is also in the planning stages. The technical infrastructure for MOSE is supposed to be located here.

Undersea Railway

Thus far, the Ponte della Libertà is the only connection between Venice and the mainland. In 2003, the city government decided to build an 8km/5mi-long underground railway. The **Sublagunare** is planned to take 9 minutes from the airport via the island of Murano to the Arsenale, leaving the city core untouched, but making it easier for the 25,000 commuters, 30,000 tourists and 20,000 students per day to come in and go home. In 2009 the construction phase, which is expected to cost €1 bil. and save commuters 10 minutes of travel time compared to the boat, was not yet in sight. Many Venetians fear that the city would only be flooded by more tourists and that the underground would become even less stable. Information about the **lagoon ecosystem** and the development of the flood protection program MOSE is available in English at www.salve.it and the office in Punto Laguna (Campo S. Stefano 2949, Mon–Fri 2.30pm–5.30pm).

The Adriatic flows through these into the lagoon twice daily; seawater flushes the channels and flows back. In order to maintain shipping and this »natural« drainage system, the bocche are kept open with major technical efforts.

Protection and hazards At the time of the maritime republic, the Magistrato alle Acque was set up in 1501 to protect the lagoon. It initiated the regular cleaning of the canals (which were used for sewage disposal). The canals were dredged to give them a minimum depth of 180cm/6ft. The rivers were redirected to prevent silting in the lagoon, and the shorelines were stabilized. The rivers that flow into the lagoon were monitored, and the drinking water supply and the well system were also very carefully monitored. Intentional contamination was strictly punished, by the death penalty in the worst case. The system of water management functioned until the unification of Italy. Then the Magistrato alle Acque was subordinated to Rome. In the early 20th century, large areas of land around Venice were then filled in, developed as an industrial site, and deep waterways dredged out for giant tankers. Since then, the aggressive **exhaust gases** and particularly the **effluents** produced by industry (especially nitrogen and phosphate compounds), but also from the households (Venice still has no sewage system) and last but not least, the excrement of the innumerable pigeons have threatened the lagoon and the city.

Significant damage is also caused by motorboats in Venice and the boats of the mainland Venetians, which are often high-powered and cause **waves** and underwater eddies. This washes the cement out of the joints of the house walls and gradually destroys walls and shorelines. Buildings and foundations sustain serious damage much faster than in older times.

This is why house façades and gondola mooring sites more and more frequently display protests: **stopp moto ondoso** – stop the waves from motorboats. But the promotion of cruise ship tourism with its day trippers (guarantied income through docking fees) is greater cause for concern. The strong waves caused by the ocean giants beat against the old city. The exhaust fumes of one ship are said to be equal to 15,000 vehicles.

MOSE The most keenly felt of all threats are the frequent floods. Since the major storm flood in 1966, when the flood waters rose to 1.94m/6ft 5in above the normal sea level, numerous ideas have been presented about how the city could best be protected. In 2003, Prime Minister Silvio Berlusconi laid the foundation stone for the project **MOSE**, which was developed in the 1970s. MOSE, actually Modulo Sperimentale Elettromeccanico, is a plan to install 78 mobile protection dams at the three entries of the lagoon. These dams could then be raised or lowered depending on water levels. In normal conditions,

Lagoon of Venice

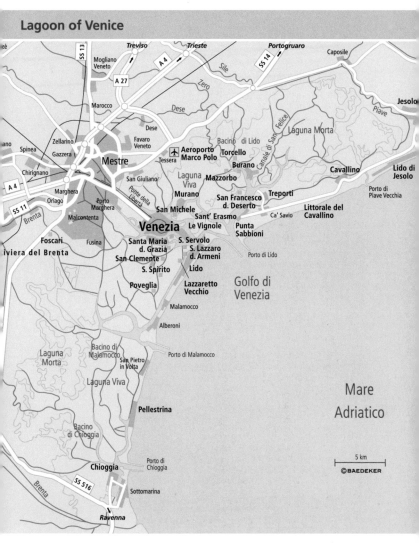

the water-filled, 5m/17ft-thick and 20m/66ft-wide bulwarks lie anchored to the ocean floor on hinges. If sea levels rise above 1.10m/3ft 7in, compressed air is forced into the gates until they stand almost upright in the water, holding back the floods. The lagoon could be closed off in this way within one hour. MOSE is intended to function

MARCO ◉ POLO INSIGHT

Venice is Everywhere

Venice of the north, Venice of the east, Venice of the west: almost every city that was built near or even in the water was given this nickname or claims to have »more bridges than Venice«. In any case, the city on the laguna has 440 bridges along with an unknown number of private bridges, so-called Pontezèlo, which lead to homes. Two thirds of the official bridges are made of stone, almost all of them have only one arch and are supposed to have more than 10,000 steps to cross them.

▶ **Ponte della Ferrovia**
At 3,500 metres (11,550 feet) the longest bridge in Venice; it was completed in 1846 and since then it has connected the city on the laguna with the mainland.

▶ **Venice's best-known bridges**

Ⓐ PONTE DI RIALTO

Ⓑ PONTE DE L'ACCADEMIA

Ⓒ PONTE DEGLI SCALZI

Ⓓ PONTE DELLA COSTITUZIONE

Ⓔ PONTE DELLA PAGLIA

Ⓕ PONTE DEI SOSPIRI

▶ **Water cities**

	AMSTERDAM	BANGKOK	BRUGES
Number of bridges	1281	unknown	80
Most famous brigde	Magere Brug	Bhumibol Brigde	St Boniface Bridge
Number of canals	156	1350	30
Elevation above sea level	0m/0ft	5m/16ft	2m/6ft
City foundation	1275	1782	1128
Area in sq km/sq mi	167/64	1565/604	138/53
Population	789,285	7,025,000	116,885
Annual income per household in €	29,600	10,500	27,600
Annual average temperature in °C	9.36	27.8	9.73

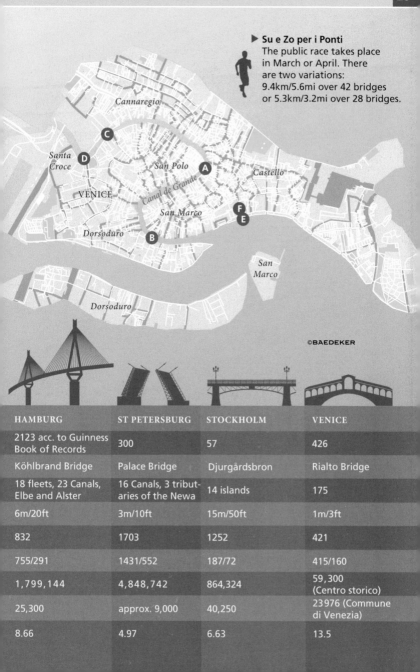

▶ **Su e Zo per i Ponti**
The public race takes place
in March or April. There
are two variations:
9.4km/5.6mi over 42 bridges
or 5.3km/3.2mi over 28 bridges.

©BAEDEKER

HAMBURG	ST PETERSBURG	STOCKHOLM	VENICE
2123 acc. to Guinness Book of Records	300	57	426
Köhlbrand Bridge	Palace Bridge	Djurgårdsbron	Rialto Bridge
18 fleets, 23 Canals, Elbe and Alster	16 Canals, 3 tributaries of the Newa	14 islands	175
6m/20ft	3m/10ft	15m/50ft	1m/3ft
832	1703	1252	421
755/291	1431/552	187/72	415/160
1,799,144	4,848,742	864,324	59,300 (Centro storico)
25,300	approx. 9,000	40,250	23976 (Commune di Venezia)
8.66	4.97	6.63	13.5

Mose Flood water safety programm

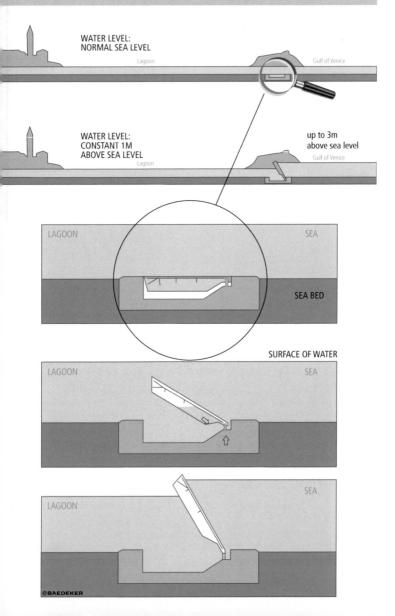

In constant flux in tidal rhythm: the lagoon

in this way up to a further increase in the water level of 60cm/2ft. This means it would provide safety from floods for the next 150 years. The Consorzio Venezia Nuova, a pool of companies which are mainly from the Veneto, was mandated to carry out the work. Building costs so far are at €5.5 bil.

It is no wonder that such amounts attract shady businesspeople. In August 2013 14 people were arrested for alleged criminal practices. Among them was the engineer Piergiorgio Baita, who holds 60 % of the stock in Consorzio Venezia Nuova. He is accused of falsifying bids, bills and the use of illegal money. Despite this construction is supposed to be finished by late 2014. Despite also the criticism of ecologists, among others. Their criticism includes the fact that the climate-related increase in sea water levels will be much higher than calculated. They also warn of the consequences of the (even temporary) separation of the lagoon from the open sea, since it depends on the cleaning effect of the tides for survival. And the poisonous industry of Marghera continues to operate.

City History

History of a Sea Power

It all started with a few merchants and fishermen who sought protection on the inaccessible islands in the lagoon. Through a brilliant combination of trade and diplomacy, the island state rose to power in the following centuries, then it surrendered in 1797 to Napoleon Bonaparte, who did not even require weapons for the conquest.

BEGINNINGS

5th century AD	Mainland Venetians fled into the lagoon from Germanic invaders
Late 7th century	Election of the first doges

According to legend Venice was founded on 25 March, AD 421, but there is no historical evidence for this date. The city was born when a storm of migrations brought about the end of the Western Roman Empire, and Germanic peoples poured into northern Italy. At that time, **mainland residents** sought **protection** in the inaccessible island world of the lagoon (lacuna, the Latin word for puddle, pond). The first settlers moved onto Malamocco (now Lido), Torcello and Murano, cleared the partly swampy islands and drained them. They probably made a rather scanty living as fishermen, coastal sailors, salt workers and vegetable growers. The Huns under Attila (452) and later the Lombards (from 568) triggered further waves of flight and settlement. A lively description originates from the Roman scholar Cassiodorus, the chancellor of the Ostrogoth king, Theodoric, who resided in Ravenna. In 537, he wrote of the Venetians: they »seem to be equally at home on the ocean and on land«. »The land is alternately covered and laid bare by high and low tide«. Their huts appear like »the nests of water birds, before which their boats are tied like horses«. Venice was not yet a city when the small lagoon population placed itself under the protective rule of the Byzantine Empire, which had grown out of the Eastern Roman Empire.

5th–6th century AD

In 697, the Byzantine exarch of Ravenna named the **first in a long series of 120 doges** (Latin: dux, leader), Paoluccio Anafesto. His first seat of government over the lagoon settlements was in Heraclea on the mainland. In 742, this was moved to Malamocco (Lido). The

Unification of the city: 7th/8th century

The winged lion over St Mark's Square

How Venice Was Built

Venice is built on 118 islands and islets located closely together in a lagoon. The first residents of these isalnds lived in huts, reminiscent of »nests of water birds« (Cassiodor). Until into the 13th century apart from the churches all of the houses were made of (lightweight) wood. To achieve more fire safety and to build with stone the Venetians developed a special building technique for the swampy ground.

❶ Venice rests on a sunken forest

Whole forests in the Carnic Alps were cut down, the logs tied together and transported to Venice as floats (zattere).

The 2 to 20 m (6.6 to 66 ft) long oak and larch logs were pounded closely together into the mud down to the lagoon's solid ground (caranto). In the slat water, where there is no oxygen or bacteria to decompose the wood the poles became as hard as stone. The builders then nailed horizontal walnut or mahogany planks on this wooden carpet or sealed them with sand, tar and oil.

❷ Actual Foundation

At the water level then the actual foundation was built, brick walling and a base of waterproof stone or marble from Istria, on which then the building was built.

According to one bill the Basilica della Salute rests on 176,627 poles, every side of the Rialto Bridge is supported by about 6000 logs. Almost 20,000 of Venice's buildings rest on this upside down sunken forest.

❸ Floor

The swaying underground also explains the Venetians' preference for mosaic and terrazzo floors as they were known in antiquity already.

Unlike marble floors they can move along with the swimming movements of the building foundations. Porphyr, serpentine, chalcedon, lapis lazuli and malachite were used. In a mortar bed of chalk and cement stones cut in to various shapes, colours and granulations were spread and polished after hardening. This can be nicely seen in the Palazzo Ducale for example.

❹ Wells

Until a water pipe from the mainland was laid in 1884 water had to be drawn for the municipal wells. Rain water was collected in cisterns dug under the streets and coated inside with clay. A layer of sand was used as a filter. The cleanliness of the water was strictly controlled..

❺ Canals

Sewage and garbage landed in the canals, which were flushed by high and low tides and the occasional storm tide. Since this was not enough they were lowered to a legal minimum of 180 cm (72 in) and cleaned regularly.

❻ The Venetian house

The floor plans of the palaces were more or less alike ▶p. 35.

The mosaic above the Porta di S. Alippio depicts the delivery of the bones of St Mark

which was harvested from the lagoon were also sold. Individual families became rich, and the city also developed into Europe's greatest financial centre.

Growing success

The growing success of Venice as a commercial power and the inflow of people from near and far ensured its rapid development. Influential merchant families dominated the economic, political and social development of the city. A powerful war fleet ensured external safety in the battle against pirates, but also steadily acquired new territory in the Adriatic, Istria and Dalmatia (AD 1000). Dalmatia provided Venice with an inexhaustible source of slaves and wood. Since this year, every year on Ascension Day the »marriage of the doge and the sea«, **sposalizio del mar** has been celebrated in front of the church S. Nicolò.

Crusades 12th/13th century

Venice, which maintained lively trade connections to the Muslim world, played a relatively small role in the first crusades to the Holy Land. This was profitable to the trade competitors Pisa and Genoa, which successfully encroached on the Venetian sphere of interest. When Constantinople gave privileges to its rival Genoa, Venetian restraint came to an end with the Fourth Crusade (1202–1204). With skilful diplomacy, the 92-year-old and half-blind Doge Enrico Dandolo obtained support for the **conquest** of the Dalmatian coastal city of Zara and particularly **Constantinople** as a reward for providing ships and crew for the transport of the crusader army (1204). The richest city of Christendom and capital of the Byzantine Empire was thoroughly plundered. Valuable art treasures, among them the four famous bronze horses of San Marco, came to Venice. At the same time, Venice secured for itself nearly half of the former territory of the Eastern Roman Empire: the coast of Epirus to the Peloponnese, Euboea, Crete, Rhodes and other islands of the Aegean. Thus **Venice** had become a **Mediterranean power**. Brief thought was given to moving into the conquered city on the Bosporus. The plan was discarded in 1224 with a majority of only two votes.

Proud maritime republic 13th–15th century

Venetian sea power now had a monopoly on all major trade routes between the Levant and the west. Such a surplus of power brought an old rival, Genoa, to the table. The struggle for first rank in the Mediterranean trade lasted until 1381, when Venice defeated its old enemy by Choggia. Venice was now a **stato da mar**, a maritime power. Venetian merchants reached far-away places on their commercial travels. Nicolò and Antonio Zeno sailed to Newfoundland, Greenland and Iceland in 1390, while Nicolò Conti crossed the Indian Ocean to the Persian Gulf and to Ceylon in the 15th century. Venetian settlements were found in the Crimea, Armenia, Syria and Egypt. In the late 15th century, Venice was the third-largest city in Europe after Paris and Naples with about 150,000 residents.

THE GOVERNMENT OF VENICE

The constitution of Venice provided inner political peace for many centuries, even among the social groups that were excluded from power. The constitution's roots are in the 11th and 12th centuries, but continued to develop in accordance with demands. It owed its success to a well-developed system of mutually controlling forces, in which the checks and balances of modern democratic constitutions were already present. The difference was that this involved »democracy« for only one class of the people, the nobility.

Organization of the republic

Venice was an **oligarchy**. Power lay in the hands of a few families who had become rich through trade. They were members of the so-called Greater Council. After its numbers had risen to several hundred, it was closed to newcomers in 1297 and known as the **Serrata**. From then on, membership was open only to those who (or whose families) were recorded in the **Libro d'Oro**, the Golden Book of the republic (at the end of the republic, this book contained 1218 names).

The Greater Council chose the members of the various committees which carried out state business, and elected the doge from among its own members. Every noble held an office in the state apparatus, usually as an unpaid servant of the state. He was not allowed to refuse a service with which he was mandated, nor a command. Persons who failed in office, whether through their own fault or otherwise, were subject to the strictest punishments. These measures promoted the development of a highly stable class of leaders which determined all the affairs of the city. Not all members of the population were satisfied with this regulation; coup attempts were inevitable. The »bourgeois« families were entered in the **Silver Book**. They had no part in government decisions, but some offices in government were open to them. The families entered in the Golden and Silver Books did not account for even 15% of Venice's total population, but controlled nearly 90% of the republic's wealth.

In AD 697, the first doge (from Latin dux, meaning leader) had been named by the representative of the Byzantine emperor. From 726 onwards, the lagoon population exercised its voting rights. In 1797 Doge Manin, the last of the long line, returned the doge's hat with the

Office of doge

Porta della Carta: Doge Foscari kneeling before the lion of St Mark

Sea Power Venice

An astonishing ascent: fishermen and saltmakers became wealthy traders and rulers over the markets of the Old World. Venice's constitution was developed in the 10th and 11th century under the influence of gaining independence from Byzantium/Constantinople

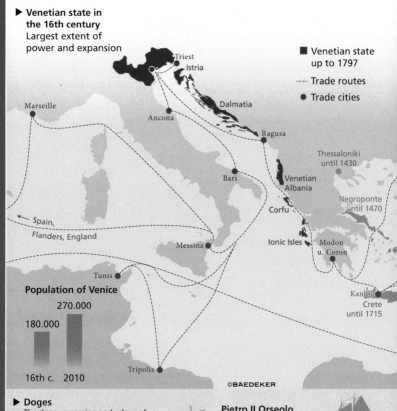

▶ **Venetian state in the 16th century**
Largest extent of power and expansion

■ Venetian state up to 1797

--- Trade routes

● Trade cities

Triest
Istria
Dalmatia
Marseille
Ancona
Ragusa
Thessaloniki until 1430
Bari
Venetian Albania
Negroponte until 1470
Corfu
Spain, Flanders, England
Ionic Isles
Modon u. Coron
Messina
Tunis
Kandia
Crete until 1715

Population of Venice

270.000

180.000

16th c.   2010

Tripolis

©BAEDEKER

▶ **Doges**
The doge, sovereign and »slave of the republic« (Petrarch) had unlimited power until 1148, after which he was watched more and more and virtually isolated. The real rulers were the around 2,000 noble members of the Great Council (established 1297) and the Council of the Ten, which was established in 1310 and was a kind of special court.

Pietro II Orseolo
991–1009
Venice's eastward expansion begins in Istria and Dalmatia as a battle against pirates.

Enrico Dandolo
1192–1205
Participation in the 4th Crusade and conquest of Constantinople in 1204 Venice rules the Mediterranean Sea.

ade routes
s an example spices from India
nd silk from China

nportant import goods
lk, furs, ivory, spices, dyes and perfume

nportant export goods
old, silver, amber, wool, wood, pewter,
on, cut jewels, glass wares, medicines
nd slaves

Constantinople
1204 to 1261

Famagusta

Cyprus
until1573

Beirut

Akkon

Alexandria

▶ Balance of power
The republic's complex system of government
was marked by constantly changing areas of
responsibility in order to prevent an
hereditary monarchy from being established
as well as to keep the balance of power
among the noble families. All state offices
that had competences connected to them
were only awarded for short periods, while
the government functions that were awarded
for life, like the doge, had hardly any
authority and were also closely watched.

Venice had a clear division of labour:

1% Nobility
Politics, administration and warfare

4% Cittadini (traders)
Finances, trade and production

95% Populani (rest of the population)
Soldiers, sailors and tradesmen

▶ Marco Polo
When the Mongols advanced as far as
Constantinople in the 13th century and
the trade routes were open all the was to
China, Marco Polo started out on a journey
with his father and uncle that took 25 years.

Venice
Jerusalem
Silk Road
Peking

acopo Tiepolo
229–1249
ne dominance of the
longols in Central
sia allows 50 years of
verland trade with China.

**Pietro Loredan
1567–1570**
Loss of Cyprus to the
Ottoman Empire (finally in the peace
treaty of 1573).

**Domenico II
Contarini
1659–1674**
After 20 years of
battles loss of Crete
o the Ottoman Empire.

**Ludovico Manin
1789–1797**
Venice is handed over to
Napoleon who
passes it on to
the Habsburgs:
end of the
Republic of
Venice

words: »It is no longer needed.« In these eleven hundred years, 120 doges who were elected for life represented the republic of Venice. Their sign of office was the famous **corno**, the doge's hat, which was decorated with gold and jewels worth 194,000 ducats. The people confirmed the election of the doge by cheering the announcement »This is your doge if you accept him«. At first, the power of the doge was nearly unlimited. In the 10th century, when Doge Pietro Candiano IV (959–976) tried to make the office of doge inheritable, there was an uprising. The Doge's Palace and the basilica went up in flames; the doge and his son, who was still a minor, were murdered. Following this, the power of the doge was increasingly restricted. He was neither allowed to travel nor to receive visitors alone. Even his letters to his wife were censored. Finally, the people were also excluded from the election of the doge. Now the announcement was only »This is your doge« (mid-12th century). A highly complicated process was intended to prevent cheating in the election of the doge. 30 people were chosen by lot from the Greater Council. They elected nine from among themselves who then chose another 40 electors. These 49 were reduced to 12 by drawing lots, and they chose another 25. These were again reduced to nine, each of which chose another five. These 45 then selected eleven men from their group, which determined the 41 final electors. The election process could take months.

Duties of the doge
The doge represented the republic, had a seat on every committee (but only one vote in elections), presided over the Greater Council, and had the duty of bringing about decisions and controlling the holders of state office. However, his authority was strictly limited: the doge and his wife had to reside in the Doge's Palace. They had to pay for their furniture and other expenses out of their own pockets. The doge was not allowed to hold private or external offices. No members of the doge's family were allowed to participate in commercial undertakings, and his sons and daughters were not allowed to marry outside the city without the permission of the Greater Council. In the absence of the councillors, the doge was not allowed to open letters from outside powers, receive ambassadors or accept gifts (unless they were flowers, scented herbs or rose water). In the 14th century, Francesco Petrarch described the situation of the doge with the words: »Doges are not rulers, not even princes, but only the glorified slaves of the republic.«

Government
If there was anything similar to a state government, then it was the **Lesser Council** which consisted of six consiglieri, representatives of the six city districts. The consiglieri discussed all state matters, monitored and represented the doge, who also had only one vote within this circle, and chaired the various bodies together with him. The two most important ones included the Quarantia (named after its origi-

nally 40 members) and the senate. The **Quarantia** was already in existence in 1179. It was initially only a court of appeals, but from about 1230 developed into a financial and legal organization. From about the same time, the **senate** mainly dealt with matters of shipping and trade. It later developed into the actually ruling parliament – responsible to the Greater Council, but entitled to make important decisions. In the first third of the 14th century, the senate gave rise to the **Collegio dei Savi**, which was mandated to prepare senate sessions and handle matters of commerce and marine duties, and in the 15th century to the **Collegio**, which, together with the doge, the Lesser Council and three representatives of the Quarantia, functioned as a sort of ministers' council. The last great constitutional organ to emerge was the **Council of Ten** (Dieci). The background was the coup attempt of Baiamonte Tiepolo in 1310. The task of the Dieci was to examine the background and the processes and punish the guilty parties. In 1335, the decision was made to maintain this type of special court. It was charged with investigating all occurrences which might endanger the security of the state. The principle of distrust which marked Venice's constitution was practically institutionalized in this body. Naturally, the names of the ten members, whom the senate elected every year, were kept secret.

> **! Secret paths** *Insider Tip*
>
> **MARCO POLO TIP**
>
> The Council of Ten usually met at night. The seat of office was the Palazzo Ducale, where the prison, torture and execution rooms were also located. However, they were very well camouflaged and not visible from the outside. A look at these rooms and the way in which this secret police worked is provided by the tour »Itinerari segreti« in the Palazzo Ducale (▸page 235).

In this way, many institutions were created which delegated and shared power and controlled each other. A network of usually unsalaried office-holders ensured that the enacted regulations were carried out precisely, and that individual groups did not become too powerful. The periods of service of the most important state offices were very short (except for the doge, who was elected for life and very closely monitored). State office terms usually lasted only a year. Furthermore, the office holders could only be elected into other offices after a waiting period. One of the most important offices was that of the cattaveri, the tax assessors. All Venetians, regardless of rank and person, had to disclose their entire financial situation to them and pay the taxes that were thus determined.

Many institutions

There are many hypotheses about why the Venetian population, the middle classes and craftsmen, but also the merchants and sailors, accepted not being directly involved in politics. Indeed there were some

Appeasement offices

fices for the upper class – e.g. the influential secret state chancellery the control of patrician noble power – »appeasement offices« and a few periods when many new citizens were ennobled. Truly outstanding wealth enabled citizens to become councillors at any period. Perhaps the so-called scuole, the typically Venetian guild brotherhoods, also played a special role.

Scuole By the 13th and 14th centuries, the constitution of Venice had largely been completed. It changed little in later times, although 95% of the population did not partake in political power. An important role in the social structure and the stability of the republic of nobles was played by the so-called scuole, which formed from the 12th century onwards – **guilds** which usually consisted of men of a particular trade. They elected their representatives, created association regulations, but also fulfilled a number of social tasks: they founded and maintained hospitals and shelters for the poor. The scuole developed into a very complex group of associations and unions and thereby offered a substitute for political activity to a large number of Venetian citizens. Longworth (»Rise and Fall of the Republic of Venice«, 1976) refers to them as the »most democratic systems of Venice«. There were numerous small scuole. The most significant ones included the Scuole di San Rocco, dei Carmine, San Giovanni Evangelista and San Giorgio degli Schiavoni. The members paid fees and supplied the men who marched in the most important processions. The large scuole had their own buildings, and it is testimony to their importance that the Scuola Grande di San Rocco has one of the most impressive cycles of paintings in the world: Tintoretto painted 56 large-format works for it. But even the interiors of the small scuole are surprising – for instance, Vittore Carpaccio created a fabulous set of paintings for the Scuola di San Giorgio degli Schiavoni. Marco Polo and many great artists were members of the scuole. The end of the republic was also their (temporary) end. Napoleon forbade the scuole as well as the monasteries. However, they were refounded (the Scuola Grande di San Rocco in 1797, others followed in the early 20th century).

FROM THE FALL OF VENICE TO THE PRESENT

1453	Conquest of Constantinople by the Ottomans – the Turks become competitors in the Aegean
1508	Founding of the League of Cambrai, an alliance against Venice
15th–16th cent.	Venice conquers its hinterland
1797	Resignation of the last doge, Venice surrenders to Napoleon without a fight

Venice was the unchallenged ruler of the seas. The merchant fleet consisted of 3,900 ships with about 17,000 sailors. Domestically the republic was stable. Only its hinterland was not secured, and so the »stato da mar« began expansion to the west in the early 15th century – finally making Venice the greatest territorial power in northern Italy.

With paid troops, led by renowned condottieri (mercenary leaders), the queen of the Adriatic conquered large parts of the mainland (terraferma): Padua, Vicenza, Verona (1405). In 1489, when the island of Cyprus fell to Venice, the city state reached its greatest size: its rule extended from the Greek islands of the Aegean west via Dalmatia and Friuli to Bergamo, north to the Alps, including a large part of Triente, and south to Ravenna. A great variety of economic activity had developed within the city. At the end of the 15th century, Venice had more printers than Rome, Milan and Florence together. Silk and cotton weaving blossomed; the glass-blowing factories on Murano grew into large-scale operations. The differentiation in crafts was far advanced, still recognizable today from the repertoire of street names – rope makers, soapers, dyers, brewers, weavers, bakers, goldsmiths, spice dealers, tanners, candle makers. This period also produced many of the magnificent churches and lovely palaces which fascinate visitors to Venice to this day.

Conquests on land 15th century

Proud condottiere: monument for Colleoni in front of Santi Giovanni e Paolo

In 1453, the Ottomans quickly conquered Constantinople, and then, one by one, the Venetian possessions of Cyprus, Crete and the Peloponnese. They even penetrated the waters of the Adriatic, and in 1499, temporarily occupied part of Friuli. At the same time (1504), France, Spain, Hungary and Austria formed the League of Cambrai with papal support. The maritime republic was able to withstand the

External threat

league, which soon dissolved due to internal troubles. Calm had only just returned west of Venice when the Turks resumed their challenge in the east. In 1517, they conquered Egypt, and from then on, controlled Venice's trade routes to Asia Minor, Persia and the Far East. The barbaric and destructive war for control of the eastern Mediterranean, which had now lasted for 300 years with interruptions, led to the destruction of the stato da mar. In 1492 the Genoan Christopher Columbus sailed to the New World, and in 1499 the Portuguese Vasco da Gama discovered the sea route across the Atlantic to India – events with far-reaching consequences, since the centre of world trade increasingly shifted to the Atlantic coast, Lisbon, London and Antwerp. The Mediterranean trade, and with it the commercial power of **Venice, increasingly lost significance**. In 1510, trade with Flanders had already stopped, and the spice trade had lessened by 60%. How desperate the Serenissima's situation was regarding these developments in the 16th century is shown by plans for the construction of a Suez canal, which, however, could not be technically realized at that time. Venice faced great difficulties: in terms of external politics, the republic was isolated from the European royal houses. But the Turkish fleet threatened not only the remaining trade activities of Venice, but also the interests of the other Mediterranean countries. Under Pope Pius V, a »Holy League« was finally formed. A fleet was created with the aid of Naples, Austria, Sicily and Genoa – a total of 450 ships with 120,000 crewmen, and on 7 October 1571, the decisive battle, the **Battle of Lepanto**, took place in the area between the Peloponnes and the island of Kefalloniá. Even though the Venetians won an outstanding victory for the last time in history, they were unable to free themselves from isolation in foreign affairs.

Long twilight There were signs of internal decay as well. Poverty became a much greater problem. Corruption and mismanagement caused the collapse of several renowned banks. Syphilis spread so severely that in 1522 the duty to report and treat it was introduced. In 1575 and 1630, Venice experienced two epidemics of the black death, from which nearly one third of the population died each time. The Turks returned, attacked Crete and drew Venice into another Mediterranean war with large losses (1644 to 1669). When the new forces of the Habsburgs pushed back the Ottoman Empire and acquired the conquered regions for themselves, Venice gave up its last trade bases in the Aegean and concentrated its efforts on preserving its independence as a small state – in the protection of its home lagoon.

End of the republic 18th century The republic of Venice had lost power, but culturally it rose to greater heights, recorded in the paintings of Tiepolo, Canaletto and Guardi as well as the writings of Casanova and Goldoni, as if carefree enjoyment could delay the imminent end of a glorious past. In the

Regatta in honour of Napoleon in 1807. The emperor is standing on the balcony of Palazzo Balbi.

early 18th century, there were still 216 Venetian patrician families, who were just able to supply members of the Greater Council and the large apparatus of officials. After 1750, in order to clean up state finances, the senate began to confiscate the possessions of the churches. The funds were used, among other things, to build the 15km/9.3mi-long, 14km/8.7mi-wide and 4.5m/15 ft-high dyke system to protect the lagoon (murazzi), a final great achievement of the republic. In 1796, **Napoleon** had declared war on Austria and marched his troops into northern Italy. In 1797, he finally stood before Venice. The Greater Council met on 17 May 1797. The last doge, Ludovico Manin, declared his resignation. With 512 yes votes and only 30 opposing votes, the end of the republic was decided. Disrespectfully, Napoleon burned the Libro d'Oro, the Golden Book of the city which contained the names of all great patrician families, and plundered the city. At that time, many works of art were taken away to Paris – among them the four bronze horses from St Mark's Basilica – buildings torn down, churches and monasteries destroyed or re-dedicated. In the same year, France ceded the entire Veneto, including Venice, to Austria.

After more than 1,000 years of independence, Venice was only a province of the distant capital Vienna. The new rulers had streets paved, gas lighting installed, sea defences strengthened, and in 1846, they built the railway bridge which connected Venice to the mainland. In the first half of the 19th century, the Serenissima bore the occupation without resistance. In the European revolution year of

**19th century
From Austria
to Italy**

1848, Venetian freedom fighters under Daniele Manin, were able to free the city from Austria for 15 months. In 1866, the Habsburgs ceded the region of Venice to the newly united kingdom of Italy. At this time, Venice was only a shadow of its former self. Marked by mismanagement and local political power struggles, the city was like a poorhouse – approximately one third of the 130,000 residents lived in poverty.

New prosperity 20th century

The desired economic and social upturn took a long time to come. In 1917, during the First World War, the construction of industrial facilities began in Marghera. The port was also moved here from Venice. In 1926, Venice, Mestre and Marghera merged. In 1933, a road traffic bridge was constructed between Mestre and Venice, parallel to the railway embankment. Despite the industrial facilities on the mainland, Venice was left unscathed by Allied bomb attacks. In the 1950s, the mainland became home to the centre of the Italian **chemical industry**.

Venice today

Insular Venice reached fame as a tourist destination in the second half of the 20th century. The re-introduction the the carnival in 1979 extended the high season to cover almost the whole year. Venice Biennale, film festival, university (about 18,000 students), numerous

The Fondaco dei Tedeschi was converted into a luxury store

cultural institutes and galleries have given the city on the lagoon an additional reputation as a world-class cultural centre. Meanwhile the city gets about 80,000 visitors a day, that is more than 29 mil annually. Tourism not only forces other economic sectors out, but also more and more Venetians. The many cruise ships blow as much emissions into the air as the industry on the mainland. The waves caused by the giant propellers shake the very foundations of the city. These problems are in addition to the many already known problems like air pollution, increased flooding and sinking foundations. The constant crush on the Canal Grande, where gondolieri, water taxis and vaporetti compete for space, claimed a fatality in August 2013 when a German tourist was fatally injured when he tried to save his daughter during a ride in a gondola after it collided with a boat.

But despite all income from tourism the city cannot seem to reduce its **€400 mil. debt**. In the »hunt« for new sources of income it began to sell the municipally owned palazzi, not only to Benetton, Prada, Bulgari, but also to enterprising Chinese. The future of the city depends on the solutions to these problems (▶MARCO POLO Insight p.22). While the former mayor and leftist-liberal philosopher Massimo Cacciari (1993-2000, 2005-2010; "Famous People) was a committed representative of a Venice that had not frozen into its own museum (he managed to get the sale of pigeon food banned on St Mark's Square), his successor, the professor of law Giorgio Orsoni (Partito Democratico) is working in the opposite direction: he supports Venice's campaign to be European culture capital in 2019. But does Venice really need it?

Venice will be a satellite station of the **World Exposition 2015** in Milan. By then the old waterway between Milan and Venice should be navigable again.

Art and Culture

Looking Back and Forward

The city is a fragile work of art in itself: made of bridges and canals, from palazzi whose paint is peeling off, and churches with shimmering gold mosaics and precious Titian madonnas and Tintoretto Lord's Suppers.

ROMANESQUE AND BYZANTINE ART

Close links to Constantinople marked the development of art in Venice. The state and court church of the doges, **San Marco**, was built with five domes in the image of the Church of the Apostles of Constantinople. After 1100 the vestibule, later the interior of the church too, was covered with Byzantine mosaics. Byzantine mosaic artists worked on them with Italian helpers. The iconography is strongly oriented to its eastern model, although the execution departs from the sense of form of Byzantine art through the lively design of the surface and the figures as well as the stylized folds. A further example is found in the Last Judgement mosaics of the west wall in **Santa Maria Assunta** on Torcello (12th century). This link between western elements of style and eastern models is an important attribute of Romanesque art in Venice.

Byzantine influence

The architecture of **Santa Maria Assunta** on Torcello shows important hallmarks of Romanesque architecture: a tall campanile towers above the column basilica, which has wooden ceilings and no transept; narrow blind arches are generously applied to structure the walls, and in the interior the wall surfaces above the narrow arcades are emphasized.

Architecture

On the basis of a Byzantine model, **Santa Fosca** was built on Torcello in the late 11th century. It has a central plan with a dome, in which the forms of the octagon, cross and circle interact to create a square interior space. The octagonal outer mantle is dominated by slender arcades on high columns.

Romanesque-Byzantine influences are evident in the cathedral of **SS Maria e Donato** on Murano: the column basilica, without a transept has a massive, broad impressive eastern façade. A two-storey arcade on double columns stands out, enclosing niches on the lower level and standing free before a wide gallery on the upper level. Between the arcades are two triangle friezes, one made of different kinds of marble. This vertical structuring with galleries that are rela-

Mosaics in St Mark's Basiica

tively far away from the wall is a characteristic of secular pre-Gothic architecture in Venice.

Sculpture   Sculpture of the 11th and 12th centuries also shows strong Byzantine influences. It is frequently difficult to decide whether the sculptures were made in Venice or imported. The screens in the cathedral of Torcello (11th century), on which a symmetrical pair of peacocks surrounded by vines picks grapes from a bowl, came from Byzantium. The symbolism refers to the renewal of life by partaking in the death of Christ. The relief with the ascension of Alexander on the northern façade of San Marco is dated to the 11th century, due to its simple form and reduced corporeality. It might have come from the Christian east.

Spolia on a column of the south front of St Mark's Basilica

Aside from the numerous imports of reliefs and sculptures, Venice possesses numerous **spolia**, pieces from older buildings. Through commercial relations, trade bases and particularly through the conquest of Constantinople in 1204, many spoils of war reached Venice. Many of the polychrome marble columns and the fine ornamentation on the pilasters of St Mark's Basilica are such plundered pieces. The two free-standing columns on the Piazzetta today are among the best-known spolia. They were brought to Venice by sea at the end of the 12th century. The figures on the columns are also spolia from the orient. The bronze St Mark's lion was originally a chimera, whose meaning was changed by adding wings and the open book. The figure of St Theodore is a Roman work, reshaped to show Christian meaning.

THE GOTHIC PERIOD

A decorative system developed in Venice during the Gothic period,   **Architecture**
particularly through the redesign of the façade of the **Doge's Palace**.
All forms show a certain grace and colour here. The arcade of the low
ground floor consist of wide pointed arches, while that of the upper
loggia is much narrower, with quatrefoils cut into the spandrels to
produce a more transparent effect.
The wall above it seems less massive
due to the white-red-green bricks
and the diamond patterns. Wide
pointed-arch windows as well as oculi with quatrefoils pierce the wall,
and the balconies have beautiful
Gothic window frames. Even the
»flame-shaped« crenellations are
perforated to form a filigree top.

The exterior of **San Marco** was also
fundamentally changed in the late
14th century, when the row of arches
on the upper floor was crowned in
late Gothic style. Figure tabernacles,
curving canopies and statues on the
gables, typically Gothic decorations,
were added. The most famous late
Gothic palace façade is that of the
Ca' d'Oro (1421 to 1440). The Gothic elements of the façade, which was
formerly partially covered in gold,
are slender arcades with various forms of tracery, balconies, friezes
and finely applied decorations as well as the polychrome work.
The Dominican church **Santi Giovanni e Paolo** and the Franciscan
church **Santa Maria Gloriosa dei Frari** are the two largest late Gothic churches in Venice. Both were built according to the scheme of
Gothic churches of the mendicant orders, as vaulted column basilicas
with transepts and side chapels in the choir.

> **?** **MARCO POLO INSIGHT**
>
> *Did you know?*
>
> Items of special interest: Venetian
> floors, which were made from the
> 9th century, first by oriental mas-
> ters, later by craftsmen from the
> region of Ravenna and from Ven-
> ice itself. Many of the motifs have
> special significance; for instance, a
> circle symbolizes the sky, a square
> the earth (paradise on earth). The
> eagle is the king of the air, the
> lion king of the desert and the in-
> carnation of majesty, courage and
> justice. Occasionally it represents
> Christ himself. The peacock stands
> for resurrection and immortality,
> while the deer embodies belief in
> God. Mythological monsters like
> the griffin or the basilisk symbol-
> ize evil.

In the field of sculpture, styles from the most diverse sources met in   **Sculpture**
Venice. Byzantine influences remained of decisive importance; elements from antiquity were taken up and combined with Gothic characteristics. The sculptural decoration on the main portal of **San
Marco** dates from the mid-13th century and shows complete indi-
viduality in its lively narrative and the detail of its depictions. The
brothers Jacobello and Pierpaolo dalle Masegne participated in im-

portant projects in Venice: their sculptures on the rood screen of San Marco (1394) show that they attached great significance to the individual design of the figures, the precise rendition of body volumes and lively gestures. On some apostles, they even worked at contrapost.

Nowhere in Venice can the development of tomb art be followed better than in **Santi Giovanni e Paolo**, for this mendicant church was a popular burial church for the doges. The design of the tomb of Michele Morosini on the right wall in the presbytery is typical for the 14th century. A pointed arch with a gable, bordered by tabernacle towers on its sides, stands high over the tomb. The deceased lies on a bed here, with an inscription between the consoles for the coat of arms. The small sculptures, angels, apostles and the Annunciation show northern influences; the mosaic of the crucifixion with the donor figures are close to the art of Giotto.

View from the Palazzo Ducale to the island San Giorgio Maggiore

Oil painting was introduced by Antonello da Messina at the end of the 15th century. The works that he produced during his stay in Venice had great influence on Venetian painting. Antonio Vivarini shared a workshop with his brother Bartolomeo. Starting with a rather decorative late Gothic style in which the figures look rigid, he refined his painting from 1400 onwards. His work displays astounding nearness to reality and empathy in characterization. Bartolomeo developed a pictorial language with depth. His work excels through strong colours and hard contours. The son of Antonio, Alvise, produced large altar and devotional paintings and had close links to Giovanni Bellini.

Painting

RENAISSANCE

In the 15th century, few new churches were built in Venice. However, the commission to sculptor and architect **Pietro Lombardo** in 1481 to rebuild Santa Maria dei Miracoli was of outstanding significance. Retaining its classical proportions, he had the entire exterior covered in polychrome marble, the lower storey rhythmically structured with pilasters and the upper storey with arcades. Marble also dominates the interior – a barrel-vaulted hall with a raised presbytery. Special emphasis is placed on the relief decorations of the pilasters, consisting of ornamental bands enriched with animals, vases, heads and masks. They have depth, and are delicate and densely worked. Aside from Lombardo, who was also responsible for the Scuola Grande di San Marco with perspective design of the reliefs at the base of the walls, important commissions had also been entrusted to **Mauro Coducci**. Among other work, he covered the façades of San Zaccaria and San Michele in Isola. Semicircular tops to façades and segments of circles are characteristic of his work. San Zaccaria shows his strict system of design, consisting of pilasters, columns and round-arch windows or blind arches as vertical elements, receiving a horizontal accent through wide cornices which separate the storeys. Round oculi are a frequent element in his façades. Both architects, Lombardo and Coducci, played a significant role in the development of the Venetian palace façade by piercing the previously closed walls with large windows. **Andrea Palladio**, in his Venetian period, devoted himself solely to religious architecture. He planned three important church façades: San Francesco della Vigna as his early work, San Giorgio Maggiore in classic monumental form and Il Redentore as his late work. They excel in terms of austere lines and clear proportions. Colossal arrangements of columns, a columned vestibule crowned by a gable and a balanced ratio of wall to column lend a special effect to the church fronts.

Architecture

Sculpture In the development of tombs, that of Pietro Mocenigo in Santi Giovanni e Paolo (1476–1481) was ground-breaking. **Pietro Lombardo** conceived a design which built on the motif of the triumphal arch. Nine warriors based on ancient models stand in the niches or support the sarcophagus, on which the deceased doge is no longer shown lying, but standing. The tomb of Andrea Vendramin by Tullio Lombardo (1493), the son of Pietro, is a further well-known monument in this church. Once more, a central arcade of columns is framed by restrained side sections. The iconographic programme combines Christian motifs with humanist ideas. An examination of the individual figures, particularly those of the warriors, suggests that the artist made a precise study of ancient sculpture. The artist lent similar vivacity to the double portrait in the Galleria Franchetti (Ca' d'Oro) by expressing emotions in the faces. **Antonio Rizzo**, the second important Venetian sculptor of the Renaissance, created the figures of Adam and Eve, which originally stood at the Arco Foscari of the Doge's Palace, in the second half of the 15th century. In the proportions, Eve in particular, with her narrow shoulders and wide hips, is characteristic of the Gothic sense of form, but it is precisely her posture and gesture that make her seem sensual and withdrawn, while Adam is moved and outward-looking, as his open mouth and right hand held in front of his chest indicate. The figures were made from models – sculptures from antiquity were surely not used. In the design of Piazza San Marco and the Piazzetta, the architect **Jacopo Sansovino**, who planned the Libreria di San Marco and the Zecca, played an important role. Even though he also worked as a sculptor, he did not himself carry out the rich sculptural decoration that he designed. Nonetheless, Venice contains significant examples of his work: the reliefs of the singers' galleries and the vestry doors of San Marco, the Madonna in the Arsenal, St John the Baptist on the font in the Frari church and the figures in the niches of the Loggetta (Pallas Athene, Mercury, Apollo, Pax) next to the Campanile, which embody the main principles of Venetian politics. In these haunting bronze sculptures, outstanding in their cohesion and the fine detail of the surface structure, the influence of ancient sculpture cannot be overlooked.

Painting One identifying characteristic of Venetian painting is the variety of colours; it can be explained by the influence of Byzantine art, the location of Venice on the water, and the numerous narrow canals in the city which create extraordinary effects of light and shade. Contrary to Florentine painting of the time, which particularly focused on narrative and pathos, Venetian painters preferred to record lyrical subjects and moods. **Giorgione's** painting *The Tempest* in the Gallerie dell'Accademia is a well-known example. The painting, which cannot be clearly decoded iconographically and may represent an allegory of

Giorgione's *The Tempest*, one of the most famous paintings in the Accademia

human life, shows a calm, peaceful scene, to which the restless, almost ominous mood of the stormy skies forms a strong contrast. Light and colour to convey mood in a sensual, poetic world are important characteristics for this painter. **Gentile Bellini**, who worked in the highly influential family studio with his father Jacopo and his brother Giovanni, had the honourable task of painting every newly elected doge. Today, few originals but many copies of these paintings survive. The portraits of the Bellini school reveal an intense concern with the individual. The sketchbooks of **Jacopo Bellini** show that he took an interest in antiquity, though more in formal terms than in terms of content. Here Venice differs from other cities of the arts such as Florence and Mantua, where mythological representations became popular as early as the second half of the 15th century. In the early Renaissance, patrons in Venice preferred paintings with Christian content. **Vittore Carpaccio** was frequently employed by the scuole to produce cycles of paintings for their meeting rooms. His paintings display a fascinating joy in narration and love of vivid details, while impressing formally through a strict composition, clear perspectives and precise modelling of figures. **Titian** painted the central altar image of the Assunta for the Frari church (1516–1518). Here, the ascension of the Virgin takes place in a space filled with light: below are the apostles, frightened, gazing after the departing Virgin with arms raised high, and in the highest zone, God receiving Mary. In this monumental work, Titian found a composition for this theme which set a standard for decades to come. While Titian worked for a variety of prominent European patrons, **Jacopo Tintoretto** concentrated on his home city of Venice. Aside from numerous commissions for secular buildings, he painted large altarpieces. His compositions emphasize the three-dimensionality of moving figures and place them in spaces with depth and a precise perspective structure. Particularly in his late period, light increasingly became a means of conveying atmosphere, drama or vision. This makes him one of the most important masters of Mannerism. In the paintings of **Paolo Veronese,** the main scene unfolds in the foreground as if on a stage, while further scenes related to the main theme take place in the background. His joy in narrative and decorative style can be seen in the church San Sebastiano, where he did the ceiling and wall paintings.

Palazzi

Strictly speaking, Venice has only one palace, the Palazzo Ducale or Doge's Palace. All buildings commissioned by well-off families were referred to with deceptive modesty as a casa (house), ca' for short. Unlike other north Italian cities, palace architecture in Venice remained unaffected by two important problems: the buildings were naturally protected by the water, and Venice was not affected by conflicts between rival families, which meant that the individual buildings could be created with a free and open design. And since Venice had numerous rich nobles and citizens, it became home to unusually large numbers of palaces. Less expensive housing was built for those with lesser financial means, as many townhouses with functional ground plans and numerous architectural refinements still show today.

Floor plans of palazzi

Palaces were both residences and places of work. This meant that their layout had some special characteristics which remained into the 18th century. On the ground or water floor, a hall extends right through the building and provides access to the adjacent rooms. From the Renaissance, these somewhat uncomfortable rooms were used as commercial space, storerooms and offices. Intermediate floors were frequently inserted next to the hall. A stairway led to the residential rooms on the first and second floors. On the first floor (piano nobile) there was a large hall with a loggia. This was a space for celebrations, feasts or theatrical performances. The sala was correspondingly furnished and decorated with paintings, weapons and trophies. The actual living rooms are on the second floor. The Venetian palazzo generally has two entrances: the fine entrance faces the water, while the simpler one is on the opposite side. From the Renaissance, the entrance area was improved and richly decorated with paintings or sculptural ornamentation. The outside stairs which were customary until that time, and of which the spiral staircase in the courtyard of Palazzo Contarini del Bovolo still provides a beautiful example today, were increasingly moved inside the house. Large inner courtyards were frequently omitted due to the high property prices.

The main façade also always faces the water. The foundation of the façade design is a base of dressed stone which terminates in a clearly marked cornice. A portal of one or more arches leads to the palace interior via a stairway. An arcade may also be built in front of the water storey. On the upper floor, the window group of the sala is the determining element. The side rooms usually had two windows placed far apart, leaving broad surfaces of wall between them. Their form depends on the period: round arches, pointed arches, tracery decoration and rectangles with triangular gables are found. The structure may be embellished with pilasters, columns or other, sometimes very detailed, decorations. The palace, originally a two-storey structure, gained another floor in the Gothic period; however it was ensured that all palazzi were of the same height. Only in the 16th century did some structures begin to exceed the uniform height. Wood remained the preferred building material until the 13th century, when the more durable stone came into favour. Brick walls became common. They were plastered and could then be painted or clad in marble or limestone. The varied colours and grains of the stone contributed to the effect of the façades.

Façade

The spiral staircase of
Palazzo Contarini del Bovolo

17TH AND 18TH CENTURIES

Painting   In Venice, in contrast to other regions, painting continued to develop, continuing the independent tradition of the city and supported by a well-off citizenry. Sebastiano Ricci, Giovanni Battista Tiepolo and his son Domenico made a significant contribution to this development. **Ricci** sought to include many ideas from Bolognese art and expanded his repertoire through travels to Rome and Florence. He influenced **G. B. Tiepolo**, who developed a style of painting that was flooded by even light with fine and highly differentiated colours. He mastered the composition of spatial depth, in which figures move lightly and playfully, and received numerous commissions, both from the church and private patrons. The frescoes of Palazzo Labia are his work. The paintings of **Pietro Longhi** depict Venetian everyday life, often in very small formats. Harmonious colouring characterizes Longhi's French-influenced art. A new genre came into being beside the description of contemporary festivities and everyday life: the vedute of Calevarijs, **Francesco Guardi** and **Canaletto**. Canaletto initially painted views of the city in strong colour contrasts, but then altered his style. His topographically meticulous pictures had become routine and rigidly formulaic by the end of his creative life.

Pietro Longhi: *The Concert*

Baldassare Longhena is regarded as the leading Venetian architect of the Baroque period and was the builder of the city's most significant Baroque church, Santa Maria della Salute. For this site, which has a prominent place in the city, he created a central plan, a domed rotunda with an ambulatory and radiating chapels. Strong architectural decoration and rich sculptural ornamentation contribute to the imposing exterior. The architects of the 18th century sought to take up the tradition of preceding centuries, the building methods of Sansovino or Palladio, thereby producing spacious buildings filled with light. **Giorgio Massari** designed Palazzo Grassi-Stucky (1749), a clear, simple building with a classical façade and an austere staircase. For the Chiesa dei Gesuati (1726–1743), he planned a façade of great sculptural effect with columns, gables, entablature and niche figures. A similarly classical columned façade was added to the church San Nicolò da Tolentino by **Andrea Tirali**.

19TH AND 20TH CENTURIES

Since Venice had only limited space, expansion through the construction of new quarters, which was common in other cities, did not occur here in the 19th and 20th centuries. Little was built, and there were few major changes to the existing building fabric. A conspicuous feature of Giudecca is the large **Molino Stucky** complex (now a Hilton Hotel). Giovanni Stucky planned to build a mill and pasta factory, and commissioned the architect Ernst Wullekopf from Hanover to provide designs. Construction began in 1896. Its historicizing neo-Gothic forms, castle-like character and brick construction reveal the north German origins of the architect. The pavilions on the site of the **Biennale** were designed by famous architects in the late 19th century and the 20th century. However, as their task was to represent individual nations in the pavilions, they did not relate to the Venetian style of architecture. **Carlo Scarpa** ran an architectural practice in Venice from 1927 and was particularly concerned with interior design. In 1952, he was entrusted with planning the restoration of the Accademia, in 1953–1960 that of the Museo Correr, and in 1961–1963 of the Galleria Querini Stampalia. Scarpa's feeling for scale and fine decoration can also be seen in the salesroom of Olivetti (1957/1958) on the north side of Piazza di San Marco. He sensitively designed the room around a central pillar, contrasted colours and materials, and skilfully combined the old with the new. **Frank Lloyd Wright**'s design for a house on the Canal Grande was rejected in 1953 after bitter negotiations.

Since 2004 practically the whole old city is under monument protection. Today Venice is trying to set accents along the outer edge of the Centro Storico through contemporary architecture and art. The Japanese **Tadao Ando** restored in 2005 on order of the French billionaire Pinault (owner of companies including Gucci, Yves Saint Laurent, since 2011 Brioni) Palazzo Grassi and in 2009 the Dogana da Mar. In 2008 Venice's fourth Canal Grande bridge was opened; Ponte della Costituzione was designed by the Spanish bridge specialist **Santiago Calatrava** (his works include Samuel Beckett Bridge, Dublin, and Kronprinzenbrücke, Berlin). **Renzo Piano** from Genua (his works include with Richard Rogers the Centre Pompidou in Paris and parts of the Potsdamer Platz in Berlin) delivered plans for the

Death(s) in Venice

Melancholy, mysterious, morbid – these attributes are frequently bestowed on Venice. Those who have experienced the city in fog or fine rain may be able to understand this. It is therefore no surprise that Venice's own particular charm has inspired writers and filmmakers: to dark stories which send a shiver down the spine of readers or audiences.

However, in other films Venice provides a joyous, romantic or exotic backdrop for pleasurable holidays, carnivals, colourful thrillers or spy films. Katherine Hepburn, in David Lean's *Summertime* (1955), plays an old maid who vacations in Venice and blossoms when she meets Rossano Brazzi, who fills the role of the Italian cavalier particularly well. In *The Venetian Affair* (1966), Elke Sommer stars in a spy story revolving around a suicide bombing. And in *The Venetian Woman* (1986), Sean Connery experiences the joys of love.

Black Comedy

However, the true Venice film is a different matter altogether. It not only presents the city's beautiful façade, but also tempts people to come and then diverts them from their course – not only in a geographical sense. Something of this atmosphere is found in *The Honey Pot* (1965), a black comedy by Joseph Mankiewicz in which Rex Harrison awaits three former lovers, plays the dying rich man to them and plans murder.

City of Errors

That the crumbling façades conceal an abyss, that the sinking city has a strange effect on visitors

and residents and may become the place for obsessions, becomes clear in Luchino Visconti's *Senso* (1953). Alida Valli plays an Italian duchess who, against her convictions, falls in love with an officer of the Austrian occupying forces (played by Farley Granger) during the Italian wars of liberation. She wants to escape him and flees through the empty alleys at night. Finally, her lover catches up with her, and later she even turns traitor. 17 years after Senso, Visconti's film of Thomas Mann's novella *Death in Venice* was a declaration of love for the city. The composer Aschenbach comes for recuperation. But Venice, which is threatened by cholera, is the wrong place. He falls in love with a beautiful boy. The magnificent images of the film exude an elegiac atmosphere, culminating in the final scenes in which the dying musician (Dirk Bogarde) lies in a deck chair on the beach, hair colour running across his face.

City of Obsessions

Obsessions and death are also at the centre of Nicolas Roeg's thriller *Don't Look Now* (1973). After the accidental death of their child, an English artist couple (played by Donald Sutherland and Julie Chris-

Scene from Visconti's film *Death in Venice* (1970), starring Björn Johan Andrésen and Silvana Mangano

tie) comes to Venice to forget. But the city brings back dreadful memories, particularly to the husband. Again and again, he sees a figure in a red coat running through the dark alleys, and believes he is seeing his child. The illusion finally leads the man, who has second sight without knowing it, to his death.

Playing with Death

The Comfort of Strangers is the name of a thriller filmed in 1990 by Paul Schrader and based on a nov-

el by Ian McEwan. In this film, a couple (Rupert Everett, Natasha Richardson) travels to Venice to refresh their slightly stale love in the place where it once began. They too go astray, lose their way and run into the arms of a man played by Christopher Walken, who, together with his wife (Helen Mirren) involves them in a game which in this city – by now this should be no surprise – can only lead to disaster. Once again, a movie plays on the mysterious, morbid atmosphere of Venice and ends in death.

restructuring of the Magazzini del Sale on the Zattere to an atelier museum for Emilio Vedova (1919 – 2006). The extension of the cemetery island San Michele is being planned by the offices of **David Chipperfield** (works include Museum Folkwang, Essen, restructuring of Museumsinsel, Berlin). The Canadian **Frank Gehry** (works include Guggenheim Museum, Bilbao) is supposed to develop the harbour basin of the airport to Venice Gateway starting in 2012 – but due to Italy's financial crisis the financing has not been cleared yet. In late 2011 the Benetton family bought Fondaco dei Tedeschi, one of the most formal grand buildings on the Canal Grande. They then commissioned the Dutch architect **Rem Koolhaas** to draw up plans for converting the house into a luxury store.

Since Berlusconi administration repealed the property taxes and thus closed of the cash flow to the communities Venice has amassed €400 mil. in debts. Huge financing gaps for monument preservation have opened up since almost all of the budget is flowing into the financing of the MOSE floodgates ("p. 26). The consequences: more and more companies are buying historic palazzi and remodelling them as they wish. So the former central post office in the Fondaco dei Tedeschi is being remodelled on plans by the Dutch star architect Rem Koolhaas into a shopping centre with bright red escalators; and the Benetton family want the faded wall frescos by Giorgione and Titian to be resurrected as trendy comic strips. Not all of the Venetians like this commercialization of public spaces. They like the cultural aide Tiziana Agostini are afaraid that »... the cultural depth of this city will be lost.«

EARLY PRINTING

In the 15th century, Venice gained importance as a major centre of printing. In 1469, Johannes de Spira (»from Speyer«) set up the first printing press in the city and introduced the Gutenberg press with moveable type. He obtained the exclusive right to carry out printing in Venice for five years. One year later already, in 1470, de Spira died, whereupon his privilege became null and void. This was a stroke of luck for numerous competitors, who immediately opened their own print works and began to produce at a lively rate. Book printing in Venice rapidly developed from an art into an important sector of the economy. The fact that individual works could be protected with copyrights by obtaining a privilege encouraged this boom. For economic reasons, privileges as wide as that given to de Spira could no longer be granted. Rights therefore extended only to one book title and included printing as well as sales. Apart from many Venetian printers, the city attracted large numbers of **German printers**. The best known printer around 1500 was **Aldus Manutius** from Bassiano, founder of the Aldine Press. He had a flourishing establishment on Campo San Luca, still commemorated by an plaque today (at the side entrance of the savings bank). In 1495, he obtained a monopoly in Greek prints, which made large sales in Venice and elsewhere. Another significant printing press was headed by **Lucantonio Giunta**, who mainly printed liturgical works in Venice and worked closely with his brother in Florence, who specialized in humanist literature. Aside from religious works, classics in various languages, humanist literature, natural science textbooks, dictionaries and, from 1501, sheet music were published. The extensive collection of manuscripts left to the city by Cardinal Bessarion constituted an important resource for the printers. Venice was able to maintain its position as a printing city without loss of quality to the end of the 16th century. Today the

Gianni Basso in his printing workshop

business card printer Gianni Basso continues the tradition of Venetian Tradizione della Stampa using lead type and hand presses (Cannaregio, Calle del Fumo 5306, tel. 04 15 23 46 81).

JACOPO, GENTILE AND GIOVANNI BELLINI

Through stays in Florence and Rome and by working at the mar-   Painters
grave's court in Ferrara and in the university city of Padua, **Jacopo**
Bellini (c.1400 – c.1470/1471), as a student of Gentile da Fabriano,
learned the powerful naturalistic painting style of the early Renaissance and combined it with the Gothic elegance that was still typical
of Venice. He painted Madonnas in nuanced colours and soft lines.
His outstanding draughtsmanship reveals his study of antiquity,
while his narrative painting skills – a mixture of rich fantasy and depictions of reality – prepared the way for Venetian historical painting.
His sons Gentile and Giovanni learned the art of painting from their
father, but were also influenced by their brother-in-law Mantegna
and became internationally known masters. **Gentile** (c.1429–1507)
was the eldest son of Jacopo and a famous portraitist, who always
succeeding in depicting his subject in a psychologically empathetic
manner. He stayed at the court of the sultan in Constantinople in
1479–1481, among other things for the purpose of portraying the Ottoman ruler. In Venice, his realistic views of the city, his keen powers
of observation in depicting rich and poor, young and old, as well as
the richness of his scenes, are impressively shown in – among other
works – the cycle on the miracles of the true cross in the Accademia.
His younger brother **Giovanni** (c.1430–1516) is the main representative of early Venetian Renaissance painting. Few other artists of the
time possessed Giovanni's drawing style and palette of luminous colours, which was not least due to the new technique of oil painting
which he learned from Antonello da Messina. His often lyrical images, ranging from half-length Madonnas to mysterious allegories,
display both intimacy of emotion and admiration for nature. The
colour harmonies, the graduated light and the atmospheric quality of
his landscape backgrounds also fascinated Albrecht Dürer, who met
Giovanni Bellini in Venice in 1506 and asserted: »He is the best in
painting«. Excellent works by Giovanni can be seen in the Accademia as well as in the Frari church and in San Zaccaria.

MASSIMO CACCIARI (* 1944)

The intellectual as mayor, the »philosopher on the doge's throne«: the
bearded Kant specialist has completed the political masterstroke of
defending his home city of Venice from 1993 – 2000 and 2005 – 2010
as a red island in Berlusconi's Italy. This also has to do with the university professor's down-to-earth roots. His local patriotic programme started with the dredging of the canals – since the end of the

Peggy Guggenheim on the roof of her palazzo (1950s)

Serenissima 200 years ago every Italian government has put it off. His scolding of tourists feeding pigeons or his relentless promoting of the rebuilding of Teatro La Fenice after it burned down is unforgettable. But his government also stands for blatant advertising on the walls of historic construction sites, the growing number of cruise ship day trippers and the conversion of living space into B & Bs. In 2010 the political thinker (*L'arcipelago*) and aesthete, who once turned Rilke's Duino Elegies into a libretto for the composer Luigi Nono, returned to the freedom of academia.

CANALETTO (ANTONIO CANAL, 1697 – 1768)

Painter Canaletto was one of the last great Venetian painters. Born in Venice, he began as a theatre painter, then studied in Rome and turned to natural observations. In Venice, he initially had great success with vedute, a style of painting in which cityscapes are painted in great detail. He was also known for working from nature instead of in studios, as was the custom then. But his work became so popular that he later had to work from drawings due to lack of time. After his second stay in Rome in 1742, he began to paint ideal landscapes. City views with authentic detail and full of atmosphere, in which people moved about in carnivals, festivals and processions, finally became his trademark. In the years 1746–1750 and 1751–1753, Canaletto stayed in England, where most of his works are today. In Venice, paintings by Canaletto can be admired primarily in the Accademia.

? MARCO POLO INSIGHT

Did you know?

More than 200 paintings by Canaletto show the city with photographic precision. He even recorded the slimy belt of algae on house walls. Precisely this detail was of interest to environmental scientists at the Istituto di Scienze dell'Atmosfera e del Clima in Padua, which, among other things, used these paintings as evidence for the scarcely perceptible sinking of Venice.

GIACOMO GIROLAMO CASANOVA (1725 – 1798)

Man of Letters and the World The Venetian Giacomo Casanova , Chevalier de Seingalt – to give him the noble title he invented for himself – gained a legendary reputation as a master of the arts of love and a frivolously cultivated lifestyle. On his journeys throughout Europe in the service of various masters, he met famous contemporaries from the worlds of politics and literature, such as Frederick the Great and Voltaire, and never failed to break the hearts of ladies. Imprisoned in Venice in 1755 for atheism, Casanova successfully made an adventurous escape from

the leaden chambers of the Palazzo Ducale in 1756. After a restless wandering life, he finally found a position as librarian to Duke Waldstein in Dux (Bohemia) in 1785. It was here that he wrote his famous memoirs, as well as a utopian novel and historical, mathematical and literary writings. As early as the mid-19th century, the adventurer, who is regarded to this day as the personification of uninhibited seduction, became the subject of literature himself.

PEGGY GUGGENHEIM (1898– 1979)

»I have always done what I want and never cared what others thought. Women's lib? I was a free woman long before the name existed.« Peggy Guggenheim lived a stormy life, personally and as a collector. In the early 1920s, the »enfant terrible of the capitalist class« joined Bohemian society in Paris and married painter and author Laurence Vail, which did not, however, prevent her from entering into close relationships with numerous artists such as Marcel Duchamp, Samuel Beckett and Max Ernst. She opened her first gallery, Guggenheim Jeune, in 1938 in London with a Cocteau exhibition. A meeting with writer and art historian Herbert Read was decisive for Peggy Guggenheim. With his aid, she wanted to open a museum in London, similar to the New York Museum of Modern Art. However, this failed due to the start of the Second World War. Instead, she returned to Paris and rapidly acquired the foundation of her collection – with the motto »Buy one painting every day.« She returned to New York in 1941. The most important events of the New York years were her marriage to Max Ernst, the founding of the legendary gallery »Art of this Century« and the discovery of Jackson Pollock. When her marriage to Max Ernst collapsed, Peggy Guggenheim moved to Venice in 1947. In 1948, she exhibited paintings from her collection in one of the Biennale pavilions, a breakthrough which brought her recognition as a collector. In 1949, she purchased Palazzo Venier dei Leoni, which still houses her collection, one of the main attractions in the venerable city.

Bohemian and collector

CLAUDIO MONTEVERDI (1567 – 1643)

The music of Claudio Monteverdi was influential far beyond the 17th century. He was born in Cremona, studied composition in his home city until 1590, and then acted as court musician and conductor in

Composer

Mantua until 1612. From 1613 until his death he held the position of musical director of St Mark's Basilica in Venice. Initially working in the polyphonic *a capella* tradition of the 16th century, Monteverdi developed increasingly free musical forms. The high points of his work are the operas *Orfeo* (1607) – which marks the beginning of opera as a genre – *Il Ritorno d'Ulisse in Patria* (1640) and *L'Incoronazione di Poppea* (1642), which influenced European opera up to the time of Richard Wagner.

MARCO POLO (C.1254 – 1324)

Discoverer   Marco Polo was the greatest adventurer of Venice and the most important European traveller in Asia in the Middle Ages. His experiences changed his contemporaries' view of the world and encouraged Europeans to explore far corners of the earth. In 1271, 16-year-old Marco Polo, with by his father Niccolò and his father's brother Matteo, two Venetian merchants, began a trading journey to Asia. The journey took 24 years. It first led via Anatolia through Persia and Turkmenistan to China. They reached Peking in 1275. Marco Polo worked for the local ruler Kublai Khan, grandson and successor of the legendary Genghis Khan, from 1275 to 1292. Kublai Khan sent Marco Polo on extensive journeys to Asiatic countries and all the way to India. He learned much, among other things the Chinese art of porcelain manufacture and the processing of silk and cotton. He saw how trade was conducted in China with »flying« money, i.e. paper money instead of coins made from precious metals. In 1292, Marco Polo received permission to return to Europe. He journeyed back through the South China Sea, past the coasts of Vietnam, Malacca, Sumatra, Ceylon and western India to Hormuz, and on via Persia, Armenia and Trabzon to Constantinople, where he boarded a ship for Venice. He dictated the report of his travels to his fellow prisoner Rustichello da Pisa while imprisoned in Genoa (September 1298 to July 1299) and soon thereafter *Il Millione* (*The Wonders of the World*) was translated into other languages, and had a great influence on geographical ideas in the 14th and 15th centuries.

SANSOVINO (JACOPO TATTI, 1486 – 1570)

Architect   Few builders have influenced the appearance of Venice as strongly as Sansovino, a native of Florence whom the Venetians commissioned from 1527 onwards to redesign the city in the High Renaissance style.

No fewer than 15 churches and public buildings were built wholly or partially by him, including St Mark's library, the mint (Zecca), the Loggetta next to the Campanile, the church San Francesco della Vigna and the Palazzo Corner. The statues of Mars and Neptune in the courtyard of the Doge's Palace and the vestry door of San Marco as well as the tomb of Doge Venier in San Salvatore also bear witness to his great talent as a sculptor.

GIAMBATTISTA TIEPOLO (1696 – 1770) AND GIOVANNI DOMENICO TIEPOLO (1727 – 1804)

As the outstanding painter of Venetian Rococo, **Giambattista Tiepolo** was commissioned by the doge and noble families to paint numerous altarpieces, murals and ceiling frescoes for churches, palaces and villas of the city and in other places in northern Italy. Further commissions led him to the residence of the Prince Bishop of Würzburg and the royal court in Madrid. Bold foreshortening and strong light effects in combination with a free, transparent application of colour are the hallmarks of his work, which can be seen, among other places, in the Accademia, in Sant'Alvise, the Scuola Grande dei Carmini and Palazzo Labia. **Giovanni Domenico** learned the art of painting from his father and was an equal partner in the most significant commissioned works until his father's death. His style is generally more anecdotal, the colouration softer, and his paintings avoid the complicated figure composition of his father's works. In old age, Domenico increasingly devoted himself to genre paintings, and painted carnival and Pulcinello scenes.

Painters

TINTORETTO (JACOPO ROBUSTI, 1518 – 1594)

Tintoretto has a place in the history of Venetian art not only as a Mannerist painter with a rich variety of ideas and as a painter of the Counter-Reformation era, but also as an artist with significant commercial abilities. The son of a silk dyer (*tintore*, the derivation of his pseudonym), he accepted every offer of work and tried to drive his numerous competitors out of business by quoting the lowest prices. Born in Venice, he only left the city of his birth once – a journey to Mantua in 1580 is proven – but was nonetheless influenced by the major artistic trends of his time. Strong contrasts between light and dark, bold foreshortening and views from below, and unusual lighting effects are characteristic for his paintings, which frequently depict dramatically composed scenes from the Old and New Testaments. In Venice, many of his altar paintings are in the Accademia collection, in the Doge's Palace, in numerous churches (Madonna dell'Orto, San Giorgio Maggiore, San Marcuola, Santa Maria della Salute) as well as in the Scuola Grande di Rocco with fabulous wall and ceiling paintings.

TITIAN (TIZIANO VECELLIO, 1488/90 – 1576)

Painter   From Cadore Valley in the Dolomites, Titian came to Venice in the early 16th century and received decisive impulses for his painting from Giovanni Bellini. After the great success of his commissioned works between 1510 and 1526, including the Assunta altarpiece and the Pesaro Madonna in Venice's Frari church, Titian rapidly rose to be a favourite painter at the courts of European princes. The d'Este, Gonzaga and Farnese showered commissions on him. François I of France held him in high esteem, and Charles V made Titian his court painter in 1533. In his late period, Titian worked almost exclusively for his son, the Spanish king Philip II. Titian's extensive works, which could not have been carried out without a large atelier of assistants, include altar paintings, mythological works, nudes and allegories as well as a considerable number of portraits. Stylistically, Titian stands at the threshold from High Renaissance to Mannerism. Colour harmonies as well as strong contrasts between light and dark, dynamic diagonal compositions, atmospheric landscapes and the ability to satisfy the need of the ruling class for official representation are the essence of Titian's fascinating works. His technique and breadth of composition set an example for the following centuries.

VERONESE (PAOLO CALIARI, 1528 – 1588)

Painter   Paolo Caliari, also called Veronese, since he was born in Verona, was the brilliant chronicler of Venetian joie de vivre. Together with Tintoretto and Titian, he is regarded as the most important painter of late Renaissance Venice. From 1553, he worked in the city, where his sensual themes even gave him trouble with the Inquisition. He was able to handle the large number of orders only with the aid of a large atelier and assistants. His large-format compositions with numerous figures, among them magnificent celebrations and banquets, are conspicuous for their richness of colour and the lively depiction of persons. In Venice, works by Veronese are to be found in the church San Sebastiano (ceiling and wall paintings), in the Gallerie dell'Accademia (*Banquet in the House of Levi*) and in the Doge's Palace (ceiling and wall paintings; here is the climax of his late work, *The Triumph of Venezia*).

ANTONIO VIVALDI (1678 – 1741)

The exceptionally gifted violinist Antonio Vivaldi was the most im-   Composer
portant Venetian composer, and his development of the solo concerto form made a major contribu-
tion to European music. In 1703,
Vivaldi was ordained to the priest-
hood, and in the same year he became the maestro di violino at the
Venetian girls' orphanage Ospedale
della Pietà, where, with few interruptions, he also worked until 1740
as a conductor and house composer.
Vivaldi's style influenced many com-
posers, including Johann Sebastian
Bach, who adapted several of Vivaldi's violin works for the organ or
cembalo. Aside from about 500 concerts (of these 241 alone for violin as
solo instrument), which excel
through rich nuances of instrumen-
tation, emotional melodies and lively rhythms, Vivaldi also composed
more than 90 sonatas, 46 operas – of
which 21 have survived – and three
oratorios. In 1740 he went to Vienna
probably because his music was no
longer modern; but he was not able
to get established here and died after
just a few months on July 28, 1741.

ENJOY VENICE

Enjoy Venetian cooking, stroll through shops with real souvenirs, wind dowen the evening in a relaxed bar ... Here are a lots of suggestions.

Accommodation

B & B in a Palazzo?

Venice has a wide range of hotels in all categories from luxury
to basic accommodation. The prices are above average, especially in the high season. This runs from carnival through
Easter to late October. At this time reservations are an absolute must

Charming inexpensive rooms are not to be had in Venice. Anyone
who has to watch his budget when booking a room could easily land
in a small, dark, run-down hotel room – even though renovations
have been noticeable for some years. A large number of Venice's historic buildings are cramped and small – the city was considered to be
overcrowded in the Baroque period already. B&Bs, which have
sprouted everywhere in recent years, make for a more pleasant experience however. **Bed and Breakfast**, English style, some with contact
to the host family is a good way to experience the Venetians' everyday
life and with a little luck, to stay in a fascinating historic setting. But
this is not without controversy because it means that more and more
living space is being dedicated to tourism.

The best places to stay

Alongside there are luxurious hotel dreams – nights in the Gritti
with its Canal Grande terrace or the Danieli make operatic dreams
come true. Venice is also a playground for aesthetes and designers.
Some of them have made their own dreams come true with enchanting »Small Charming Hotels«. An example in the up-market segment
is the Ca' Maria Adele with its moorish candle holders, while a more
inexpensive location is the guesthouse of the glassblower clan Orsoni. True in general is: the further from St Mark's Square and the
Rialto Bridge, the more imaginative the accommodations and guest-
houses. Another alternative is rooms or apartments rented by the
week.

The wise will visit the Serenissima of the laguna during the **low season**. Winter prices can fall to as little as 30% of the high season prices!

Since Venice has many visitors throughout the year, especially during
the main season, for carnival and for major events, it is recommended to make reservations in advance. Individual travellers can obtain
help from the reservation centre VeneziaSì of the hotel association
Associazione Veneziana Albergatori (AVA), call centre tel. 04
15 22 22 64 and 199 17 33 09 (daily 8am – 11pm), www.veneziasi.it.

Booking

**One of the most beautiful places for breakfast: the terrace of Hotel
Bauer with a view of Santa Maria della Salute**

The VeneziaSì offices in Venice will also help find a hotel room: at the Piazzale Roma (Garage Comunale, Garage S. Marco), in S. Lucia railway station, in Marco Polo Airport as well as at the traffic circle Villabona Sud / Marghera. Other accommodation addresses at www.venicehotels.com.

Recommended hotels

Price categories

€ Double room up to €150
€€ Double room €150–250
€€€ Double room €250–400
€€€€ Double room over €400

Since the summer of 2011 Venice also has a tassa di soggiorno (= **hotel tax**). It varies from 2 to 4 euros, depending on the hotel category.

❶ etc. ▶Plan p. 80/81
No number: outside of plan limits

❶⑦ Danieli €€€€
Castello, Riva degli Schiavoni 4196,
tel. 04 15 22 64 80
www.danieli.hotelinvenice.com
One of the most famous hotels in the world in the 14th-century palazzo of Doge Enrico Dandolo; exquisite furnishings and perfect service right on Piazza San Marco. Diners in the much-lauded panorama restaurant have an unforgettable view across the lagoon to San Giorgio Maggiore and the Lido.

㉒ Luna Baglioni €€€€
San Marco, Calle Larga dell'Ascensione 1243
tel. 04 15 28 98 40
www.baglionihotels.com
Oldest hotel in Venice, magnificent furnishings; perfect service.

⑲ Londra Palace €€€/€€€€
Castello, Riva degli Schiavoni 4171
tel. 04 15 20 05 33
www.hotellondra.it
Elegant four-star city hotel with British atmosphere – Tchaikovsky composed his fourth symphony here. View of the promenade and the lagoon.

㉖ Gritti Palace €€€/€€€€
San Marco, Campo Santa Maria del Giglio 2467
tel. 04 17 94 611
www.hotelgrittipalacevenice.com
The palace was built in the early 16th century for Doge Andrea Gritti. In 1585, it was given to Pope Sixtus V. Writers like Hemingway described this legendary hotel with the exclusive restaurant Club del Doge.

㉙ Molino Stucky €€€ – €€€€
Giudecca 810
tel. 04 12 72 34 90
www.molinostuckyhilton.it.
Venice's largest and newest luxury hotel is housed in a restored 19th-century mill and has 380 rooms! Fantastic view from the terrace bar. The northern European style brick building was built in 1896 by the Hanover architect Ernst Wullekopf for the pasta producer

Hotel Londra Palace on Riva degli Schiavoni

Gustavo Stucky and was empty for almost 50 years after 1954 until the Hilton chain restored it.

Excelsior €€€ – €€€€
Lungomare Marconi 41, Lido
tel. 04 15 26 02 01
www.hotelexcelsiorvenezia.com
Open April – October
Luxury oasis in neo-Moorish style on the south side of the Lido; boat transfer from the Lido to Piazza San Marco.

San Clemente Palace €€€€
Island of San Clemente
tel. 04 12 41 34 84
www.sanclementepalacevenice.com

Luxury hotel in a 17th-century convent on a private island south of Giudecca.

⑩ Concordia €€ – €€€€
San Marco, Calle Larga 367
tel. 041 52 06 85 66
www.hotelconcordia.com
The only hotel with a view of St Mark's Basilica. Magnificent decor, cosy and comfortable

㉔ Flora €€ – €€€€
San Marco, Calle Larga XXII Marzo 2283a
tel. 04 15 20 58 44
www.hotelflora.it
Romantic 17th-century palazzo, wonderful gardens.

Hotels

Where to sleep
1. Domus Orsoni
2. Florida
3. Giorgione
4. Ca' Bonvicini
5. Al Ponte Antico
6. Rialto
7. Ca' della Musica
8. Locanda Silva
9. Serenissima
10. Concordia
11. Casa Verardo
12. Bisanzio
13. La Residenza
14. Cavalletto & Doge Orseolo

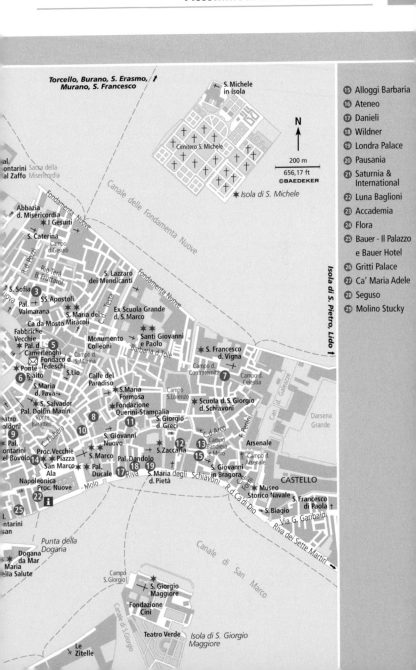

Torcello, Burano, S. Erasmo,
Murano, S. Francesco

S. Michele
in Isola

Cimitero S. Michele

N

200 m
656,17 ft
©BAEDEKER

Isola di S. Michele

Canale delle Fondamenta Nuove

al.
ontarini
al Zaffo

Sacsa della
Misericordia

Abbazia
d. Misericordia
I Gesuiti

Fondamenta Nuove

S. Caterina

Campo
d.Gesuiti

R. d. Pozzi

Rio Tera
B. Fruttarol

S. Sofia 3
Pal.
Valmarana

SS. Apostoli

uova

S. Lazzaro
dei Mendicanti

Fondamenta Nuove

S. Maria del
Miracoli

Ex Scuola Grande
d. S. Marco

Ca da Mosto

Fabbriche
Vecchie
Pal. d. 5
Camerlenghi

Monumento
Colleoni

Santi Giovanni
e Paolo

Fondaco d.
Tedeschi

Campo d.
S. Marina

Barbaria d. Tole

S. Francesco
d. Vigna

Ponte
Rialto 6

S.Lio

Calle del
Paradiso

Campo d.
Confraternita 7

Campo d.
Celestia

S.Maria
d. Fava

S.Maria
Formosa

Campo
S.Lorenzo

Scuola d. S. Giorgio
d. Schiavoni

Can. d. Galeazze

S. Salvador
Pal. Dolfin Manin

Fondazione
Querini-Stampalia

S. Giorgio
d. Greci

Darsena
Grande

Ponte
Barattieri

8

eatro
oldoni 9

Chiovere

10

S. Giovanni
Nuovo

S.Zaccaria

C.d. Arco

Campo
Bandiera
e Moio

Arsenale

R. Penini

Pal.
ontarini
el Bovolo 14

Proc.Vecchie
Piazza
San Marco
Ala
Napoleonica
Proc. Nuove

S. Marco
Pal.
Ducale 17

12
18 19
Riva

13
15

S. Giovanni
in Bragora

Campo d.
Arsenale

11

S.Maria degli
d. Pietà

Schiavoni R.d.Ca di Dio

CASTELLO

22 i

Museo
Storico Navale

S. Biagio

S. Francesco
di Paola

Punta della
Dogana

Via G. Garibaldi

25

I.
ntarini
san

Dogana
da Mar
Maria
ella Salute

Campo
S.Giorgio

Canale di San Marco

Riva dei Sette Martiri

S. Giorgio
Maggiore

Fondazione
Cini

Canale di S.Giorgio

Teatro Verde

Isola di S. Giorgio
Maggiore

Le
Zitelle

Isola di S. Pietro, Lido

15 Alloggi Barbaria
16 Ateneo
17 Danieli
18 Wildner
19 Londra Palace
20 Pausania
21 Saturnia &
International
22 Luna Baglioni
23 Accademia
24 Flora
25 Bauer - Il Palazzo
e Bauer Hotel
26 Gritti Palace
27 Ca' Maria Adele
28 Seguso
29 Molino Stucky

㉕ Bauer – Il Palazzo e Bauer Hotel €€ – €€€€
San Marco,
Campo San Moisè 1465
tel. 04 15 20 70 22
www.bauervenezia.it
Luxury accommodation on the Grand Canal a few steps from Piazza San Marco, panorama restaurant.

! *Nice discounts* **Insider Tip**

MARCO POLO TIP

Booking via Internet can pay – many places offer Internet last-minute discounts. An easy-to-use portal is Hotel Reservation Service (www.hrs.de). After opening the site set the language in the upper right-hand corner.

❸ Giorgione € – €€€€
Cannaregio, Campo Santi Apostoli 4587
tel. 04 15 22 58 10
www.hotelgiorgione.com
Very romantic atmosphere in a 15th-century palace.

❺ Al Ponte Antico € – €€€€
Cannaregio,
Calle dell'Aseo 5768
tel. 04 12 41 19 44
www.alponteantico.com
Lovingly converted palazzo on the Grand Canal with a view of the Rialto bridge.

❻ Rialto € – €€€€
San Marco,
Riva del Ferro 5149
tel. 04 15 20 91 66
www.rialtohotel.com
Nice four-star hotel right by the Rialto Bridge.

⑫ Bisanzio € – €€€€
Castello, Calle della Pietà 3651
tel. 04 15 20 31 00
www.bisanzio.com
Elegant hotel in a 16th-century building; only 300m/330yd from Piazza San Marco.

⑭ Cavalletto & Doge Orseolo € – €€€€
San Marco, Calle Cavalletto 1107
tel. 04 15 20 09 55
cavalletto.hotelinvenice.com
Top address in the romantic location of a gondola harbour behind the Procuratie Vecchie.

⑯ Ateneo € – €€€€ **Insider Tip**
San Fantin, San Marco 1876
tel. 04 15 20 07 77
www.ateneo.it
Small, pretty hotel with a family atmosphere.

⑳ Pausania € – €€€€
Dorsoduro, Fondamenta Gherardini 2824
tel. 041 52 22 08 36, 27 rooms
www.hotelpausania.it
Lovingly restored 14th-century palace; begin the day restfully on the breakfast veranda in the garden.

㉑ Saturnia & International € – €€€€
Calle Larga XXII Marzo,
San Marco 2398
tel. 04 15 20 83 77
www.hotelsaturnia.it
14th-century palace of a Venetian admiral; beautiful inner courtyard and roof terrace. Family-run

⑪ Casa Verardo € – €€€
Castello 4765, Ponte Storto
tel. 04 15 28 61 38

www.casaverardo.it
Mr & Mrs Mestre has transformed a 16th-century noble palazzo into a Residenza d'Epoca. Fortuny lamps and Rubelli fabrics, breakfast terrace with canal view. House dog Leone is also a real Venetian and named after the St Mark lion.

⑱Wildner € – €€€
Castello,
Riva degli Schiavoni 4161
tel. 04 15 22 74 63
www.hotelwildner.com
Good price, central location.

㉓Pensione Accademia Insider Tip
€ – €€€
Dorsoduro, Fondamenta Bollani 1058
tel. 04 15 21 01 88
www.pensioneaccademia.it
Popular, very pretty accommodation with a view of the canal or a romantic garden.

㉗Ca' Maria Adele €€€
Dorsoduro 111
tel. 04 15 20 30 78
www.camariaadele.it
Modern Venice between orientalism, Baroque and minimalism.

Pensione Accademia seen from the Grand Canal

Townhouse with 12 elegant rooms right next to S. Maria della Salute, once housed the offices of the salt monopoly. Doge's room, Moorish hall, fireplace room, black hall and oriental hall are open to all guests as elegant meeting places. An aesthetic experience

❶ Domus Orsoni € – €€
Cannaregio 1045, Guglie
tel. 04 12 75 95 38
www.domusorsoni.it
Affordable elegance. In the location of the only glass-blowing oven in Venice gold and glass mosaics have been produced for more than 100 years. Family Orsoni has designed the individual rooms and bathrooms uniquely with modern mosaics and will proudly explain the technique. Traditional terrazzo floors, garden and mosaic hall

❷ Florida € – €€
Cannaregio, Calle Priuli 106/A
tel. 041 71 52 53
www.hotel-florida.com
Pleasant house with 25 rooms, quiet situation near the railway terminal.

❽ Locanda Silva € – €€
Castello, Fondamenta del Remedio 4423
tel. 04 15 23 78 92
www.locandasilva.it
Between St Mark's Basilica and Campo S. Maria Formosa on a small canal; no elevator, spotless rooms, friendly staff.

❾ Serenissima € – €€
San Marco, Calle Goldoni 4486
tel. 04 15 20 00 11

www.hotelserenissima.it
The privately managed hotel (no restaurant) is ideally located between the Rialto bridge and Piazza San Marco. It has been in the ownership of the Del Borgo family for over 40 years. Modern art hangs on the walls: the father of the present-day owner was a passionate collector.

㉘ Seguso € – €€
Dorsoduro, Zattere 779
tel. 04 15 28 68 58
www.pensioneseguso.com
Setting of Patricia Highsmith's *Those Who Walk Away*, wonderful view of Giudecca.

⓭ La Residenza € – €€€
Castello, Campo Bandiera e Moro 3608
tel. 04 11 28 53 15
www.venicelaresidenza.com
Stylishly furnished patrician palace.

BED & BREAKFAST
❹ Ca' Bonvicini €
S. Croce 2160,
tel. 04 12 75 01 06
www.cabonvicini.it
Elegant B & B with tastefully furnished rooms.

⓯ Alloggi Barbaria € Insider Tip
Castello 6573
tel. 04 15 22 27 50
www.alloggibarbaria.it
Spartan furnishings in a family-run B&B with a lively Venice blog. Barrier free

❼ Ca' della Musica €
Castello 2954,
Calle del Morion
tel. 04 12 77 04 49

Signora Aurelia is an opera director and Italian language trainer for tenors. She rents out 4 individually furnished rooms in her 13th-century palazzo.

Hotel Villa Mabapa € – €€
Riviera S. Nicolò 16,
Malamoco (Lido)
tel. 04 15 26 05 90
www.villamabapa.com
This villa combines four-star comfort with plenty of 1930s charm; 300m/330yd from the beach and ten minutes by boat from Piazza San Marco. Beautiful restaurant terrace.

B & B Tra Mare e Laguna €
Lido, Via P. Orseolo II 2
tel. 04 12 42 02 04
www.bb-venezia.de
Centrally located accommodation with carefully designed rooms.

BEACH RESORTS OUTSIDE VENICE
Sole € – €€
Sottomarina di Choggia
Viale Mediterraneo 9
tel. 041 49 15 05
Fax 04 14 96 67;
62 rooms
www.hotel-sole.com
Hotel directly behind the beach of Chioggia seaside resort. Beautiful rooms, ample breakfast buffet, own garage.

> **MARCO ⊕ POLO TIP**
>
> *Inexpensive and stylisch* **Insider Tip**
>
> In Villa Revedin near Osoppo 28km/16mi north of Udine, ca. 60km/36mi from Venice, the »sweet life« of Renaissance patricians can be experienced – at a comfortable price. The hotel (A) has a good fish restaurant. Via Palazzi 4, Gorgo al Monticano, tel. 04 22 80 00 33 33, www.villarevedin.it

Holiday Park Pra' delle Torri €
Caorle, Viale Altanea 201
tel. 080 01 81 39 14
www.pradelletorri.it
A paradise for families – everything from a golf course to a car racetrack and giant water slides.

Union Lido Park Hotel Ca' di Valle €
Cavallino, Via Fausta 258
tel. 0 41 96 80 43, 0 41 96 88 84
www.unionlido.com
Perfect hotel for a high-class family vacation, near the beach in extensive holiday village.

Igea €
Padua, Via Ospedale 87
tel. 04 98 75 05 77
www.hoteligea.it
Directly at the Ospedale Civile and easy to find; the centre is within walking distance.

Youth hostels & other accommodation

Youth Hostel – Albergho della Gioventù
The youth hostel is on the island of La Giudecca ►MARCO POLO Tip p.216

Domus Cavanis **Insider Tip**
Dorsoduro, Rio terá Foscarini 912
tel. 0 41 74 09 18, 39 39 27 84 24
www.domuscavanis.org
Excellent location between the

Accademia and the Gesuati church. Simple, well-furnished rooms, double rooms from €60, breakfast in Hotel Belle Arti opposite

Istituto Canossiano San Trovaso
Dorsoduro, Fondamenta de le Romite 1323
tel. 04 12 40 97 11
www.romite1323.com
College run by nuns that also offers accommodation to women (double room without breakfast €110).

Foresteria Valdese in the Palazzo Cavagnis
Castello, Calle Lunga Santa Maria Formosa 5170
tel. 04 15 28 67 97
www.foresteriavenezia.it
Beautiful Waldensian guest house near San Marco (double rooms €110 to €135).

CAMPING · CAMPEGGI

There are many 1 to 4-star camping sites on the Cavallino peninsula and near Mestre or Marghera. The tourist office (▶Information) and www.camping.it provide information. Unauthorized tenting is prohibited. Drivers with caravans or motor homes are permitted to spend one night on a parking lot or at a service station where this is not expressly prohibited.

Mestre – Ca' Noghera
Camping Village Alba d'Oro ★★★★
Via Triestina, S.S. 14, km 10
tel. 04 15 41 51 02
Open year-round

Fusina
Camping Fusina★★
Via Moranzani 93
tel. 04 15 47 00 55
www.camping-fusina.com
Open year-round

Mestre
Campeggio Rialto★
Via Orlanda 16, Campalto
tel. 04 15 42 02 95
www.campingrialto.it

Tessera
Campeggio Marco Polo★
Via Triestina 164
tel. 04 15 41 60 33
Open Feb – Nov

Oriago
Campeggio Serenissima★★
Via Padana 334/a
tel. 0 41 92 18 50
Open April – Oct.

Punta Sabbioni
Marina di Venezia★★★★
Via Montello 6, Cavallino Treporti
tel. 04 15 30 25 11
www.marinadivenezia.it
Open late April – Sept

AGRITURISMO

There are also a few providers of »country holidays« around Venice. Information www.agriturist.it, www.agriturismo.it and www.agriturismo.com.

PRIVATE ACCOMMODATION, APARTMENTS, B & B

Alloggi Temporanei
Castello, Calle Sant'Antonio 5448/a
tel. 04 12 41 14 56

www.mwz-online.com
This agency offers approx. 100
addresses, ranging from individual rooms to spacious apartments.

Private Venice
Campo S. Samuele 3226/b
tel. 04 12 41 14 56
www.privatevenice.com
Small selection of apartments in
palazzi.

Bed & Breakfast
Further information on the many
B&B offerings (▶ Information) and
online, including

www.bed-and-breakfast.it
www.bbitalia.it
www.bbvenezia.com
www.venicehotel.com
www.bedandgo.com

Children in Venice

Never a Dull Moment

With its crooked alleys, innumerable bridges, old palaces and the lagoon, Venice has many attractions for young visitors.

And instead of using cars, locals and visitors alike travel on boats on the waterways. There are plenty of other differences to everyday life back home. A good preparation is the **bestseller** *The Thief Lord* by **Cornelia Funke**, the story of a group of children in winterly Venice. The trick is to find the right balance between culture and entertainment. Here are a few suggestions: aside from trips by vaporetto, traghetto or gondola, the highlights include counting stone lions, taking a boat trip to the islands of Burano and Murano to watch glass blowers at their work, or swimming on the Lido, Lido di Jesolo or Litorale del Cavallino. Just observing everyday life can be very fascinating for children. The market boats with their little watch dogs on the way to the Rialto market, finding out what fire boats look like, where to learn to row will certainly interest the little visitors. However, the 400 bridges are a major obstacle to parents with children in prams, and the canals without railings are a safety risk. In the labyrinth of alleys and in view of the unguarded canals and bridges keeping an eye on toddlers becomes a full-time job. Put a business card from your hotel into each bambino's pocket.

> **MARCO ⊕ POLO INSIGHT**
>
> **?** *Looking for lions*
>
> Venice is said to have about 2,000 lions of St Mark, some big, some small, some with wings and some without. They are found on house walls, bridges, towers, gates and balconies, in paintings and on coats of arms. Sometimes it is necessary to look closely, since they are well hidden.

Insider Tip

There are numerous discounts for children in public transport (up to four years of age) and in museums. For teenagers and young adults, there is the **Rolling Venice pass** (►Prices and Discounts p. 313).

Discounts for children

Offers for Bambini

Sala del dinosauro
The dinosaur hall is an attraction of the Museo di Storia Naturale in the Fontego dei Turchi (►p. 176).

Kids day al Guggenheim
Free workshops for children aged from 4 to 10 years at the Guggenheim every sun afternoon. Infor-

One of about 2,000: the lion of St Mark on the Piazzetta

mation and registration on the Friday before
tel. 12 40 54 44/401, www.guggenheim-venice.it/education/kids_day.html

Fanfaluca
Rio Marin, S. Croce 779
tel. 04 15 28 71 03
Fashion, toys and accessoires for elegant mammas and their bambini.

Il nido delle cicogne
S. Polo 2806, tel. 04 15 28 74 97
In the stork's nest there is fashion made in Italy for children and toddlers.

Kirikù'
S. Polo 1465
tel. 04 12 96 06 19

www.kiriku.it
A must for little fashion victims. Focal point is casual and international labels.

Fate e Folletti ai Frari
S. Polo 373, tel. 04 12 41 34 17
Fairies and fools are the themes of this shop for children's clothing near the Frari church.

Artusi Emporio del Giocattolo
Mestre, Via Antonio Olivi 45
tel. 0 41 95 73 07.
www.artusigiocattoli.it
Since 1947 an institution in toys with a giant selection from miniferraris to dolls. The family-run business could be a reason to make an excursion to Mestre on the mainland.

Venice is not just a tourist attraction. There are signs of everyday life, too, like here in sestiere Castello

Bambolandia
S. Polo 1462
tel. 04 15 20 75 02
Beatrice Perini creates artistic dolls
by hand. A gift with lasting value.

Biking along the Lido
To Forte S. Nicoló and the beaches
or to Malamocco.
Adresses for bike rentals
►MARCO POLO tip p. 225

The Childrens Lagoon
In the lagoon centre, Campo S.
Stefano 2949
www.salve.it (►p. 25)
Every fall starting in September
there are workshops for children
in English and Italian.

Traghetto
Ferry rides across the Canal
Grande for a small fee. But it's important to keep your balance and
also an eye on the little kids.
(► p. 316).

Rowing on the Canal Grande
tel. 04 15 22 80 45
www.incantesimoveneziano.com
1-hour boat ride with rowing
course for 6-13-year old children
(2 – 5 children per gondola).

Pra' delle Torri
Family-friendly holiday park in
Caorle (►p. 85).

Carnevale dei Bambini
Even the carnival sceptics in Venice join in and dress their bambini
as »principessa«, »saraceno« or
»orsotto« (princess, Saracen or
teddy bear). On Campo S. Polo in
the last two weeks of the carnival
season masked actors fascinate
the children from 2.30pm on. Little athletes and ballerinas can try
out the ice-skating rink. Since
2010 a »carnevale dei ragazzi«
with an enchanted forest and
treasure hunt is held on the
grounds of the Biennale
(www.labiennale.org).

Going Out

Nightlife in Venice used to have the dubious reputation of consisting of nothing more than bars in luxury hotels, but that's changed.

The students of Università Ca' Foscari and young people from Vene-to on the mainland, who flock into the Centro Storico on the week-ends, have brought about a network of scene clubs around the open-air meeting place Campo Santa Margherita and in the side canals of Cannaregio. English-style pubs are in fashion. Unlike night cafes, lounges and in-bars, they are often overfilled. Most night-spots close no later than 1am, but there are some exceptions in the trendier quar-ter of Dorsoduro and Cannaregio. But it remains a fact: because of the high population density and the narrow alleys, where each noise echoes, and the increasing age and noise-sensitivity of the residents – very few younger people can afford the high rents or expensive property – Venice is no Mecca for night owls. Cultural alternatives can be found in the theatre, cinema and concert scene. La Fenice, which has been rebuilt several times, is one of Europe's leading opera stages and is worth seeing for the architecture too. An evening with *Troubadour* or *Turandot* can be an unforgettable Venice experience. Concerts with Venetian *settecento* music are held regularly in church-es like San Vidal or San Salvador. Clubbers had better head to the mainland, the beach resorts or Treviso.

Venice's nightlife

MUSIC

Concerts are held in Venice all year round; they are often the oppor-tunity to see palaces from the inside that are usually not open to the public. Since 1930 the Festival of Contemporary Music (Festival In-ternazionale di Musica Contemporanea) has been held every year in late Sept/early Oct as part of the Biennale.
The chamber orchestra performs works from the Baroque, classical and romantic periods. The concerts are held in the Palazzo delle Pri-gioni (next to the Doge's Palace) and the church Santa Maria For-mosa. Info and tickets: tel. 0 41 98 81 55, www.collegiumducale.com. These internationally successful musicians play about 200 times a year in the church San Vidal; their repertoire consist especially of Baroque works including ones by Vivaldi, Bach, Tartini. Info: tel. 04 12 77 05 61, www.interpretiveneziani.com.

Café Florian is one of the oldest, most beautiful and most expensive coffee houses in the world

Gondola rides with music on the Canal Grande and the side canals in Venice are the epitome of romance, but this does not come without a price (info at the tourist office ▶Information).

The daily newspapers Il Gazzettino and La Nuova Venezia as well as the Italian-English brochures LEO Bussola, Venezia News (www.venezianews.it), Un Ospite di Venezia (www.unospi tedivenezia.it), Venezia da vivere (www.veneziadavivere.it) and Meeting Venice (www.meetingvenice.it) have information on events, opening times etc. The latter can be found in all APT offices ("Information) as well as hotels
.

Nightclubs, theatres and more

❶ etc. ▶Plan p.114/115
No number: outside of the plan limits

CINEMAS
❻ **Videoteca Pasinetti**
Palazzo Mocenigo
S. Stae 1990
tel. 04 15 24 13 20
City art house cinema opened in 2008.

❼ **Cinema Giorgione**
Cannaregio 4612
tel. 04 15 22 62 98
Venice's best cinema.

CASINOS
❸ **Palazzo Vendramin**
Cannaregio 2040
tel. 04 15 29 72 30
www.casinovenezia.it
Sun – Thu 3pm – 2.30am, Fri, Sat until 3am
Men are required to wear suit-coats and ties in this high class palazzo. Shuttle service at no charge.

Venice Casino
Via Paliaga 4/8 (at Marco Polo airport)
tel. 04 12 69 58 88
www.casinovenezia.it

Sun – Thu 11am – 2.30am, Fri, Sat until 3am
The informal alternative. American-style games and roulette.

BARS, NIGHTCLUBS, DISCOTHEQUES
❶ **Paradiso Perduto**
Cannaregio, Fondamenta della Misericordia 2539
tel. 041 72 05 81
Student atmosphere, live music Sunday evenings, jazz Monday evenings.

❽ **Muro Rialto Vino e Cucina**
San Polo,
Campo Bella Vienna 222
tel. 04 15 23 47 40
At the Rialto Market. Downstairs: busy, elegant bar; upstairs: good restaurant.

❿ Bacaro Jazz
San Marco,
Salizzada del Fontego dei Tedeschi 5546
tel. 041 28 52 49
Both the jazz music and the drinks are very popular – and very expen-

A legend: Harry's Bar

sive. Fortunately the bartenders know their business.

⑪ Devil's Forest
Rialto, Campo San Bartolomeo
tel. 04 15 23 66 51
Pub with live music.

Madigan's Pub
Dorsoduro, Rio Terra Canal
3053/A
tel. 04 15 20 59 76
Always packed long after midnight, a hint of Irish character.

⑰ Martini Scala
San Marco, Campo San Fantin
1983
tel. 04 15 22 41 21
Piano bar; snacks available until
3.30am.

㉑ La Fenice
San Marco, Campiello della Fenice
1939
tel. 04 15 22 38 56
Artists' favourite next to the Teatro La Fenice, with stylish dining.

㉒ Harry's Bar
San Marco, Calle Vallaressa 1323
tel. 04 15 28 57 77
Restaurant opened by Giuseppe Cipriani and Harry Pickering in 1931 and immortalized by the steadfast drinker Ernest Hemingway in his novel *Across the River and into the Trees*; the cocktail bar is open until 2am, and the gourmet restaurant on the first floor of the building attracts a famous clientele – so cocktails and snacks come at a price.

Teatro La Fenice, Venice's legendary opera house

㉓ Club Piccolo Mondo
Dorsoduro, Calle Contarini Corfù
1056a
tel. 04 15 20 03 71
A stylish club with all the current
hits.

Acropolis
Lido, Lungomare Marconi 22
tel. 04 15 26 04 66
Popular place for disco fans.

**THEATRES,
CONCERTS**
❶ etc. ▶Plan p. 114/115
No number: outside of the plan
limits

❶ Teatro Malibran
Info and tickets:
tel. 0 41 24 24
www.teatrolafenice.it
Opera, ballet, concerts.

❷ Teatro Goldoni
San Marco, Calle Goldoni 4650
tel. 04 12 40 20 11
www.teatrostabileveneto.it
Comedies, especially (naturally) by
Carlo Goldoni.

❸ Teatro Avogaria
Dorsoduro,
Campo S. Sebastiano 1617

tel. 04 15 20 61 30
www.teatro-avogaria.it
Experimental theatre and pieces
in dialects.

❹ Teatro La Fenice
San Marco, Campo S. Fantin
1965
Opera, ballet
▶Sights from A to Z

A Whirl of Festivals

The carnival in Venice ends on Ash Wednesday. But there are other festivals all year round; they are merry, historic or contemplative – something for every taste.

Festa del Redentore is especially popular among Venetians, when on a mild July night everything that floats is put to water and to anchor in front of La Giudecca, sing Venetian barcaroles, watch the fireworks and toast with prosecco. **Festa della Madonna della Salute** is also a real local meeting place with a pontoon bridge and a meal of mutton. Mulled wine (vin brulé) is served at the **witches' regatta** (Regate delle Befane) on January 6, when the gondolieri wear *streghe* costumes. The opulence of the **Regata storica** with its magnificent boats and rowing competitions attracts so many guests that the police turns the streets of Venice into one-way streets to channel the pedestrian traffic. The **carnival**, which was revived in 1979, has become the absolute tourist attraction – many Venetians leave town during these weeks.

Popular festivals

The daily newspapers *Il Gazzettino* and *La Nuova Venezia* as well as the Italian-English brochures *LEO Bussola*, *Venezia News* (www.venezianews.it), *Un Ospite di Venezia* (www.unospi tedivenezia.it), *Venezia da vivere* (www.veneziadavivere.it) and *Meeting Venice* (www.meetingvenice.it) have information on events, opening times etc. The latter can be found in all APT offices ("Information) as well as hotels.

Event information

HOLIDAYS
1 January: New Year's Day (Capo d'anno)
6 January: Epiphany (Epifania)
Easter Monday (Pasqua)
25 April: Liberation Day 1945 (and the day of San Marco)
1 May: Labour Day (Festa del primo maggio)
2 June: National holiday (Festa della Repubblica)
15 August: Ascension of the Virgin (Ferragosta; family holiday, the climax of Italian summer holidays)

1 November: All Hallows (Ognissanti)
8 December: Immaculate Conception (Immaculata Concezione)
25/26 December: Christmas (Natale)

CALENDAR OF FESTIVALS
JANUARY
Early in the morning of 1 January, people gather on the beach of the Lido – brave souls even take their first swim of the year.

The Regata storica commemorates Venice as a glorious sea power

Madcap Days

January and February are not usually the most popular months in which to travel, not even for Italy. But Venice makes an exception. Because: The first few weeks of the year are also the most crazy ones – carnival!

It is Sunday morning, still ten days before the start of Lent. A dense crowd on St Mark's Plaza stares up to the Campanile, to the large dove that, according to ancient tradition, is pulled up from its belfry to the upper arcades of the doge's palace. Right on the dot at 12 noon, it begins: Colourful balloons rise into the sky and gaudy confetti rains down on the crowd – the Venice carnival is underway once again. There are concerts and costume competitions on stages around the city; the international art scene shines in the theatres and palaces; and on the floating raft in front of the Piazzetta, the Venetian past is reawakened to life. The celebrations continue in the alleys and on the canals of the city on the lagoon until far into the night – until Shrove Tuesday, when a **gigantic fireworks** display ends the foolishness for another year.

Feasting Before the Fast

The first documented record of the Venetian carnival comes from the year 1094. The original heathen purpose of the ceremony was to celebrate the **arrival of spring** after a long winter. The term carnival from the Latin carne vale (= flesh fare well), which arose along with Christianity, initially referred to the last meal before Lent but soon represented all carnival celebra-

tions before Ash Wednesday, since all meat, butter and eggs had to be used up before the fast. Oxen were butchered, sword fights were carried out and masterful acrobatic achievements were performed on St Mark's Plaza in the presence of the doge, high dignitaries and foreign state guests; and of course there was ample gambling which was only permitted during the carnival period, although this lasted almost six months due to special laws. The **processions on the water** with beautifully decorated gondolas were especially elaborate. When the last doge stepped down in 1797 and the French entered Venice, Napoleon banned the infamous Carnevale.

Rebirth

Nearly two centuries passed before resourceful tourism managers rediscovered the legendary masked celebration and revived it in 1979. Venice quickly became a bastion of the carnival. The nearly extinct trades of costume creator and mask-maker experienced a real Renaissance. The **masks** made from paper-mâché, ceramics, or leather have long since become a symbol of the city.

Traditional Costumes

Wearing masks probably originated mainly from **contact with the** orient and Muslim attire. Strictly speaking, masks were only permitted during the carnival; however, the elegant Bautta, a black hood made from velvet or silk that left the face exposed, was also permitted for special festivities. The Bautta was worn with the tricorn (tricorno) and a long black coat (tabarro). The actual mask was white or black and hid the top half of the face; for those who wanted to remain completely incognito, a lace handkerchief on the lower edge of the mask also covered the mouth and chin. The domino, a white cloak similar to a monk's cowl that completely hid its wearer from view, was of Spanish origin. The moretta, a small oval velvet mask, was only worn by women. The mattacini, **colourful fool's costumes** with large feather hats, were very popular. The medico della peste was created as a result of the devastating plague epidemics repeatedly visited upon Venice. With this costume, the coarse plaid and a slouch hat drawn low over the face left only the eyes exposed; the mask with the characteristic over length hooked nose was supposed to filter the mephitic air, and the long staff allowed patients to be examined from a safe distance.

Everyone participates in the carnival in Venice

Arleccino and Co.

The carnival scene was enriched by the figures of the **Commedia dell'Arte**, the most famous among them being the Arlecchino in a colourful costume who is known for his antics. Arlecchino and the imaginative servant Brighella perform as the two Zanni. The female counterpart is Colombina, an adroit maid, while Pulcinella from the back country of Naples embodies the braggadocio. The symbol of the clever Venetian businessman is the Pantalone with a goatee, clad in red knee-breeches, red doublet and a black coat, the beloved moneybag on his belt. The Dottore, a jurist with a hammer nose, is regarded as the parody of intellectual vanity. A special role plays the Capitano with his colourful striped uniform, sword, and wide-brimmed feather hat as a symbol of the revolution against foreign rule and the **epitome of the carnival freedom** to speak one's mind. Although a lot Venetians flee to the mainland to get away from the turbulence of the carnival, many continue to participate in the lively activities; others get together for private balls while the official masked spectacle takes place on and around St Mark's Plaza as a media event. Every carnival has a **different motto**, and it remains a fixed part of the Venetian calendar in spite of any criticism. The best thing to do is to just go along with it and indulge in the ancient longing to slip into the role of another.

No limits to the imagination

Regate delle Befane
»Witches' Regatta« on the Grand Canal on 6 January, the day of Epiphany (Epifania).

FEBRUARY
Carnevale di Venezia
Carnival begins 14 days before Ash Wednesday and lasts until Shrove Tuesday. The burning of Pantalone on a pyre symbolizes the end of carnival. Then revellers go to Riva degli Schiavoni to the church of Santa Maria della Pietà, where the Ash Wednesday concert (Concerto delle Ceneri) takes place at midnight – the only concert where it is allowed to wear masks.

MARCH
Su e Zo per i Ponti   *Insider Tip*
Marathon for all age groups across the city on a Sunday in mid-March.

Easter: Benedizione del Fuoco
The »blessing of the flame« on the late afternoon of Maundy Thursday is a highlight of Holy Week. In the complete darkness of St Mark's Basilica, the holy flame is first lit in the atrium, then the procession walks through the basilica and lights all candles until the whole church is bathed in light.

APRIL
Festa di San Marco
Feast of the city patron on 25 April. At the time of the republic, this was a state ceremony with solemn processions and Risi e bisi. Today, high mass is celebrated in St Mark's Basilica. In the afternoon, the gondoliers hold their

Regatta dei Traghetti on the Grand Canal. According to an ancient tradition, Venetians give their sweetheart a rosebud, the so-called bocolo.

MAY
Sposalizio col mare
In accordance with tradition, the symbolic marriage of the Serenissima to the sea is celebrated on the Sunday after the Ascension of Christ. Until the end of the republic in 1797, the doge had himself rowed out from the Lido, where he tossed a gold ring into the waters. A 14-day fair attracted merchants from all over Europe; the festivities ended with a banquet for the diplomatic representatives. Today, there is a historic procession on Piazza San Marco, with the mayor as the doge, accompanied by representatives of the church and armed forces. From Riva degli Schiavoni, thousands observe the crossing of the fleet to the Lido, where a simple laurel wreath is now symbolically dropped into the water.

Vogalonga   *Insider Tip*
Rowing regatta (no competition!) on the Sunday after the Ascension of Christ, starting at 8.30am in the Bay of San Marco, via various islands in the lagoon – Sant'Erasmo – San Francesco del Deserto – Burano – Mazzorbo – and returning to the bay of San Marco. Info: www.vogalonga.it.

JUNE
Biennale d'Arte
International art exhibition
▶MARCO POLO Insight, p.215

Fireworks of the Festa del Redentore

Sagra di San Pietro di Castello

In the last week of June, small booths are set up in the piazza before San Pietro, serving wine and Venetian specialities; the Sunday ends with a large prize draw.

JULY
Festa del Redentore

The festival of the Saviour on the third Sunday commemorates the end of the plague epidemic in 1576. It begins on the previous evening with a parade of decorated boats on the Canale della Giudecca and a great firework display. On Sunday, believers cross a temporary bridge to the island of Giudecca, where mass is held in the Redentore church. Traditional dishes are served on the boats and in the alleys. The celebration ends in the early morning hours on the beach of the Lido, where sunrise is greeted with singing and dancing.

AUGUST
Mostra Internazionale d'Arte Cinematografica

International film festival on the Lido, a media event with lots of celebrities from the world of cinema.

Concerto dell'Assunta

Concert on 15 August, the day of the Assumption of the Virgin, in the Basilica Santa Maria Assunta on Torcello.

SEPTEMBER
Regata Storica

The historic gondola regatta on the Grand Canal on the first Sunday in September is a reminder of the great days of Venetian maritime power. Historic figures such as the doge, his wife the dogaressa, the queen of Cyprus and ambassadors take part in a magnificent procession before the start. Four different races take place between 2.30pm and 7pm: the youth regatta, the women's regatta, the regatta with caorlina (type of boat from the neighbouring Caorle) and a regatta with small gondolas. The goal is the Ca' Foscari, where the victors are also honoured. On the second Sunday in September, the boats of the historic regatta are paraded on the Brenta canal.

Sagra del Pesce di Burano

On the third Sunday, fish and wine stands are set up in Burano before the Burano regatta takes place.

Festival di Musica Contemporaneo

Festival for contemporary music, until October.

OCTOBER

Festival del Teatro

Theatre festival throughout the city

Sagra del Mosto di Sant'Erasmo

Insider Tip

Wine festival of the island S Erasmo on the first Sunday with new wine (mosto) and snacks, music, dancing and the only regatta in which women and men participate jointly.

Marathon in Venice

On the second Sunday: the starting point is Strà on the mainland.

The route crosses the Ponte della Libertà to the finishing line Riva dei sette Martiri (info: www.venicemarathon.it).

NOVEMBER

Festa dei Morti

On the first Sunday of the month, lovers give their sweethearts so-called fave – small, coloured cakes of shortcrust pastry.

Festa di San Martino

On 11 November, St Martin's day, children parade through the city. They drum on pots with wooden spoons and sing about the good deeds of St Martin. They are given a small tip for their performance – or more often, to get them to stop. Bakeries sell St Martin on horseback in the form of a pastry with coloured sugar glaze.

Festa della Madonna della Salute

To commemorate the end of the plague epidemic of 1630, a large procession of pilgrims goes from St Mark's Basilica over a pontoon bridge on the Grand Canal at the level of Campo Santa Maria del Griglio to the church Santa Maria della Salute on 21 November. The traditional dish on this day is castradina, made from mutton and savoy cabbage.

Food and Drink

Food Culture in Venice

You can get pizza in Venice, you can get spaghetti in Venice, you can get Coca-Cola in Venice and chips and kebab are becoming more common too. And then there is the authentic Cucina veneziana.

There are tourist restaurants that serve a menù turistico with »Italian food«, but fortunately there are more and more trattorias and osterias that offer regional cooking. **Venetian cooking** has many different fathers and mothers and is among the **most exciting in all of Europe**. The palette of Oriental spices plays as much of a role here as do the products and cooking methods of the Greek islands, which were ruled by Venice for centuries – like pot roast with onions. But the terraferma of the Veneto and the Alpine foothills offer typical products like red Treviso radicchio, yellow asparagus, air-dried goose breast. Add to this the wealth of fish from the lagoon and the tender spring vegetables from islets like San Erasmo. Jewish recipes give the »cucina veneziana« its own note – artichokes and aubergines are said to have come into the European kitchen via the ghetto. And something else is Venetian: eating with a fork. The Byzantine princess Theodora, who married Doge Domenico Selvo (1071 – 1084), provoked people with this »devil's tool«. But by the Renaissance the custom had prevailed as can be seen on the banduet paintings by Veronese.

La cucina italiana

Venice has a wide selection of places to eat. They range from exquisite gourmet restaurants to boring »calorie filling stations« for tourist groups. The variety in prices is just as great – the restaurants in less-visited city quarters are less expensive than those around Piazza San Marco. There are different types of restaurants: apart from the ristorante, there is the more popular **trattoria** and **osteria** and of course the **pizzeria**, where the waiter will not look askance if you ask for the bill, »il conto per favore«, after only a pizza and a glass of beer. For a snack or a cup of coffee in between, go to a **caffè** or stand at the counter of a **bar** or a bacaro (►MARCO POLO Insight p. 116).

Trattoria, osteria, ristorante?

A Venetian meal begins with **Antipasto** (starter), e.g. a selection of seafood like shrimp, jackknife clam (capelunghe), lagoon crabs (canoce) and squid (sepie) or the »local dish« sarde in saor (sapore = Aroma), sardines stewed in sour onions with pine nuts and tiny raisins. The meat of a granseola is considered to be a delicacy. Air-dried San Daniele ham from Friuli is also popular. The first course (**primo**

Order of courses

Fish is essential for Venetian cooking

MARCO POLO INSIGHT

? *Quick snack*

Tramezzini are soft, white triangular sandwiches. They come with a wide range of filling, including shrimps with mayonnaise, tuna and tomato, and egg.

piatto) is often an excellent risotto. Many are vegetarian, with maybe zucchini, radicchio from Treviso or dwarf artichokes. A very tasty specialty is risotto nero (it is coloured black with squid ink).Of the pastas linguine (wider than spaghetti) suit seafood best, like shell fish (ganassete), Venus clams (vongole) or lagoon clams (cape rossoi). Fresh gnocchi is more traditional than pasta, and can be served with rabbit sauce (al sugo di coniglio). There is no lasagne in Venice: here it is called pasticcio and can be filled with fish or radicchio. Soups are less unique, except for the tripe soup (zuppa di trippa).

The second course (**secondo piatto**) could be a fritto misto (baked shrimps and squid). Freshly grilled fish is expensive, but the selection is very extensive (coda di rospo/monkfish, branzino/sea bass, orata/dorade, pesce di S. Pietro/john dory etc.). It is usually charged by weight. A stock fish casserole Vicenza-style (baccalà alla vicentina) is excellent. The typical meat dish is veal liver roasted in white wine and onions (fegato alla veneziana) with polenta. In the winter there is also pot roast (pastizada). During the hunting season there are lagoon duck to be tasted. Among the side dishes (**contorni**) the bitter, dark-green rucola salad, roasted radicchio and forest mushrooms from the Veneto Alpine foothills are recommended.

The most local **dessert** is the sweet, yellow biscuits (buranei) that are duipped into a sweet dessert wine. After espresso a glass with raisins soaked in grappa or sgroppin (vodka mixed with lemon sherbet).

Dining habits

Regardless of the locality, there are some ways in which Italian dining habits differ from those in other countries. For instance, it is not the custom in Italian restaurants to choose your own table. Wait until the waiter directs you to a table. In some cases, the price for service (servizio) as well as the bread and place setting (pane e coperto) are additionally billed. Italians do not eat breakfast in the true sense. In the morning, it is »un caffè e via«, a strong coffee and let's get going. Most hotels do now offer breakfast (**colazione**). However, this is usually insubstantial (and somewhat costly). For a much more interesting environment, go to a bar and order a bun or sandwich (panino or tramezzino) – the »normal« Italian types of coffee are better than the tourist coffee in most hotels. Lunch (**pranzo**) is usually available between 12.30pm and about 2.30pm, while dinner (**cena**) is available from 7pm to about 10pm.

Tips

In hotels and restaurants, service is included in the price; however at least 5 to 10% of the invoice amount is expected as a tip. In bars or cafés, service is frequently not included. In such cases, 10 to 15% is given as a tip. For taxi trips, round up the sum.

Spriz, an aperitif of white wine, Campari, Aperol and sparkling water, is a Venetian speciality but know n beyond its borders now. Wine is the favourite drink, of course. In the past Venetians drank sweet Cyprus wine and their own Malvasia. In the 19th century they drank red wine from Dalmatia; only in 1866 did they go over to Italian wines because of the customs duties. The hour of the wine traders from Apulia had come and wine rooms opened, which in part are still run by their decendants. It was only in the EU that wine growing on a large scale began in Veneto, Friuli and the local Piave regions.

The best-known white wines from Venetia are the dry Breganze Bianco, Bianco di Conegliano, Bianco di Custoza, Gambellara and Soave; the fragrant Friulani and Verduzzo; and Reciotto, a dessert wine. The dry red wines of the Veneto include Barbarano Rosso, Breganze Rosso, Cabernet di Treviso, Friularo, Bardolino, Merlot, Ricioto Amarone and Valpantena as well as the heavy, aged Amarone. Reciotto, Rubino della Marca and Rubino del Piave have a rather flowery bouquet. The sweet Moscato di Arqua is a dessert favourite. Table wines are served open in litre, half-litre and quarter-litre carafes (un litro, mezzo litro, un quarto) and by the glass (un bicchiere). Do not fail to try Prosecco di Valdobbiadone e Conegliano DOC, an outstanding aromatic product of the Venetian wine region

Drinks, wine

▶Language

Throughout Italy, meals end with caffè espresso. However, foreign visitors to Venice favour cappuccino, a caffè with plenty of hot milk and the famous milk foam on top, or latte macchiato (»spotted milk«, that is, a lot of milk and not much caffè). The focal point of the caffè bar is an espresso machine. Seating is rare – customers stand at the counter – furnishings are sparse, but choosing the right coffee is a science. Espresso, which is simply referred to as »caffè« in Italy, is available as double (doppio), corrected (corretto) with grappa, cognac or bitters, and even weak and diluted (ristretto). A simple milky coffee is caffè latte or macchiato (spotted).

Menu

Caffè and cappuccino

Recommended restaurants

Price categories
For a menu consisting of primo (pasta or risotto) and secondo (meat or fish) without drinks:
€ Menu up to €25
€€ Menu €25 – 40

€€€ Menu €40 – 50
€€ €€ Menu over €50

❶ etc. ▶Plan p. 114/115
No number: outside of plan limits

LUSSO ED ELEGANZA

㉘ Trattoria da Arturo €€€€
San Marco, Rio terà degli Assassini 3656
tel. 04 15 28 69 74 (closed Sun)
A tiny gem of a restaurant with matchless fillet of beef (no fish on the menu). Cash only!

MARCO ⊕ POLO TIP

! *Special recommendations* Insider Tip

Al Fontego dei Pescatori: traditional fish recipes, creatively applied.
Due Colonne: excellent pizza; outdoor tables in summer.
Harry's Dolci onGiudecca: magnificent view and slightly lower prices than its »big brother«.
Al Ponte del Diavolo on Torcello: the shady terrace is especially beautiful.
La Bitta: Terraferma-recipes from the Veneto.

㉜ La Colomba €€€€
San Marco, Piscina Frezzeria 1665
tel. 04 15 22 11 75 (closed Wed)
Works of Carrà, Chagall, De Chirico, Oskar Kokoshka and others grace the walls of the restaurant; the owner, who had an interest in art, let the artists, who were little known at that time, pay him in paintings instead of lire – to the benefit of later visitors.

㉝ Antico Martini €€€€
San Marco, Campiello della Fenice
tel. 04 15 22 41 21
www.anticomartini.com
(open daily)
This elegant restaurant first opened in 1720. The prices are high, the cooking does not always live up to them. The wine bar next door Vino Vino with snacks is really nice.

❽ Poste Vecie €€€
San Polo, Pescheria Rialto 16020
tel. 0 1 72 18 22
www.postevecie.it (closed Tue)
High class restaurant, the oldest in the city (16th century). Stylish dining room, an enchanting garden, normal food.

㊱ Ai Gondolieri €€€
Dorsoduro, Fondamenta Zorzi Bragadin, San Vio 366
tel. 04 15 28 63 96 (closed Tue)
Well-stocked wine cellar; try the raviolini filled with guinea fowl in saffron, veal cheeks with rosemary and the homemade sweets.

TRATTORIE

❶ Da Marisa €/€€
►MARCO POLO tip p. 213

t Osteria La Zucca €€
Santa Croce 1762
Campo S. Giacomo dall'Orio
tel. 04 15 24 15 70
www.lazucca.it (closed Sun)
Open kitchen and door to the canal. The kitchen focuses on vegetarian dishes like pumpkin flan or perfect risotti. A light meat specialty is rabbit in prosecco.

㉞ Quattro Ferri €€
Dorsoduro, Campo S. Barnaba 2754/b
tel. 04 15 20 69 78
Pleasant trattoria with typically Venetian dishes, including fish lasagna, stuffed clams, »schie« (tiny clams) or innards.

㉟ La Bitta €€

Dorsoduro, Calle Lunga S. Barnaba 2753
tel. 04 15 23 05 31 (closed Sun)
No fish, but delicious vegetable and goose dishes from the Veneto. One of the most honest restaurants in Venice.

㉕ Trattoria da Ignazio €€/€€€

San Polo, Calle Saoneri 2749
tel. 04 15 23 48 52
www.trattoriadaignazio.com
(closed Sat)
The typically Venetian riso e bisi tastes as good here as the squid rings cooked in their own ink. Inner courtyard.

❺ Osteria Antico Giardinetto €€€

San Polo, Calle dei Morti 2253, S. Croce 30135
tel. 0 41 72 28 82 (closed Mon)
Very pretty family-run restaurant with outstanding Venetian cooking.

FISH

⓱ Pronto Pesce €/€€   *Insider Tip*

S. Polo 319, Campo delle Beccarie
tel. 04 18 22 02 98
www.prontopesce.it (closed Sun, Mon)
Excellent fish snack bar at the pescheria of the Rialto Market.

❷ Al Fontego dei Pescatori €€/€€€

Cannaregio 3726, Calle Priuli
tel. 04 15 20 05 38
www.alfontego.com (closed Mon)
Bruno Paolato's place for fish and vegetable gourmets waits with ideas like hops risotto with scampi. Small garden, good wines.

❿ Antiche Carampane €€/€€€

San Polo, Rio Terra delle Carampane 1911
tel. 04 15 24 01 65
www.antichecarampane.com
(closed Sun, Mon)
»No Pizza, No Lasagne, No Menù turistico«. Extremely cosy. Don't miss the clam soup and the croccantini with sweet wine.

⓭ Fiaschetteria Toscana €€€

Cannaregio, San Giovanni Crisostomo 5719
tel. 04 15 28 52 81
www.fiaschetteriatoscana.it
(closed Tue, Wed midday)
Venetian cooking despite the name. Tasty lagoon fish and wonderful desserts.

㉙ Corte Sconta €€€

Castello, Calle del Pestrin 3886
tel. 04 15 22 70 24 (closed Sun, Mon)
Fish and seafood, particularly popular in the moleche season. Elegant osteria, it is expected that you order a three-course menu

⓯ Osteria da Fiori €€€/€€€€

San Polo, Calle del Scaleter 2202
tel. 041 72 13 08
Modern interpretations, Michelin star for a long time. Traditional dishes such as mantis crabs, cod puree, wolf fish in balsamico or breaded artichokes.

SNACKS & BACARI

❹, ⓫, ⓬, ⓰, ⓲, ㉓, ㉖, ㉗, ㉚, ㉛, ㉟   For the descriptions to these numbers ▶MARCO POLO Insight p.116

A Selection of Venetian Dishes

The Rhodian specialties are more hearty: they go from favá (flat peas) to moussaká, a casserole made with aubergines, zucchini and potatoes, which is popular all over Greece.

Sarde in saor: One of venice's most popular antipasti goes back to an Oriental recipe for marinading fried fish (in sapore) . The most important ingredients are pine nuts, onions and small, dark currants, whcih were once brought in from the Ionian Islands. The original recipe for sarde in saor can still be found on Ithaka or Zakynthos as savouro.

Insider Tip

Bigoli in salsa: Tasty cucina povera. In this »poor« recipe bigoli pasta (authentic when made from buckwheat) is sautéed in sardine paste with olive oil and sweet cooked onions. But serving it with grated cheese is a severe *faux pas*.

Fegato alla veneziana: Tender veal liver is blanched slightly sweet with white wine and onions, so that it remains as tender as possible. It is served with the classic Veneto side dish: stirred polenta porridge made from corn meal.

Pasta con fasoi: Broken pasta with white beans (fagioli). Once a hearty soup for gondolieri, today a popular winter dish. It can taste wonderful with a good olive oil, but often becomes a pasty appetite killer.

Risi e bisi: A spring recipe for the feast of the city's patron, St Mark on April 25, of which the doge used to get the first portion:
750 g sweet peas (with pods)
400 g Italian risotto rice (Arborio or Vialone Nano)
100 g butter
75 g finely diced streak y bacon
2-3 Shallots (finely chopped)
1 bunch parsley (or fennel greens)
Remove peas from pods and cook the pods with salt to make a vegetable broth by passing the pods through a strainer. In a pot sautée the shallots with a little butter, add the bacon and lett them cook for about five minutes. Add the rice and continue cooking while stirring and continuously adding broth until all'onda thick and creamy (about 15-20 minutes). Add the finely chopped greens, the remaining butter and freshly grated Parmesan cheese if necessary. A Pinot Grigio from the Soave region fits well.

Pasticcio al radicchio: There is no lasagne in Venice: here it is called pasticcio, a name that was picked up in modernGreek, but which goes back to Renaissance recipes. Pasticcio is especially tasty when it is made with bitter red radicchio leaves from Treviso. Other variations are filled with fish or artichoke.

Restaurants, Cafés and other places for entertainment

Restaurants

1. Da Marisa
2. Al Fontego dei Pescatori
3. Osteria La Zucca
4. Al Prosecco
5. Antico Giardinetto
6. Giardino di Giada
7. Boldrin
8. Poste Vecie
9. Pizzeria Due Colonne
10. Antiche Carampane
11. Do Spade
12. Bancogiro
13. Fiaschetteria Toscana
14. Ganesh Ji
15. Osteria Da Fiore
16. Do Mori
17. Pronto Pesce
18. Al Portego
19. Antica Pizzeria La Corte
20. Alla Madonna
21. Ai Rusteghi
22. L'Olandese Volante
23. Al Mascaron
24. Alla Botte
25. Da Ignazio
26. Al Volto
27. Fiore
28. Da Arturo
29. Corte Sconta
30. Da Codroma
31. Al Bacareto
32. La Colomba
33. Antico Martini
34. Quattro Feri
35. La Bitta
36. Ai Gondolieri
37. Cantinone

Bars, Cinemas and Cafes

1. Paradiso Perduto
2. Planet Internet
3. Palazzo Vendramin/Casino
4. Casanova
5. Grom
6. Videoteca Pasinetti
7. Cinema Giorgione
8. Muro Rialto Vino e Cucina
9. Rosa Salva
10. Bacaro Jazz
11. Devil's Forest
12. Rizzardini
13. Boutique del Gelato
14. Café Noir
15. Madigan's Pub
16. Net House
17. Martini Scala
18. Florian/Lavena/Quadri
19. Gran Caffè Chioggia
20. Grom
21. La Fenice
22. Harry's Bar
23. Club Piccolo Mondo
24. Nico
25. Harry's Dolci

Theatres and other stages

1. Teatro Malibran
2. Teatro Goldoni
3. Teatro Avogaria
4. Teatro La Fenice

Liquid Shadows

The bacari (the 1st syllable is stressed) are part of everyday Venetian life: Simple stand-up bars where one can enjoy a few snacks, the genuine cicheti, along with a glass of the normally open house wine from mid-morning until late into the night.

The name »Venetians« is a derivation of »Enetians« (Greek Enos = wine). **Bacari**, reminiscent of the sensuous god of wine Bacchus, is what the typical Venetian wine taverns are called. Here one can enjoy a glass of wine at an ancient wooden counter; mainly fresh, light selections such as a Pinot Bianco, Tocai, Chardonnay, or Merlot. This is accompanied by simple **cicheti**, appetizing titbits which are usually home-made according to traditional recipes; croquettes with tuna, stockfish and herb canapés, fried rice and meatballs, anchovy rolls and pickled calamari, stuffed olives, grilled eggplant and artichokes as well as pickled sardines with onions, raisins and pine nuts, the typical Venetian Sarde in saor.

The wine is served »in the shade« of a 100ml/3.5fl oz glass called an **ombra**. It is said that the wine used to be sold on the Piazza San Marco, and that the wine sellers always followed the shade (= Ombra) of the Campanile in order to keep the wine cool. A bacaro is an extremely democratic event. Here, one guest is as good as another and differences in social standing do not apply; there are no language problems, nobody gives you a hard time, but there is lots of communication.

Giro de ombre

These taverns are usually closed on Sundays; numbers ►map p. 114)

④ Al Prosecco S. Croce, Campo San Giacomo dall'Orio 1503, tel. 04 15 24 02 22. Enoiteca (!) popular with Venetians with a garden, an attractive selection of wines and a high level of quality. Bio-prosecco and smoked fish crostini.

⑪ Do Spade, San Polo, Calle delle Do Spade 860, closed Sun/Mon midday, www.cantinadospade.it. The ancient wine tavern »To the Two Swords« is also located next to the Rialto market; it is said that in 1744, Casanova spent an unforgettable night of love with a local beauty in the room of the Bacaro with the same name during the carnival; try the stuffed pig's feet, smoked bull's neck filet, or the spicy tramezzini.

⑫ Bancogiro ►MARCO POLO Tip p. 255

⑯ Do Mori, San Polo, Calle dei do Mori 429. *Insider Tip* One of the oldest and best bacari on the Rialto market; try the tingly layered prosecco cartizze and select from up to 100 different (tiny) delicacies such as steamed artichoke hearts and stockfish tramezzini.

⑱ Al Portego Castello, San Lio 6015. Pretty bacaro with first-class pea risotto and irresistible baicoli.

Very old wine room »To the Two Swords« (Cantina Do Spade)

㉕ **Al Mascaron**, Castello, Calle Lunga Santa Maria Formosa 5225, tel. 04 15 22 59 95; one of the most inventive wine taverns (not exactly cheap). Recommended: Spaghetti with lobster and the traditional castradina con verze sofegae (= smoked mutton with braised savoy cabbage and bacon).

㉖ **Al Volto**, San Marco, Calle Cavalli 4081; a popular place for Venetian youth; well-stocked wine cellar and excellent selection of crostini.

Insider Tip

㉗ **Fiore**, San Marco, Calle delle Botteghe 3461. Rich selection of cicheti, including spicy meatballs and fried fish.

㉚ **Da Codroma**, Dorsoduro, Fondamenta Briati 2540 (closed Thur). Traditional osteria which is popular with students as a hangout and for graduation parties, with various snacks and panini.

㉛ **Al Bacaretto**, San Marco, Calle delle Botteghe 30124; with much sought after tables inside and outside; mixed crowd; imaginative Cicheti.

㊲ **Cantinone** ►MARCO POLO tip p. 260

❼ Boldrin €
Cannaregio, Salizzada San Canziano 5550
tel. 04 15 23 78 59 (closed Sun)
Popular enoteca with culinary delicacies.

㉑ Ai Rusteghi €
San Marco, Campiello del Tentor 5513
tel. 04 15 23 22 05 (closed Sun)
Behind Campo San Bartolomeo a paradise for snack fans is hidden. In this tiny osteria there is an unbelievable selection of crisp, tasty panini. Getting fed in Venice doesn't get any cheaper than this.

㉒ L'Olandese Volante €
Castello, Campo San Lio 5658
tel. 04 15 28 93 49 (closed Sun)
Sit on the small campo with an aperitif or a beer – they have a giant selection – and eat one of the creative sandwiches, salads or pasta dishes.

㉔ Alla Botte €
San Marco, San Bartolomeo 5482, Calle della Bissa
tel. 04 15 20 92 99 (closed Thu, Sun evening)
Typical bacaro just afew steps from the Rialto Bridge, simple, a little cramped. Good selection at acceptable prices.

⑳ Trattoria alla Madonna €€/€€€
San Polo, Calle della Madonna 594
tel. 04 15 22 38 24
www.ristoranteallamadonna.com
(closed Wed)
Very popular old restaurant which specializes in fish, two minutes from the Rialto bridge (market side).

PIZZA
❾ Pizzeria Due Colonne €
San Polo Campiello S. Agostin 2343
tel. 04 15 24 06 85 (closed Sat noon, Sun noon)
Excellent pizza; in summer, there are also tables on the quiet Campo S. Agostin.

⑲ Antica Pizzeria La Corte Ex Birreria €
San Polo, Campo San Polo
tel. 04 12 75 05 70
www.birrarialacorte.it (closed Tue)
Very good pizza, modern furnishings. In the summer, tables on the Campo.

ETHNIC RESTAURANTS
❻ Giardino di Giada €
San Polo, Calle dei Botteri 1659
tel. 0 41 72 16 73. (closed Tue)
Considered to be Venice's best Chinese restaurant. Many Venetian guests.

⑭ Ganesh Ji €
S. Polo, Fondamenta Rio Marin 2426
tel. 0 41 71 98 04 (closed Wed, Thu)
Meticulous Punjabi cooking since 1997. Popular with students.

BURANO
Trattoria da Primo e Paolo €€
Piazza Galuppi 285
tel. 0 41 73 55 50 (closed Mon)
Cosy eatery, home cooking and fish dishes.

Riva Rosa €€/€€€
Via S. Mauro 296
tel. 0 41 73 08 50
www.rivarosa.it (Mi. und Mo. bis
Do. abends geschl.)
Top quality fish from the lagoon
like risotto with mackerel or white
shrimp with white polenta.

Da Romano €€€
Via Galuppi 221
tel. 0 41 73 00 30
www.daromano.it (Di. geschl.)
Good standard, popular restaurant with typical Venetian dishes.

Al Gatto Nero €€€€
Fondamenta della Giudecca 88
tel. 041 73 01 2 (expensive)
Cosy trattoria on the other side of
the canal at the fish market.
Excellent fish dishes and local specialities.

MURANO
Antica Trattoria Muranese €
Fondamenta Riva Longa 18
tel. 0 41 73 96 10 (closed Tue and
Wed midday)
Pleasant trattoria with a lovely
garden.

SANT'ERASMO
Ristoro Ca' Vignotto €€
Via Forti 71, tel. 04 15 28 53 29
www.vignotto.com (closed Mon.
and Sun to Wed evenings)
Alessandro and Gabriele spoil
their guests with outstanding
cooking, the castraure (young artichokes) are especially delicious.

TORCELLO
Al Ponte del Diavolo
€€/ €€€
▶MARCO POLO tip p. 289

LE VIGNOLE
Trattoria alle
Vignole €
tel. 04 15 28 97 07
Open: April – Sept,
closed Mon
Popular restaurant with day-trippers on the vegetable island. Fish
and grilled meat. Call ahead.

CAORLE
Enoteca Enos €
Via della Serenissima 5
tel. 04 21 21 21 99
www.enotecaenos.com
(in the summer daily)
More than 30 wines by the glass,
finger food from Veneto and
lunch snacks. An institution since
1958. Jazz evenings.

CAVALLINO
Da Achille €€
Piazza S. Maria Elisabetta 16
tel. 041 96 80 05 (closed Mon)
An institution in Cavallino. Won-
derfully fresh fish and clams.

CHOGGIA
Ristorante and Trattoria
Eden €€
Calle Airoldi 152/B
tel. 04 15 50 04 25 (closed Mon)
Simple restaurant in a side alley of
Corso del Popolo. Good fish at
moderate prices.

JESOLO
Antica Jesolo €€
Piazza 1 Maggio 2
Jesolo Paese
tel. 04 21 95 14 70
(closed Mon)
Inexpensive restaurant with sophisticated cuisine and pizza from
wood-burning oven, terrace.

CAFÉS AND ICE CREAM PARLOURS

The first person to speak, or rather write, about coffee in Italy was Gian Francesco Morosini, who was the ambassador of the Serenissima to the sultan of Constantinople from 1582 to 1585: »In Turkey, they drink a black water made from a seed called 'cave'; it is said that it can keep people awake.« The **first caffè** of the city is said to have served the bitter Turkish beverage as early as 1647. Drinking coffee became very fashionable; in the 18th century, there were eight coffee houses on Piazza San Marco alone. In Venice today there is a caffè bar on every major piazza, with a large selection of beverages ranging from coffee and tea to juices and beer, aperitifs and wine. Snacks are often sold as well – freshly baked goods in the morning, buns or sandwiches at noon, cream tarts, biscottini and other sweets in the afternoon.

CAFES AND ICE CREAM PARLOURS

❺ , ⑳ Grom
Dorsoduro, Campo S. Barnaba and
Cannaregio 3844 (Ca' d'Oro)
www.grom.it
Venice branches of the Turin ice cream parlour that uses the best ingredients like Piemont hazelnuts, Amalfi lemons and highland cocoa.

❾ Rosa Salva Insider Tip
Castello, Campo SS. Giovanni e Paolo 6779
www.rosasalva.it
Pretty, old café with excellent dolci – meanwhile also visited by Commissario Brunetti fans. More branches: S. Marco, Calle Fiubera/C. Forner, San Salvador 5020 and Isola di San Giorgio.

⑫ Rizzardini
San Polo 1415, Campiello dei Meloni
Mon, Wed – Sun 7am – 8pm
Wood-panelled pasticceria and tiny bar. Wonderful home-baked

dolci and salted almonds to go with your sprizz.

⑬ La Boutique del Gelato Insider Tip
Castello, Salizzada S. Lido 5727
Considered to be the best ice cream parlour in Venice.

⑱ Florian / Lavena / Quadri
Piazza San Marco
The three famous, but also expensive cafés are still among the most beautiful in the world.

⑲ Gran Caffè Chioggia
San Marco, Piazzetta 11
Formal, expensive, with a view of the Doge's Palace.

㉔ Nico
Dorsoduro, Zattere ai Gesuati 922
Inimitable ice cream specialities. Try the tartufo!

㉕ Harry's Dolci
▶MARCO POLO Tip p.216

INTERNET CAFES
❷ Planet Internet
Cannaregio 1519

Rio terà San Leonardo (open daily 9am – 11pm)

④ Casanova
Cannaregio 158/a, Lista di Spagna
Disco and music bar as well as Internet café (Internet daily 9am – 2am, club Thu – Sat until 4am)

⑭ Cafè Noir
Dorsoduro, Calle San Pantalon 3805

Daily 7am–2am
This cyber-café is where Venice's Internet fans meet for surfing or next door for a cup of tea or a beer.

⑯ Net House
San Marco 2967/2958
Campo Santo Stefano/Calle de le Botteghe
(open daily round the clock)

Shopping

All is Art ...

Venice is famous for its masks, fine Burano lace and artistic glasswork from Murano. There is also a wide range of unusual textiles, in some cases made to old designs (Fortuny), but also to modern designs (Rubelli).

Shopping in Venice is much more than just shopping. It is a lesson in aesthetics and culture that inspires respect for manufacture and fashion. In no other small city in the world have as many craftsmen and small shops survived: frame gilders, cabinet makers who decorate Baroque chests with rocailles, silk-makers, paper makers, restorers of historical musical instruments, jewellers who make Moor's head brooches out of onyx and gold, the colourful sparkle of Murano glass goblets and the lustre of mirrors and murrina necklaces. Of course, Italy's greatest couturiers from Armani to Versace have flagship stores here, but there is also fashion »made in Venice«. Like velvety papusse in all colours of the spectrum – gondolieri slippers and a silk scarf by Fortuny will give you a unique look, especially when you wear your own hand-made Venetian mask to the local ball at home.

More than just shopping

> **? MARCO ⊕ POLO INSIGHT** *Mask-making*
>
> To make leather masks, a wooden model is needed; for paper masks, a plaster model. The model is stuffed with many layers of papier machè, which has been soaked in glue. Visitors to Alberto Sarria's shop can watch how he and his colleagues produce traditional and modern masks (San Polo, Ruga Rialto 777, where the small theatre is occasionally used for performances; and Santa Croce 1807, near S. Stae vaporetto stop, tel. 04 15 20 72 78, www. masks venice.com).

The city is expensive. This is especially true in the stores around Piazza San Marco, the so-called Mercerie between the Rialto and Piazza San Marco, as well as in Calle Larga XXII Marzo. But it's fun to hunt for a pair of chic boots in the more reasonable boutiques in one of the less luxurious shopping streets such as Lista di Spagna or Strada Nova in Cannaregio, or to be waited on in one of the wonderful old lingerie shops or to buy a simple espresso machine in one of the labyrinthine houseware shops. However, it is useful to know that many of the goods on offer are no longer produced in native studios, but in countries with low wages.

Shopping streets

Very few people know how to make marbled paper by hand

Venetian Crafts

»Venice is a completely unbelieveable city. Nothing here is natural, everything is art.« Massimo Cacciari

(Marbled) Paper

Ebru – is what the Turks called the marbled paper they invented. Delicate and beautifully patterned, it has been handmade in Venice since the 17th century. Among the masters of his craft is Alberto Valese. Each sheet of his high-quality paper is unique, made by dotting, spattering or spraying the colour. The custom of drawing flowers onto the glue layer came from Turkey. If the marbled pattern is inter-rupted regularly by dark stripes, then the paper is made in the Spanish style. The versatility of marbled paper can be seen in the selection in Valese's shop. Valese's »Lightstones« – lights made from marbled paper, which can easily be confused with real stones – show also how modern it can be.

Ebru-Alberto Valese
San Marco, Campo S. Stefano
tel. 04 15 23 88 30
www.albertovalese-ebru.it

Stefano Nicolao
Cannaregio 2590
tel. 04 15 20 70 51
www.nicolao.com

Stefano Nicolao – King of Costumes

He studied art and architecture, worked as a theatre set designer and belongs to the small circle that revived the Venetian carnival in 1979. In his picturesque studio in the Sestiere Cannaregio Stefano Nicolao produced masks and costumes that seem to spring from his unquenchable fantasy, but which are still based on historical fact. Tens of thousands of robes and hoops, masks and coats are crammed into his stock, neatly sorted by centuries. His costumes can also be rented.

Stefano Nicolao shows an historical costume

Good shopping addresses

ANTIQUES
Antiquus
San Marco, Calle del Botteghe 2973, tel. 04 15 21 01 06
High-quality Murano glass antiques, also rarities from England and France.

Grafica Antica
San Marco, Calle Larga XXII Marzo 2089, tel. 04 15 22 71 99
Old engravings and historic city views of Venice.

ART GALLERIES
Il Capricorno
San Marco, San Fantin 1994
tel. 04 15 20 69 20
Renowned avant garde.

Totem – Il Canale
Dorsoduro, Accademia 878/b
tel. 04 15 22 36 41
Contemporary art from northern Italy.

Il Traghetto
San Marco, Campo Santa Maria del Giglio 2460
tel. 04 15 22 11 88
Modern art from Italy and North America.

BOOKS
Goldoni
San Marco, Calle dei Fabbri 4742
tel. 04 15 22 23 84
The bets »normal« bookseller, Venice literature.

Librairie Française
Castello, Campo Santi Giovanni e Paolo 6358, tel. 04 15 22 96 59
Books in various languages.

Toletta
Dorsoduro, Sacca della Toletta 1214
tel. 04 15 23 20 34
Good modern used bookshop.

CARNIVAL
Bac Art Studio
Dorsoduro, San Vio 862 (east of the Accademia)
tel. 04 15 22 81 71
Beautiful prints about the carnival.
▶Masks and costumes

DEPARTMENT STORE
Coin
Cannaregio, Fontego Salizzada San Crisostomo 5787 (at the Rialto)
The only department store; a stylish range of goods.

FABRICS
Mario Bevilacqua
San Marco, Fondamenta Canonica 337b
tel. 04 15 28 75 81
Brocade fabrics, tapestries and finest scarves.

Frette
Calle Larga XXII Marzo 2070
tel. 04 15 22 49 14
Bed-linen to die for.

Fortuny
▶ p. 288

Rubelli
San Marco 3877
Palazzo Corner Spinelli
tel. 04 15 23 61 10
Wondrous designer fabrics.

Traditional glass-making on Murano Island

FASHION
The winter end-of-season sales run from January until about 2 weeks before carnival begins; enough time to shop for practically the latest fashion.

Borsato
San Marco, Calle Vallaresso 1318
tel. 04 15 22 55 25
Selected alta moda.

Camiceria San Marco
San Marco, Corte Barozzi 2137
tel. 04 15 22 14 32
First-class tailored shirts and finest fabrics.

Fiorella Show by Fiorella Mancini
San Marco, Campo San Stefano 2806
tel. 04 15 20 92 28
Unusual fashions. The androgynous doge figures as window dummies are a curiosity.

Giuliana Longo
San Marco, Calle del Lovo 4813
tel. 04 15 22 64 54
Interesting hat creations, gondolier's caps.

FOOD AND DRINK
Mascari
▶MARCO POLO Tip p.255

Aliani Gastronomia
San Polo, Ruga Rialto 654
tel. 04 15 22 49 13
The displays are a joy to the eye – ham and biscotti, pasta and other delicacies, nothing but the best.

Giacomo Rizzo Insider Tip
Cannaregio, Calle S. Giovanni Crisostomo 5778
tel. 04 15 22 28 24
Pasta in the craziest shapes and colours (like gondolas) since 1905.

Rizzo
San Marco, Calle dei Fabbri 933/A
tel. 04 15 22 33 88

A treasure trove of culinary traditions of Venice; giant selection of specialized bakery items.

GLASS
Barovier & Toso
Murano, Fondamenta dei Vetrai 28
Palazzo Contarini
tel. 041 73 90 49
www.barovier.com
The workshops of the famous glass blowers use traditional techniques and modern designs.

Cenedese
Piazza San Marco 40/41
tel. 04 15 22 93 99
Best Murano glass shop in Venice.

Eugenio Ferro
Murano, Fondamenta Navagero 75
tel. 041 73 92 99
Lamps and chandeliers.

Nason & Moretti
Murano, Calle dietro gli Orti 12
tel. 0 41 73 90 20
www.nasonmoretti.it
Modern glass art for the table.

Gambaro & Poggi
Murano, Fondamenta Manin 1
tel. 0 41 73 65 76
Classically transparent or trendy colours – Mario Gambaro and Bruno Poggi have been creating vases, pitchers, glasses, lights and other treasures for almost 30 years.

Glimpse of Venice
Dorsoduro, San Vio 723
tel. 04 15 22 56 28
Large, colourful selection from various producers.

Venini
San Marco, Piazzetta Leoncini 314
tel. 04 15 22 40 45
Murano vases and other items by Carlo Scarpa and Tapio Wirkkala.

GONDOLA ROWLOCKS
The traditional forcole, as the rowlocks of Venetian gondolas are called (►MARCO POLO Insight, p.264), are sold at:

Carli S.d. Brandolisio
Castello, Calle Rotta 4725
tel. 04 15 22 41 55

Spaziolegno
Castello, Fondamenta del Tintor 3865, tel. 04 15 22 56 99

Saverio Pastor
Dorsoduro, Fondamenta Sorenzo detta Fornace 341 (between the Collezione Guggenheim and the Salute church)
tel. 04 15 22 56 99
www.forcole.com

Casellati
San Marco, Calle Larga XXII Marzo, tel. 04 15 23 09 66
Largest antique dealer in the city.

HERBS   Insider Tip
Il Melograno
Campo S. Margherita 2999
tel. 04 15 28 51 17
Oldest and best-stocked herbalist in Venice.

JEWELLERY
Salvadori
San Marco, Mercerie San Salvador 5022
tel. 04 15 23 06 09
Exclusive jewellery since 1857.

!
MARCO ◉ POLO TIP

Banco 10   Insider Tip

A charity shop that supports reha-
bilitation: fashion, clothing and
handbags from the tailoring shop
of the women's prison on Giudecca. Even Teatro La Fenice has had
theatre costumes made here, Castello, Salizada S. Antonin 3478a,
Mon–Sat 10am – 5.30pm, tel.
04 15 22 14 39.

Paropamiso
Castello, Campo S. Marina 6051
tel. 04 15 23 58 88
Unusual pearl jewellery, including
foreign items.

LACE
Jesurum
Piazza San Marco 60/61
tel. 04 15 22 98 64,
Mercerie del Capitello 4856
tel. 04 15 20 60 85
The best place to get first-class
lace.

Kerer
Castello, Calle Canonica 4328a
tel. 04 15 23 54 85
A famous shop.

Merletti d'arte Martina
Burano, Strada San Mauro 307
tel. 0 41 73 55 23
www.martina-lace.com

La Perla
Burano
Via Baldassarre Galuppi 287
tel. 0 41 73 00 09

LEATHER GOODS AND SHOES
Rolando Segalin
San Marco, Calle dei Fuseri 4365
tel. 04 15 22 21 15
The best made-to-measure shoes,
since 1932, from creative to crazy.

MARBLED PAPER
Legatoria Piazzesi
San Marco, Campiello della Feltrina 2511
tel. 04 15 22 12 02
Imaginative paper prints and pup-
pet theatres.

Paolo Olbi
Cannaregion, Campo S. Maria
Nuova (near the church S. Maria
dei Miracoli) and Calle Bandi 5478
San Polo, Calle della Mandola
3653.
In addition to handmade paper,
there are also beautifully bound
books and albums.

Carteria Tassotti
S. Marco 5472
Calle de la Bissa
tel. 04 15 28 18 81
Luxurious Bassano paper

MARKETS
The largest market is open Mon
– Sat 7am – 1pm (fish market
also closed on Mondays) around
the Rialto bridge. In the Castello
district, in Via Garibaldi, fruit,
vegetables, fish and household
goods are sold on weekdays from
7am. Smaller markets with vegetable, fish and flower stands are
open in the mornings in Cannaregio on the Ponte delle Guglie, in
Dorsoduro on Campo Santa
Margherita and in the San Marco
quarter on Campo Santa Maria
Formosa. On Campo San Barnaba, fruit and vegetables are sold
from boats.

MASKS AND COSTUMES
Alberto Sarria
Studio and shop, ▶MARCO POLO
Tip p.123

Laboratorio Artigiano Maschere
Castello, Barbaria delle Tole 6657
tel. 04 15 22 31 10
Masks patterned by old engravings.

Tragicomica
San Polo, Calle dei Nomboli 2800
tel. 041 72 11 02
Gualtiero dall'Osto makes masks
and costumes, for the Arena in
Verona or the Teatro San Carlo in
Naples among others.

La Venexiana
Castello, Ponte Canonica 4322
tel. 04 15 23 35 58
Magnificent theatre and carnival
masks.

METAL GOODS
Valese
San Marco, Calle Fiubera 793
tel. 04 15 22 72 82
Gondola irons, door knockers etc.

WOOD ART
Livio de Marchi
Livio de Marchi, San Marco, San
Samuele 3157a
tel. 04 15 28 56 94
www.liviodemarchi.com
Everything wooden – from curtains
to furniture, from cars to books.

! MARCO ⊕ POLO TIP

Lanterns from Venice Insider Tip

They are a unique product – traditional Venetian lanterns of glass
and wrought iron frames whose
production demands great skill. A
unique souvenir from Venice as
well as a testimony to ancient
craftsmanship, available solely
from La Fucina del Ferro Battuto,
Cannaregio, Strada Nova 4311,
tel. 04 15 22 24 36.

Through Venice

Venice's Centro Storico is easy to explore with a city map and a good guidebook. But if you have special interests or little time or just like to be led then individual guided tours make for a special experience.

No visit to Venice is complete without at least one trip around the city by vaporetto, the »water bus«. Lines 1 and 2 travel the Grand Canal (▶Sights, Grand Canal) in both directions between Piazza San Marco and the railway terminal. Line 1 serves all stops, Line 2 only the most important ones. There is enough time on the way to see the patrician palaces and churches or take a break at a station. Since 2012 there is an extra line called **Vaporetto dell'Arte** (▶Transport, p. 314)

Canal Grande in a vaporetto

Lines 41/51 goes around the centre of Venice counter clockwise, Lines 42/52 clockwise – the latter stops at the Lido, the former stops at Murano. The tour with the 41 takes two hours (incl. Murano). It starts at Riva degli Schiavoni (S. Zaccaria) eats of the Doge's Palace. Then it goes around S. Elena Island and on to Fondamenta Nuove, from there to the north past the cemetery island San Michele to the islands of Murano, which is circled (from here go on to Burano and Torcello). After returning to Fondamenta Nuove it goes on to the district of Cannaregio with the basilica Madonna dell'Orto and through the Canale di Cannaregio to the north end of the Grand Canal, leaving it again at Piazzale Roma to head through the western harbour to the Guidecca Canal, reaching the Piazza San Marco again opposite San Giorgio Maggiore.

Vaporetto tour

A special feature of Venice is the lagoon, a labyrinth between the ocean and the land with canals, salt marsh and gardens, islands and islets. Excursions, some with sail and motor boats are organised by »Nonno Renzo« in Chioggia (www.escursioninonnorenzo.it, tel. 32 98 18 64 06). Excursions with ACTV ferries are offered by the guides mentioned previously.

Excursions into the lagoon

The recommended tour guides on p. 132/133 have various tours on offer; they are also open to suggestions like: Venice with children. How did Venice function as a sea power? Venice's city quarters. Architectural tour. Contemporary art in Venice. Biennale. In Commissario Brunetti's footsteps. Venice and music. Excursions into the lagoon.

Recommended theme tours

For romantics: a ride in a gondola

Active in Venice

There are supposed to be 398 bridges in Venice … There is a race called »Su e Zo per i ponti« – »up and down the bridges«. In the full 9.4km/5.6mi version runners cross 42 bridges and in the short version (5.3km/3.2mi) 28 bridges!

But you don't have to have run the race (www.suezoperiponti.it) to be justifiably worn out after a day full of art treasures and shopping – walking around Venice all day is an athletic feat in itself. But it goes faster too: there's a running conversation online about different jogging routes. The most important question: how late in the morning can you still jog across St Mark's Square before it's overrun by tourists?

Sports or Culture?

Apart from that decide beforehand what you really want to do. Venice's Centro Storico is simply made for art, dolce vita and shopping. Anyone who really wants to be active should head for the water or the islands. Various rowing clubs offer courses in Venetian rowing – but you usually have to join the club to take part. **Voga alla veneta** is not exactly easy. The rowers stand facing the direction of travel and the row rests in a forcola, an open oarlock.

Moreover, rowing or angling is a good way to experience the fascinating island world of the laguna.

Swimming in Venice

The closest beach is on the ▶Lido, Venice's green lung. Here you can swimm, stroll, bike or play gold along long sandy beaches. But the beaches (stabilimenti balneari) belong to the hotels or commercial owners. At the latter you can rent a changing cabin (capanna), umbrella (ombrellone) and lounge (sdraio). There are public beaches at Alberoni at the south-west and near S. Nicolò Airport at the northeast end of the Lido. Relaxed beach life can be had at ▶Lido di Jesolo or in Sottomarina (▶Chioggia). For water temperatures ▶When to go, p.318.

PERSONAL TOURS
Agency
Agents for authorised English-language guides (guide turistiche) – make sure to reserve in advance:
Associazione Guide Turistiche
San Marco 750
tel. 04 15 20 90 38
www.guidevenezia.it

Our recommendations
Dr. Christina Gregorin
tel. 04 15 20 24 34
www.walksinsidevenice.com
Contemporary art, literature, crafts and slow tourism

Dott. Fiona Giusto
guideinvenice@libero.it
www.venicetours.it

TOURS

Not sure where to go? Here are a few suggestions for beautiful routes that touch the main points of interest in the historic city centre and the lagoon.

Tours Through Venice

Five tours on foot and a small excursion by boat will take you to the lagoon and the main attractions of Venice.

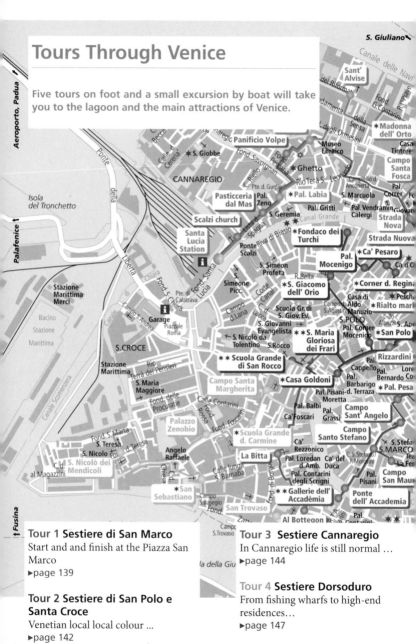

Tour 1 **Sestiere di San Marco**

Start and and finish at the Piazza San Marco

▶page 139

Tour 2 **Sestiere di San Polo e Santa Croce**

Venetian local local colour ...

▶page 142

Tour 3 **Sestiere Cannaregio**

In Cannaregio life is still normal ...

▶page 144

Tour 4 **Sestiere Dorsoduro**

From fishing wharfs to high-end residences…

▶page 147

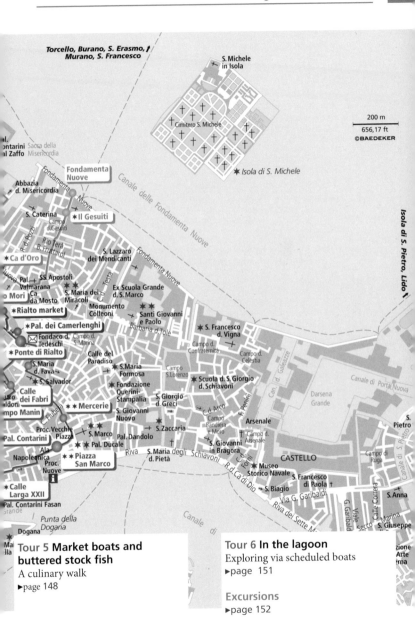

Torcello, Burano, S. Erasmo,
Murano, S. Francesco

S. Michele
in Isola

Cimitero S. Michele

200 m
656,17 ft
©BAEDEKER

★ Isola di S. Michele

Canale delle Fondamenta Nuove

ntarini Sacca della
al Zaffo Misericordia

Isola di S. Pietro, Lido

Fondamenta
Nuove

Abbazia
d. Misericordia

Fondamenta Nuove

S. Caterina   Campo
d. Gesuiti

★ Il Gesuiti

R. d. Pozzi

Rio Terà
B. Friulatol

★ Ca d'Oro

S. Lazzaro
dei Mendicanti

Fondamenta Nuove

SS. Apostoli

Terà

Pal.
Valmarana
o Mori   Ca
da Mosto

★ ★
S. Maria dei
Miracoli

Ex Scuola Grande
d. S. Marco

★ Rialto market

Monumento
Colleoni

★ ★
Santi Giovanni
e Paolo

★ S. Francesco
di Vigna

★ Pal. dei Camerlenghi

Barbaria d. Tole

Campo d.
Confraternita

Campo d.
Celestia

Canale di Porta Nuova

Fondaco d.
Tedeschi

Campo d.
S. Marina

★ Ponte di Rialto

Calle del
Paradiso

★ S. Maria
d. Fava

S. Maria
Formosa

Campo
S. Lorenzo

Scuola d. S. Giorgio
d. Schiavoni

Can. d. Galeazze

Darsena
Grande

★ S. Salvador

★ Fondazione
Querini-
Stampalia

S. Giorgio
d. Greci

C. d. Pignati

Calle
dei Fabri

Ruga

aldoni
po Manin

★ ★ Mercerie

S. Giovanni
Nuovo

Campo
Bandiera
e Moro

Arsenale

S.
Pietro

Proc. Vecchie

Ala
Napoleonica
Proc.
Nuove

★ ★
Piazza

Pal. Contarini

C. Fiubera

★ S. Marco

Pal. Dandolo

★ ★ Piazza
San Marco

Pal. Ducale

★ S. Zaccaria

Campo d.
Arsenale

Canale di Porta Nuova

Campo di
Ruga

★ Calle
Larga XXII

Pal. Contarini Fasan

Riva

S. Maria degli
d. Pietà

S. Maria
in Bragora

R. d. Ca' di Dio

CASTELLO

★ S. Francesco
di Paola †

S. Anna

Punta della
Dogana

Dogana

Canale di

Riva dei Sette M.

Via G. Garibaldi

Viale G. Garibaldi

Secco Marina

S.
Giuseppe

Out and About in Venice

How long
to stay

Is a day trip to Venice worth it? Of course! But it only provides a first impression – no more, no less. Two to three days are the minimum for a short visit. One week is recommended – this allows time to get to know **the different sides of the city**. Palaces, museums and churches with more than 1000 years of architecture, sculpture and painting display **the cultural side of** Venice. At the Biennale and film festivals, the city hosts the **»jet set«**. And in quieter corners, away from the main tourist routes, the **everyday world** of Venice is waiting to be discovered. To see what makes this city unique, a quick trip to the **lagoon** and the islands is a »must«. One week also leaves enough time for trips further afield. Depending on tastes and interests, the options include a **leisurely boat trip** on the Brenta canal, an ancient waterway with long idyllic stretches. For sun, sea air, **sandy beaches** and a swim in the Adriatic, go to the Lido or on the peninsula of Litorale del Cavallino.

Venice is about 1.4 x 4.3 km (0.8 x 2.5 mi) in size and a compact city. Before or after viewing the **main sights**, allow **chance** take over for a while: »It's all right to get lost in Venice – you won't get far in any case. The worst thing that can happen is that you will find the edge and end up looking at the lagoon.« (Tiziano Scarpa, *Venice is a Fish*). It is not possible to get lost. Venice grew out of numerous small islands with their own core consisting of a church, campanile and campo (piazza). Find your way either by the city map, or after searching briefly at a corner for a yellow sign or arrow giving the direction to »Rialto«, »San Marco«, »Ferrovia« (railway station) or »Accademia«, or allow a friendly Venetian to show you the way.

! Don't miss! *Insider Tip*

MARCO ⊕ POLO TIP

- A trip by vaporetto on the Grand Canal
- Piazza San Marco at the south end of the Grand Canal, the heart of the city
- Have a look from the Campanile; it offers a unique view across the city and the lagoon.
- Basilica di San Marco & Palazzo Ducale
- Sample the legendary coffee houses around Piazza San Marco.
- Walk through the Mercerie, the shopping paradise between Piazza San Marco and the Rialto.
- Gallerie dell'Accademia, a treasure chest of Venetian painting
- Boat trip to the lagoon and islands

Sestiere di San Marco   Tour 1

Start and finish: Piazza San Marco
Duration: 1 day

The start and finish of this first tour is Piazza San Marco (St Mark's Square), undeniably one of the most famous squares in the world. The Sestiere di San Marco, the »sixth of the city« that surrounds it, has been the heart of Venice since its foundation. Its luxury hotels, restaurants and shops make it the tourist centre of Venice.

Start at the always busy ❶****Piazza San Marco**, the »most beautiful salon in the world« (Napoleon). To get your bearings, take the elevator to the top of the **Campanile**, which provides a marvellous view across the older part of the city and the lagoon. Next, visit the **Basilica di San Marco** and **Palazzo Ducale** (Doge's Palace), centre of power for centuries. Now leave Piazza San Marco and window shop while slowly walking west along the elegant shopping street ❷****Calle Larga XXII Marzo** to ❸**Campo San Maurizio**. Surrounded by proud patrician palaces, ❹***Campo Santo Stefano**, one of the most spacious squares in the city with numerous cafes, bars and restaurants, is the next stop and a good place for a break before making a detour to the south. A wooden bridge, ❺**Ponte dell'Accademia**, leads across the Grand Canal to the ❻****Gallerie dell'Accademia**, the most significant collection of Venetian paintings. In the Palazzo Venier dei Leoni, slightly down the canal, the **Collezione Peggy Guggenheim** has a fine exhibition of modern art and a chic museum café. Return to Campo Santo Stefano, past the church of the same name to the pretty ❼**Campo Sant'Angelo** and ❽***Palazzo Pesaro degli Orfei**, where there is a museum about the Spanish painter Mario Fortuny, the creator of sensual dreams in silk plissé. At ❾**Campo Manin**, where a monument to the patriotic lawyer Daniele Martin stands, it is worth taking a quick walk to ❿*** Palazzo Contarini del Bovolo**, where the inner courtyard has a lovely spiral staircase dating from around 1500 (currently closed for restoration).

Via Campo San Luca, walk past the stores on ⓫**Calle dei Fabbri** to the Grand Canal or the ⓬***Ponte di Rialto**, which was the only bridge across the canal until the 19th century. Return to Piazza San Marco along the ⓭****Mercerie**, which lure passers-by into shopping heaven. Everything is available here – fashionable clothing stores, carnival masks and costumes, the finest Burano lace, artistic Murano glass as well as jewellery. At the end, relax in one of the cafes around

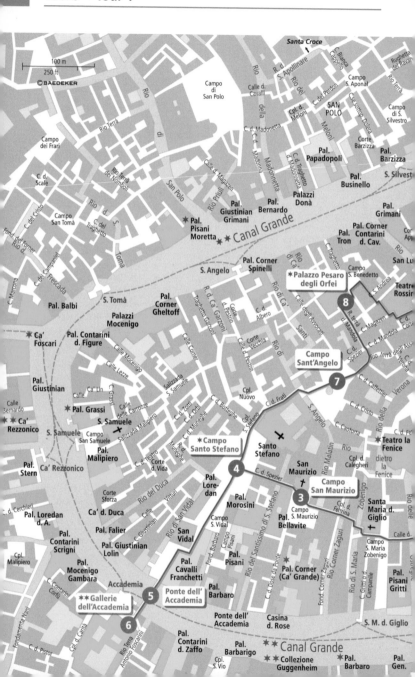

100 m
250 ft
©BAEDEKER

Santa Croce

C. Bianca
Cappello
R. d.
C. d. Perdon
C. de

SAN
POLO
Campo
di San Polo
Calle d.
Cavalli
Campo
S. Aponal
Rughetta
del Ravano
Campo
di S.
Silvestro

Rio
di
Rio Terra
del Nomboli
C. d.
Scale
C. del Cristo
Campo
San Tomà
C. d. Traghetto
C. del
Traghetto
San Polo
Rio Terra
Rio d'
Calle d. Magazen
Rio Frescada
C. Madonetta
C. d. Madonetta
C. d. Madonetta
C. d. Traghetto
di Madonetta
della
Madonetta
Meloni
Col. d.
Meloni

Campo
dei Frari
Pal.
Papadopoli
Corte
Barzizza
Pal.
Barzizza
Pal.
Businello
S. Silvest

Fond. dei Frari
C. Ai Campaniel
Palazzi
Donà
Pal.
Giustinian
Grimani
Pal.
Bernardo
Pal.
Grimani

★ Pal.
Pisani
Moretta ★★
✦ Canal Grande
Pal. Corner
Contarini
d. Cav.
Pal.
Tron
Pal. Corner
Spinelli
S. Luca
Cor
App

C. Marcona
Pal. Balbi
S. Tomà
Pal. Corner
Gheltoff
S. Angelo
Rio di Ca'
★Palazzo Pesaro
degli Orfei
Campo
S. Benedetto
S. Andrea
Teatro
Rossin

★ Ca'
Foscari
Palazzi
Mocenigo
Pal. Contarini
d. Figure
C. di Ca. Garzoni
Traghetto di Ca.
Calle d. Pestin
C. d.
Albero
Rio degli Avvocati
Santi
R. terra
di Mandola
C. d. Magazen
Cord

Pal.
Giustinian
Calle Mocenigo
Calle Lezze
Corte
Vecchia
Campo
Sant'Angelo
Calle d. Pestin
C. d. Caffettieri
C. d. Mandola
C. d. Spezier
Rio Terra degli Ass
Calle Verona

Calle
Bernardo
★ Pal. Grassi
Ca' Lin
Calle delle Carrozze
C. Grassi
Salizada S. Samuele
Cpl.
Nuovo
C. d. Botteghe
Ca'
S. Stefano
C. d. Frati
S. Angelo
C. d. Cristo
Rio della
C. Fet

★★ Ca'
Rezzonico
S. Samuele
Campo
San Samuele
S. Samuele
C. d. Zorzi
C. d. Orbi
C. d. Muneghe
✦
★Teatro la
Fenice

Pal.
Stern
Pal.
Malipiero
Teatro
Corte
d. Vida
★ Campo
Santo Stefano
Santo
Stefano
San
Maurizio
Rio Malatin
Cpl. d.
Caleghei
dietro
la
Fenice

Ca' Rezzonico
Corte
Sforza
Rio del Duca
Ca' d. Duca
C. d. Spezier
San
Maurizio
Campo
San Maurizio
Santa
Maria d.
Giglio

Cpl.
Malipiero
Pal. Loredan
d. A.
Pal.
Falier
Pal.
Loredan
Pal.
Morosini
Campo
S. Maurizio
Bellavite
Cpl. d.
Feltrina
Calle d.

C. d. Cerchieri
Pal.
Contarini
Scrigni
Pal. Giustinian
Lolin
Campo
S. Vidal
San
Vidal
Campo
Pisani
Rio del Santissimo di S. Stefano
Campo
S. Maria
Zobenigo
Pal.
Pisani
Gritti

Pal.
Mocenigo
Gambara
Accademia
Pal.
Cavalli
Franchetti
Pal.
Pisani
Pal. Corner
(Ca' Grande)
Fond. Corner Zaguri
Rio Corner Zaguri
Rio di S. Maria
Pal.
Pisani
Gritti

C. d. Contarini
Corfù
Rio Terra
Antonio Foscarini
★★ Gallerie
dell'Accademia
Ponte dell'
Accademia
Pal.
Barbaro
Ponte
dell'
Accademia
Casina
d. Rose
Rio di Doxe la Ponte
Campanile
S. M. d. Giglio

Fondamenta Nani
C. d. Pistor
Pal.
Contarini
d. Zaffo
Pal.
Barbarigo
Cpl.
S. Vio
★★ Collezione
Guggenheim
✦✦ Canal Grande
★Pal.
Barbaro
Pal.
Gen.

8
7
4
3
5
6

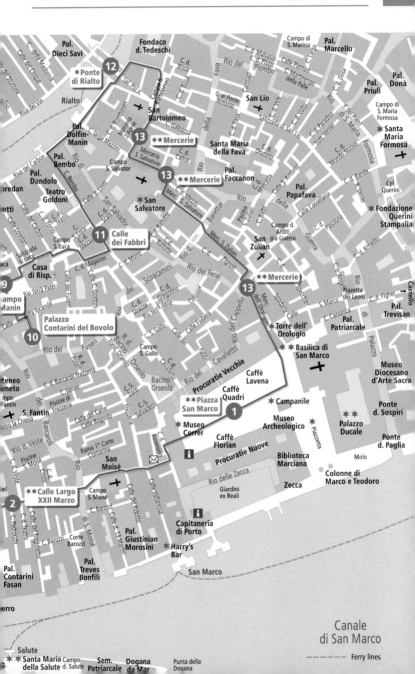

Pal. Dieci Savi

Fondaco d. Tedeschi

Campo di S. Marina

Pal. Marcello

✳Ponte di Rialto

12

Rialto

Pal. Dolfin-Manin

San Bartolomeo

13

✳✳Mercerie

Santa Maria della Fava

Pal. Faccanon

Pal. Bembo

Campo S. Salvator

Pal. Dandolo

Teatro Goldoni

✳San Salvatore

13

✳✳Mercerie

Pal. Papafava

Casa di Risp.

11 Calle dei Fabbri

San Zulian

✳Santa Maria Formosa

Pal. Priuli

Pal. Donà

Campo di S. Maria Formosa

Cpl. Querini

✳Fondazione Querini Stampalia

Pal. Trevisan

9

ampo Manin

Palazzo Contarini del Bovolo

10

Piazzetta dei Leoni

Pal. Patriarcale

Museo Diocesano d'Arte Sacra

✳✳Mercerie

13

✳Torre dell' Orologio

✳✳Basilica di San Marco

teneo eneto

mpo antin

S. Fantin

Procuratie Vecchie

Caffè Lavena

Caffè Quadri

✳✳Piazza San Marco

1

✳Museo Correr

Caffè Florian

Bacino Orseolo

San Moisè

✳✳Calle Largo XXII Marzo

2

Pal. Contarini Fasan

Pal. Treves Bonfili

✳Campanile

Museo Archeologico

Piazzetta

✳✳Ponte d. Sospiri

Palazzo Ducale

Ponte d. Paglia

Molo

Procuratie Nuove

Biblioteca Marciana

Zecca

Colonne di Marco e Teodoro

Giardini ex Reali

Rio delle Zecca

Capitaneria di Porto

Pal. Giustinian Morosini

✳Harry's Bar

San Marco

Canale di San Marco

✳✳Santa Maria della Salute

Sem. Patriarcale

Dogana da Mar

Punta della Dogana

– – – – Ferry lines

❶**Piazza San Marco** and listen to the house musicians over a cappuccino or aperitif while enjoying the unforgettable atmosphere of the square.

Tour 2 Sestiere di San Polo and Santa Croce

Start and finish: Ponte di Rialto
Duration: 6 hours

The second walk leads through the city districts of San Polo and Santa Croce, which are more down-to-earth than San Marco and lie in the upper loop of the Grand Canal. This area contains not only the economic heart of Venice – the Rialto market – but also the fantastic Frari church and the Scuola Grande di San Rocco. Narrow alleys, homes and workshops existing side by side, and many campi and campielli – larger and smaller squares – are features of both districts.

The starting point is the Grand Canal footbridge, ❶*Ponte di Rialto**, between **Fondaco dei Tedeschi** (left bank, Sestiere San Marco) and the lovely ❷**Palazzo dei Camerlenghi** (San Polo). On weekdays from the early morning, ❸*the Rialto market** with its colourful fruit and vegetable stands begins right behind the bridge. A visit to the market is one of the most enjoyable experiences in Venice. The church of San Giacomo di Rialto at the busy Ruga degli Orefici is said to be the city's oldest church. Continue past the Fabbriche Nuove to the **Pescheria**, where fishermen offer their wares every morning (except Sunday and Monday).

Head across Campo S. Cassiano and past the mighty Baroque palace ❹*Corner della Regina** to the imposing ❺*Ca' Pesaro**, where the first floor houses the **Galleria d'Arte Moderna** and the third floor the **Museo d'Arte Orientale**. Only a few steps farther, ❻ **Palazzo Mocenigo** presents a collection of precious fabrics and costumes. Information about the flora and fauna of the lagoon is found in the Museum of Natural Science in the ❼*Fondaco dei Turchi**.

Churches and piazzi

Next go south along narrow canals to the church ❽*San Giacomo dell'Orio** with its impressive ceiling. At noon, the piazza of the same name is like a playground; its inviting cafés are a good place for a break. The next goal is Campo San Polo, one of the largest squares in

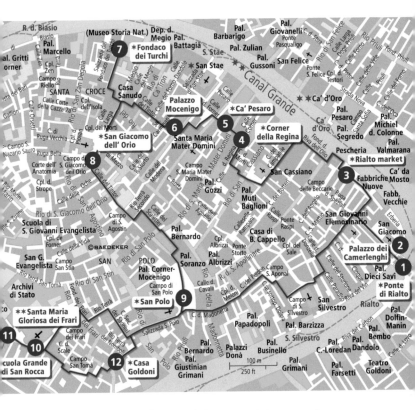

Venice, which is named after St Paul. In summer it is a venue for open-air cinema. ❾*San Polo church, for which the piazza is named, has a Last Supper by Tintoretto.

A visit to the famous Frari church, properly called ❿**Santa Maria Gloriosa dei Frari**, with masterpieces by Titian, Bellini and Donatello, is a must for art lovers. At 70m/233 feet, its bell tower is one of the tallest in Venice.

In the immediate neighbourhood is the ⓫**Scuola Grande di San Rocco** with paintings by Tintoretto. The return route to the **Ponte di Rialto** passes ⓬*Casa Goldoni, once the residence of the illustrious comic poet. A **gondola trip** through the canals is a wonderful end to the day. Or simply stroll through the crooked alleys, across the innumerable bridges and magical piazzas, and let the special charm of Venice away from the main tourist track cast its spell on you.

Santa Maria
Gloriosa

Tour 3 Cannaregio

Start: Santa Lucia railway station
Duration: 3 hours
Finish: Fondamenta Nuove

This walk leads through Cannaregio in the north-western part of Venice. Before the construction of the railway bridge, this sestiere was the main entrance to the city. Here, visitors still find the everyday world of Venice, some handsome churches, palaces and the oldest ghetto of the world.

❶ **Santa Lucia railway station** (1954; it bears the house number 1 of this city quarter) stands on the site of the monastery Santa Lucia which were torn down to build Ponte della Libertà (the construction of this connection between the mainland and the city began in 1841). They are commemorated in the church **Santa Maria degli Scalzi** (1654; B. Longhena). Follow the always lively Lista di Spagna to Campo Santa Geremia; here stands the magnificent ❷ ***Palazzo Labia** (mid-17th century), which has been the local seat of RAI and which is used for events. On **Ponte delle Guglie**, cross the Canal di Cannaregio and on the opposite side, walk through Sottoportego del Ghetto into the first and oldest ❸ ****ghetto** in Europe (▶MARCO POLO Insight p. 209). Leaving Campo Ghetto Nuovo, cross Rio della Misericordia and turn left into Calle Turlona. Continue across Rio della Sensa to Palazzo Michiel (16th century), left again into Calle dei Riformati to Fondamenta dei Riformati and the former Carmelite nunnery (ex Monastero delle Carmelitane Scalze) and ❹ **Sant'Alvise** church. Zigzag – across Rio di S. Alvise into Calle di Capitello, left into Fondamenta della Sensa and Calle Loredan – to Fondamenta Madonna dell'Orto. Immediately after crossing Rio Madonna dell'Orto,

! *Off Piazza San Marco* Insider Tip

MARCO⊕POLO TIP

The Comune di Venezia along with the Touring Club Italiana has put together a couple of walking tours in order to present some of the less well-known treasures of the city on the lagoon. The map with descriptions is available at the tourist offices. The following tour is based on the tour »From Santa Lucia railway station to the Fondamenta Nuove«.

you reach the small Corte Cavallo, horse court, the former site of the foundry in which Verrocchio had his equestrian monument of Bartolomeo Colleoni cast in 1496. Slightly east, the former Scuola dei Mercanti (remodelled in 1570 by Palladio) and the beautiful brick church ❺ ***Madonna dell'Orto**, a place of pilgrimage for Tintoretto fans, lie on Campo della Madonna dell'Orto. Cross Campo dei Mori, (piazza of the Moors) named after the four statues on the house walls, pass the

Inside Tip

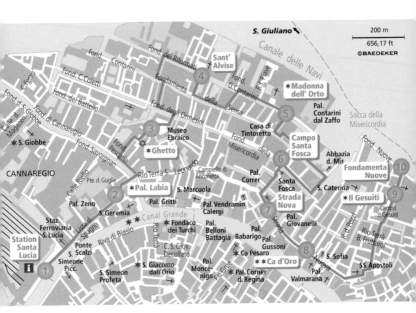

house where Tintoretto died and reach Campo dell'Abbazia with the Chiesa Santa Maria della Misericordia, founded in the 10th century, and the Scuola Vecchia, the former meeting house of the silk weavers' guild. Cross Rio dell'Abbazia, pass the Scuola Nuova della Misericordia, built in 1583 by Sansovino but not completed, and Palazzo Lezze (1670; Longhena) to the little church of San Marziale (1721) with a richly decorated Baroque interior. From here, cross two bridges to ❻**Campo Santa Fosca**, where a monument (1892) commemorates Father Paolo Sarpi, a supporter of Venetian independence. from Rome Here is the lively ❼**Strada Nova**, which was laid out in 1868–1871 parallel to the Grand Canal as a link between the railway station and the centre of Rialto. (pedestrian highway) Palazzo Correr Contarini at the very beginning of Strada Nova dates from the 15th century; just a little further, on the opposite side of the street in a walled garden, is Palazzo Giovanelli (15th century). From Rio di Noale there is a beautiful view of its façade; the outside stairway dates from the 19th century. At the Renaissance church of **San Felice** (one of Tintoretto's oldest paintings, *St Demetrius and a Donor from the Ghissi Family* hangs inside); continue to the elegant ❽**Ca' d'Oro**. Strada Nova joins **Campo dei Santi Apostoli**, where the church has an eye-catching campanile. This is a convenient place for a short detour to the church of **Santa Maria dei Miracoli**. Behind the choir of Santi Apostoli church the street called first Rio Terà dei Santi Apostoli, then

Salizzada Seriman that leads to Campo dei Gesuiti. On the left, take a look at Palazzo Zen (1534, ascribed to S. Serlio, while the Oratorio dei Crociferi with a significant cycle of paintings by Palma the Younger (1583–1591; accessible only by appointment) and the Jesuit church **❾ *I Gesuiti** are further along on the right. A short side trip across Calle Larga dei Botteri (just behind I Gesuiti) leads to the home and workshop of Titian (behind a brick wall). Take **Salizzada degli Specchieri** to **❿ Fondamenta Nuove**, the »new quay« founded in 1589, to look across at the cemetery island **San Michele** and at **Murano**. Boats to the lagoon islands also depart from here.

Dorsoduro – »Hard Back«   Tour 4

Start: Santa Lucia railway station   **Duration:** 3 hours
Finish: Zattere

Unlike the other sestiere of Venice, Dorsoduro, the district between the Grand Canal (north-east) and the Canale della Giudecca, stands on tree-trunk piles arranged in spirals (not in rows). It has a varied character. The western part was originally occupied by fishermen, sailors and workers. Some of the industrial or church buildings here now house parts of the university. Campo Santa Margherita is a favourite meeting place. East of the Accademia, Dorsoduro has become one of the most popular (and most expensive!) residential areas.

This tour also starts from **❶ Santa Lucia railway station**. Past the Chiesa degli Scalzi, cross the bridge of the same name to the south bank of the Grand Canal. Following the signs for »Frari«, first walk along a narrow alley and then along a canal to the south-east. After several changes of direction, you will reach a church decorated with paintings by Titian and named **❷ **Santa Maria Gloriosa dei Frari**. Another highlight is close by – the **❸ **Scuola Grande di San Rocco** with paintings by Tintoretto. Follow Scuola Grande and Calle San Pantalon to the extensive **❹ Campo Santa Margherita**, one of the most popular piazzas in the city with many cafes and bars, where there is a small fruit and vegetable market in the mornings. The **❺ *Scuola Grande dei Carmini** at its southern tip is worth visiting for the ceiling painted by Giambattista Tiepolo. Now follow the canal on the rear side of the Scuola. At the beautiful **❻ Palazzo Zenobio**, cross the canal. The Fondamenta Briati becomes Fondamenta Barbarigo and joins Corte Maggiore. Cross the canal again. From Fondamenta della Teresa there is a view of the so-

Insider Tip

Santa Maria dei Miracoli, a masterpiece of the early Renaissance

called **Case Tron** opposite, 18th-century townhouses with seven chimneys. This is the start of the old workers' quarter Santa Marta, which dates from the first decades of the 20th century. Slightly farther west, the route ends at a cotton-spinning factory, today part of the architectural college. Here stands one of Venice's oldest churches, ❼ **San Nicolò dei Mendicoli**, in its present form dating from the 16th century. Return via Fondamenta Lizza and a bridge to the church San Angelo Raffaele. It is decorated by a lovely scene from the legend of Tobias by Franceso Guardi (1750). For the Renaissance church ❽ **San Sebastiano**, Veronese, who is also laid to rest here, created a major cycle of paintings.

From Campo San Sebastiano, cross the canal of the same name and go south a short distance on Fondamenta San Basilio. Turn left into the narrow Calle della Chiesa, follow Fondamenta Ognissanti and Rio Ognissanti to Campo ❾ **San Trovaso** with San Trovaso church and the Squero di San Trovaso, one of Venice's oldest gondola workshop. Only a few minutes' walk farther south, a view opens up across the Canale della Giudecca onto the island of **Giudecca** with the massive Molino Stucky and the Redentore church. Here is ❿ **∗Zattere**, Venice's »sun promenade« with numerous bars, ice cream salons and restaurants. From here, it is approximately 1.5km/1mi to the **Dogana da mar** at the eastern tip of Dorsoduro.

Tour 5 Market Boats and Buttered Stockfish – a Culinary Stroll

Start: Santa Lucia railway station   **Duration:** 1/2 day
Finish: Campo S. Barnaba

In the morning on the railway station steps on the Canal Grande. Venice awakens. The commuters from Mestre, waiters and policemen, maids and postal employees stream into the Centro Storico.

Before you're drawn along onto the »pedestrian highway« Lista di Spagna, take a look at Murano glass that you cannot drink out of: in the ❶ **Scalzi church** in mystical darkness in a side chapel on the left two deep-blue candelabras glow – not everyone sees this.

To the Ghetto

The first break is made standing up and is a good chance to hear the local Venetian dialect with its many vowels: the hectic but elegant ❷ **Pasticceria dal Mas** (Lista di Spagna 150a, Mon, Wed – Sun 7.30am – 8pm) makes excellent cappuccino and is a candidate for the best cornetti and apple pastries in town. From here take a detour through the *ghetto, which has displayed its identity more strongly in recent years, in food as well. It is still too early for traditional Venetian-Jewish goose salami, which is harder to find than the new snackbars with Israeli food, but the ❸ **Panificio Volpe** (bakery, Calle del Ghetto Vecchio 1143, Sun 9am –1pm, Mon –Fri 7.30am –1.30pm, 5pm – 7.30 pm) Israeli baked goods are sold. If the dolci just taste Italian to the uninitiated it is a sign of how closely connected Venetian Jews were with their homeland even in everyday things – many of the ghetto's synagogues even look more like rococo theatres at first glance.

Insider Tip

Return to the main traffic route ❹ **Strada Nuova** for the long walk to Campo S. Sofia. Of course, we won't miss the chance to cross to the ❺ *Rialto market in a ferry gondola. Anyone who has started out early enough can watch the market boats being unloaded; on most of them small, yapping lapdogs like the one in the courtesan paintings by Vittore Carpaccio ride along. Hats off to the strenuous logistics of this market, one of Italy's most beautiful and lively! Under the open columned hall of the **Pescheria** the daily catch from not only the lagoon and the Choggia fishermen is sold: schie shrimps and moleche crabs, squid, dragonhead and above all the glittering dorades and John Dory fish. And »frog's tails«: coda di rospo is the name of the rare, but somewhat creepy looking fish (monkfish or lotte). Under awnings sellers offer appetizing artichoke stems from San Erasmo, dark violet Castelfranco radicchio that can be grilled, prepared salads for rock-bottom rpices, but also porcini from the Alpine foothills, Sicilian oranges or even bright orange persimmons.

To Rialto Market

After this much stimulation you need some refreshment. In Venice with its old Austrian traditions the first enoteca open at 8am for the first glass of ombra. Insiders like to join the crush in the dark ❻ **Do Mori** (▶S. MARCO POLO Insight p. 116), whose brightly polished copper kettles make it look like an Alpine cheese dairy. The wine selection goes from a reasonable verduzzo to the finest prosecco denomination Cartizze. Along with your drink don't miss the fluffy stockfish with herbs: mild and without the bothersome saltfish aroma, the baccalà mantecato here tastes like the best French brandade de morue.

Insider Tip

For the senses Why not follow the stream of visitors and meander through the narrow alleys called ruga with their countless pretty, small shops towards the Frari church? This is also the chance for the first espresso (say caffè) of the day. ❼ **Rizzardini** (▶Food and Drink, p. 120) is one of the »antichi pasticceri veneziani« where Venetians like to drink a quick vermouth and munch on some salty almonds standing up. There is absolutely no room to sit down in the tiny wood-panelled confiserie, but the Venetian dolci like zaeti can be bought in pretty packages to take along.

The route continues past the **Frari church** and **university Ca' Foscari**
to **Campo S. Barnaba**. One of the most famous photo settings of the
city awaits here: On Rio S. Barnaba opposite the church of the same
name fuit and vegetables are sold under a huge awning from a freight
boat. A scene that is reminiscent of the harbour pictures by Claude
Lorrain or Canaletto. A few steps further the wine shop **❽ Al Bottegon** (Cantina di Vini Già Schiavi, Fondamenta Nani, Mon –Sat
8.30am –10pm) right next to the bridge has developed into one of the
most popular bacari in the city. How about a glass of Incrocio Man-
zoni (a cross between riesling and pinot blanc) and a wedge of asiago
cheese from the Carnic Alps as an aperitif?

Enough standing and walking. Nearby is a refreshingly un-touristy
Trattoria **❾ La Bitta** (Calle Lunga S. Barnaba 2753, ►Food and Drink,
p. 111) with seating. The family-run restaurant specializes in vegetable
risotti, pasta made with pumpkin, and Venetian liver. Buon appetito!

Insider
Tip

By Ferry to the Lagoon

Tour 6

Start: Fondamenta Nuove
Duration: 1 day
Finish: S. Zaccaria

**Morning fog, salt corroded piles, oysters farms and long-leg-
ged birds: it is the lagoon that makes Venice so extraordinary.
Here are suggestions for an »exploration« by ferry. Up-to-
date ferry timetables are available at the ferry terminals; Fondamenta Nuove (Cannaregio) and San Zaccaria (San Marco)
are the most important. Various lines can be combined. For
further information see the websites www.actv.it, www.turis-
movenezia.it (»Itinerari«) und www.hellovenezia.com (»Trans-
ports/Excursions«)..**

The well-known islands of Murano, Torcello and Burano can be reached
by public ferry. Line 7 passes the cemetery island * **San Michele** on the
way to towards ** **Murano**, home to glass-blowing workshops since
1291. Continuing to Mazzorbo, the boat also passes uninhabited islands
such as San Giacomo in Paludo, where pilgrims stopped on their way to
the Holy Land from the 11th century, and Madonna del Monte, seat of a
14th-century Benedictine monastery. **Mazzorbo**, which was probably
settled as early as the 6th century, still has 350 inhabitants. Of the former
five churches and six monasteries, only Chiesa di Santa Caterina (late
13th century) remains. It is possible to walk to the neighbouring island
of Burano from here via a wooden bridge.

More islands

Next, the boat visits the fishing island of ** **Burano**, whose colourful houses glow from afar. To visit * **Torcello**, it is necessary to change boats here. The adjacent island, which is now home to not even 50 people, was once the most important settlement in the lagoon. Now you can return from Burano via Mazzorbo and Murano directly to Fondamente Nuove. However, it is also possible to go from Burano via Treporti and Punta Sabbioni, two stops on the Cavallino peninsula, to the **Lido**, returning to San Marco in Venice (San Zaccaria quay) from there.

!

MARCO ⊕ POLO TIP

Quiet lunch

Anyone who wants to eat lagoon duck away from the tourist bustle should go to Antica Trattoria Maddalena immediately next to the dock Mazzorbo (Fri–Wed 12.30pm–3pm, tel. 0 41 73 01 51). In the summer make reservations for Sunday if you want to sit on the terrace or in the garden.

Anyone who would like to get out into nature should visit the lagoon's »vegetable islands« (**Le Vignole** and **Sant' Erasmo**). Line 13 from Fondamente Nuove, ending in Treporti, connection to Line 14. * **San Francesco del Deserto**, the monastery island to the north-east ahead of Sant'Erasmo, is accessible only by water taxi or private boat, e.g. from Burano.

Excursions

For visitors with time and interest, here are some suggestions for further trips outside Venice.

The islands of **Giudecca** and M**San Giorgio Maggiore** are also worth a trip. From the campanile of San Giorgio Maggiore, there is a wonderful view over the city and the lagoon. For perfect sunbathing go to the sandy beaches of the **Lido**, where world-class films and actors are awarded the Golden Lion at the Palazzo del Cinema every year in late August/early September. Beach-lovers flock to the nearly 20km/12mi-long peninsula **Litorale del Cavallino** and the M**Lido di Jesolo**, which have excellent camping and bathing areas (there are bus and boat connections between Piazzale Roma, San Zaccaria and Jesolo and Cavallino/Treporti). The splendour of past days comes to life on a boat trip along the Brenta canal to the most beautiful **villas of Venetia**. From March to October, various operators run boats between Venice and Padua (information in the tourist offices of Padua and Venice). Barely 40km/25mi inland, the lively old university town of **Padua** with its art treasures is also worth a longer visit. It is reached most quickly and easily by train or bus (information: Turis-

The typical colourful houses of Burano

mo Padova, www.turismopadova.it, Galleria Pedrocchi, Mon – Sat
9am – 7pm,   tel. 04 98 20 16 76, infopedrocchi@turismopadova.it;
info booth on the plaza in front of the railway station, tel.
04 98 20 16 72).

SIGHTS FROM A TO Z

St Mark's Basilica, the maginficent doge's palace, the palaces of nobles on the grand canal – these are only a few of the highlights of Vencie.

Arsenale

✦ K/L 12/13

Location: Rio dell'Arsenale
Quay: Arsenale

From the beginning, the power of Venice was based on the arts of shipbuilding and navigation. Consequently the arsenal, the shipyard, was a the »heart« of the maritime republic.

A fort in the middle of the city

It was founded in 1104. In the following centuries, it was constantly expanded and fortified. Aside from merchant ships with capacious holds and slender, nimble war galleys, it also produced slinging machines, catapults and later, cannon. At its height, the shipyard employed up to 16,000 workers. As keepers of secrets, the arsenalotti enjoyed high regard and such privileges as an old age pension and free housing. The organization of the work was reminiscent of conveyor-belt production. This made it possible, as early as 1188, to produce up to 100 new galleys for the high seas within half a year. In 1571, the year of a battle against the Turkish fleet, 100 galleys were built in 60 days. Until the end of the 18th century, the Arsenale was regarded as one of the largest and most productive shipyards in the

The »factory hall« of the trading metropolis could be considered to be the first industrial business of the Middle Ages

world, admired by visitors almost as much as St Mark's Basilica or the Doge's Palace.

The Dante bust commemorates the visit of the Florentine poet **Dante Alighieri**, who immortalized the Arsenale in his Divine Comedy: »As the Venetians in the Arsenale boil the thick tar in wintertime in order to seal their leaking ships which are no longer seaworthy, while one builds a new ship and another tightens the ribs of a ship which has made numerous journeys, one hammers on the bow and one on the stern, one carves paddles whilst another twists ropes, yet another repairs top and mizzen sails, it is there that not through fire, no, but through the art of God, a thick black porridge boils, rendering the stony banks sticky all around.« (XXI Canto. The verses are inscribed on a marble plate to the left of the entrance).

The Arsenale was a forbidden area. At first it was accessible only through one sea and one land entrance (the one to the northern part of the lagoon was only made in the 19th century). The land entrance **(Ingresso di Terra)**, a large gate in the form of an ancient triumphal arch (1460), is one of the first Renaissance monuments in the city. The two lions were brought from Greece as spoils of war by Francesco Morosoni in the 17th century. The sitting lion originally guarded the port of Piraeus, the recumbent lion came from Delos and was once set up on the Sacred Way between Athens and Eleusis. | *Ingresso di Terra*

The Arsenal is now about 46ha/113ac in size, a third of which has been leased by the military. It is usually not accessible, except during the Biennale. The oldest international exhibition of contemporary art takes place every two years, in part in the Arsenal (▶p. 215).

In the maritime museum – the former hardtack store of the Arsenale opposite the church of San Biagio – much can be learned about the history of Venice as a sea power. Exhibits include spoils from the innumerable maritime wars of the republic, many different models of ships, navigation instruments, uniforms and documents about shipbuilding and types of ships. One of the main items of interest is the gondola collection, including a 17th-century Bucintoro – the magnificent state galley of the doge burned out in 1798. | ***Museo Storico Navale*** / *Insider Tip*

🕐 Mon–Sat 8.45am –1.30pm, admission €1.55

Behind the bridge is the start of the unusually wide Via Garibaldi, built in 1808 under Napoleon. On the very first house, on a marble plate commemorates Giovanni and Sebastiano Caboto, who discovered Newfoundland, Labrador and Greenland in 1497. The street, which is lined by many small shops and cafés and barely touched by tourism, leads to Isola di San Pietro with the cathedral ▶San Pietro di Castello, until 1807 the seat of the clerical head of the city. Halfway there is the entrance gate of the ▶Giardini Pubblici. | *Via Garibaldi*

★★ **Basilica di San Marco**

✦ H 12

Location: Piazza San Marco
Quay: Vallaresso San Marco, San Zaccaria
🕐 Mon – Sat 9.45am – 16.45/17pm, Sun from 2pm
www.basilicasanmarco.it; appointments for tours: www.venetoinside.com

The unique Basilica di San Marco (St Mark's Basilica) with its five domes, traceried arches and windows, the core which goes back 1000 years, is the church of the doge, the state church of the republic, the monumental shrine for St Mark and, since 1807, a cathedral too.

Unique St Mark's

The magnificent décor of the basilica is partly the result of a law of Doge Domenico Selvo, who ordered the entire city to participate in adorning St Mark's Basilica in 1075: he required everyone who came home from a voyage to bring a precious ornament for the »house of Saint Mark«. This explains the numerous architectural fragments and ornaments from the orient, the columns, reliefs, sculptures and jewellers' work from a large variety of materials.

Building history

Today's building is the third on the site. The first St Mark's Basilica was built after the arrival of the relics of St Mark, which two sailors took from Alexandria in 828 (►History p.34). The church was destroyed by a fire in the Doge's Palace in 976, and rebuilt. This building was torn down in the 11th century and replaced by the existing church. Its initiator was Doge Domenico Contarini (1043–1070), for which reason it is often known as the **Contarini church**. The layout was that of the preceding buildings: a Greek cross with two aisles, with a dome above the crossing and four smaller domes over the arms of the cross. In 1094, the basilica was consecrated in the presence of Holy Roman Emperor Henry IV and made the state church. After the conquest of Constantinople in 1204, the domes were raised, the north vestibule added and the west front designed as a columned façade. The brick building, which had been nearly undecorated until then, was richly adorned inside and out with marble, mosaics and innumerable pieces of booty. A last construction phase, the Gothicization of St

! MARCO ◉ POLO TIP

Don't miss *Insider Tip*

- the stone floor of San Marco (most of it is unfortunately hidden under carpets) and the mosaics
- the Pala d'Oro behind the high altar
- the four horses of San Marco on the loggia of the basilica
- attending one of the infrequent concerts or mass (e.g. on Sunday at 10.30am), in order to appreciate the unique acoustics of San Marco without walking around

Mark's Basilica, began in the second half of the 14th century and lasted into the 16th century. On the exterior the upper storey, in particular, was altered (windows were embellished with tracery, arches with decorative gables and tabernacles with statues, etc). Inside, additional structures such as the Cappella Mascoli and the Cappella Zen were built.

OUTSIDE APPEARANCE

St Mark's Basilica has three façades: the main façade to Piazza San Marco, the southern façade to the Piazzetta and the sea, and the north façade to Piazzetta dei Leoncini. Two round-arched portals decorated with mosaics in deep niches dominate the west façade. Precious spolia columns in various colours are arranged on the sides of the portal in two rows, one above the other. The larger central portal penetrates the ****West façade**

balustrade of the terrace, on which bronze copies of the horses of Saint Mark stand. The central arch is emphasized by its size and the angel stairway which leads to the statue of Saint Mark. The mosaics of the lunettes in the side niches of the portals show the story of St Mark's relics, beginning on the far right with the removal of the body from Alexandria, veneration of the relics and their arrival in Venice – all work of the 17th and 18th centuries. The only mosaic from the 13th century is above the outer left portal, the Porta di San Alippio. It shows the transfer of the saint's body into St Mark's Basilica and the external appearance of the church in the 13th century before it was altered in the Gothic style. The lunette of the main portal shows Christ as the judge of the world with the Judgment Day (1836). The mosaics of the upper storey depict scenes from the passion of Christ to his ascension (17th century). The inner surfaces of the arches are ornamented with Byzantine-Roman reliefs. The cen-

Detail of the angel stairway

tral arch shows many different crafts (mid-13th century). The reliefs in the spaces of the outer arcade arches depict scenes from the legend of Hercules (13th century).

The three **flagstaffs** of cedar wood before the west façade were placed there in 1376. In 1505, they received fine iron bases from the workshop of Alessandro Leopardi. The reliefs of the central pedestal show Justice between elephants (a symbol of strength and wisdom) and Pallas (symbol of plenty). The southern pedestal depicts nereids and tritons, the northern one Neptune, to whom a satyr offers the fruits of the earth – a demonstration of Venice's rule on water and land.

South façade

The former Porta da Mar, the entrance from the sea which was used for ceremonial purposes, was removed in 1503 in favour of the Cappella Zen (inside the church the portal, which is decorated with mosaics of the legend of St Mark, is still visible). The traceried gate to its right leads into the narthex of the baptistery. Next to it are the smooth, marble-clad outer wall of the Tesoro (treasury). For the second storey, the scheme of the west façade was used, but with more window openings and marble-clad tympana. Note the two griffins on the first arch, which may originally have been integrated into the portal, and the Byzantine Madonna mosaic (13th century) before which two lamps are lit every evening.

The marble columns before the south façade, the so-called **Pilastri Acritani**, were probably made in Constantinople in the 6th century. At the south-west corner of the Tesoro, towards the Doge's Palace, the **tetrarchs**, four embracing men of porphyry, are built into the wall. These are also spoils from Constantinople, made in the 4th century in the Eastern Roman Empire. They may represent the jointly ruling emperors Diocletian, Maximian, Valerius and Constantius. Legend regards them as four thieves who were turned to stone during an attempt to rob the treasures of San Marco.

The structure and design of the **north façade** are similar to the west façade. A Romanesque relief above the Porta dei Fiori (4th arcade) tells of the birth of Christ.

**Vestibules

The vestibules (narthexes) of St Mark's Basilica originated in different phases of construction: the west wing with the main portal was part of Contarini's church, while the north wing was not added until the 13th century. Main items of interest include the polychrome marble floors (from the Contarini period in the west section and from the 13th century in the north section) and the 13th-century vault mosaics. The themes come mainly from the Old Testament (while the mosaics inside the basilica are from the New Testament) and begin in the southern arch of the west vestibules with scenes from Genesis,

The mysterious tetrarchs

and continue in the following arches with the stories of Noah, Abraham, Joseph and Moses. Some niches contain doges' tombs from the 12th century. The southern Porta San Clemente is particularly noteworthy. Its bronze door, which originated in Constantinople, reached Venice in the 11th century. A copy of it was used as a central portal in the 12th century. The grille door which separates the Cappella Zen from the narthex is also from Byzantium.

INTERIOR

**Mosaics The spatial effect of the interior is determined by the five domes which rest on massive columns and are connected to wide barrel vaults. San Marco has more mosaics than any other church in the West. They cover an area of 4,240 sq m/45,640 sq ft and mainly date from the 12th and 13th centuries, but were partly replaced between 1500 and 1750 according to new designs by Titian, Tintoretto, Veronese and Tiepolo, among others. The main themes are developed between the apse and the exit, beginning with Christ Pantocrator in the east and closing with the apocalypse in the west. Between them are the events from the passion to the ascension of Christ. The wall surfaces of the north and south arms of the transept show stories of saints and the parents of Jesus.

Pentecost Dome Closest to the main entrance is the Pentecost Dome, probably the oldest in the church (late 12th century). The Holy Spirit floats at its centre as a dove, sending fiery tongues over the twelve apostles enthroned at the lower edge of the dome.

Ascension Dome In the central dome (12th century), Christ floats in a circle of stars borne by angels, below it the Virgin at prayer with two angels and twelve apostles separated by olive trees. The pendentives are occupied by the four evangelists.

Passion Vault In the Passion Vault, between the Pentecost Dome and the Ascension Dome, the capture and crucifixion of Christ and Christ in limbo are shown (around 1200).

Choir dome The dome over the choir shows Christ giving blessing, surrounded by prophets and the Virgin. The mosaic dates from the 12th century. Parts of it were renewed after the fire in 1231; this is visible in the gold ground, where the old parts appear different from the new parts. The apse mosaic with the Pantocrator is dated 1506. Unfortunately, the mosaics in the right aisle of the choir are very difficult to decipher. They provide a lively description of the **legend of St Mark** and are among the oldest mosaics in the church.

Basilica di San Marco

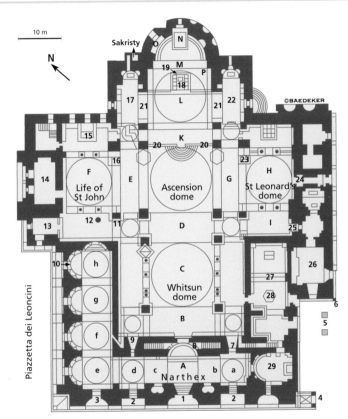

10 m

N

Sakristy

Piazzetta dei Leoncini

Palazzo Ducale

©BAEDEKER

O N
19 M
18 P
17 21 L 21 22
15
16 K
20 20
14 F
Life of
St John
E Ascension
dome
G H
St Leonard's
dome
24
13 12 11 D I 25
10 h
g D 26
f C
Whitsun
dome
27
9 B 28
8 7 29
e d c b a
3 2 A 1 2 4
Narthex 5
6

Piazza San Marco

1 Main door
2 Iron grille by Venetian
   master Bertuccius (c. 1300)
3 Porta di S. Alippio
4 Pietra del Bando
5 Pilastri Acritani
6 Sculpture: the tetrarchs
7 Porta di San Clemente
8 Stairs to Museo Marciano
9 Porta di San Pietro
10 Porta dei Fiori
11 Altar of the Annunciation
   Romanesque holy
   water basin with angels
   (12th century)
12 Capella dei Mascoli
13 Capella di Sant' Isidoro

14 Capella della
   Madonna Nicopeia
15 Altare di San Paolo
16 Capella di San Pietro
17 High altar
18 Pala d'Oro
19 Iconostasis
20 Reliquary shrines
21 Capella di
   San Clemente
22 Altare di San Giacomo
23 Connection to Doge's
   Palace
24 Entrance to treasury
25 Treasury (tesoro)
26 Baptistery
27 Baptismal font (1546)

28 Capella Zeno
   (for Cardinal G. B. Zeno,
   † 1501)

MOSAICS

a Genesis
b Noah's ark
c Story of Noah and
  the Tower of Babel
d Story of Abraham
e-g Story of Joseph
h Story of Moses

A Paradise
B Apocalypse
C Whitsun

D Scenes of Christ's
  passion
E St Michael with sword
F Life of the Virgin
G Washing of feet,
  Temptations in the
  wilderness
H Four miracles of Jesus
I Miracle of columns
K Miracles of
  St Peter, resurrection,
  etc
L Christ and Prophets
M Lamb of God
N Christ as Pantocrator
O Sansovino door
P Legend of St Mark

** *Venice's State Church*

The doges house chapel, state church and monumental shrine for the patron saint of Venice – St Mark's Basilica, with its huge domes, is one of the most impressive building monuments in Venice.

Opening times: Mon– Sat 9am – 5pm (Nov. – Easter until 4.45pm), Sun 2pm until 5pm. April to Dec. reservations accepted until two days before your visit at the latest (www.alata.it, www. veneto inside.com). Guided tours April – Oct. Mon to Sat 11am. No large bags or photographing allowed inside.

❶ Portals
The round arches of the portals on the west façade of St Mark's are set deep. The decoration: columns of precious marble in various colours and mosaics as well as – in the centre main entrance – stone masonry from the 13th century.

❷ Façade mosaics
Traders brought the remains of St Mark from Alexandria to Venice under a load of pork. The story of this »kidnapping« is depicted in the mosaics above the portals of the west façade.

❸ Baptistry
Mosaics and reliefs on the baptismal font show the life of John the Baptist.

❹ Tetrarchs
Mysterious 4th century figure group made of porphyry: four men in a tender embrace.

❺ Tesoro
The booty that the Venetians brought back after looting Constantinople in AD 1204 are the basis of the church treasure today.

❻ Miraculous find
St Mark's remains were lost in the fire of 976. This mosaic shows the miracle of their rediscovery.

❼ High altar
The crowning glory of the high altar, which is made up of older pieces, is the canopy, which rests on four columns.

❽ Domes
They were raised after the conquest of Constantinople in 1204, and have been visible from St Mark's Square since then; they give the building an Oriental flair.

Detail of the floor mosaic

Choir stalls and magnificent mosaics inside St Mark's Basilica

The high altar, which was newly made from old pieces, houses the bones of St Mark, which were formerly kept in the crypt and could be seen through a window in the altar. The four columns of the canopy with reliefs are noteworthy. They show scenes from the lives of Jesus and the Virgin Mary. It is not certain whether the reliefs are 6th-century Byzantine or 13th-century Venetian work.

*Canopy and high altar

The famous 2.50m/8ft-high and 3.50m/11-ft wide altarpiece is behind the high altar today. Its front, a masterpiece of the goldsmith's art, is covered in precious stones, pearls and about 250 small enamel medallions. The first version of the Pala d'Oro was created in the late 10th century in Constantinople. It was enlarged in the 12th and 13th centuries, and received its final appearance in 1345 under Andrea Dandolo, who had the individual parts newly arranged and mounted by the goldsmith Gian Paolo Boninsegna. The small, round medal-

**Pala d'Oro

MARCO⊕POLO TIP

A better view

Insider Tip

The distance and the dim lighting make it difficult to get a good look at the mosaics, especially the details. Binoculars are very helpful. Climb up to the galleries (to the left of the main entrance) to get closer to the wonderful mosaics.

lions which were placed within the frames are among the oldest works. The rectangular panels, labelled in Latin and showing scenes from the lives of St Mark and Christ, were probably made in Venice in the early 12th century. The mount with the archangel Michael at the centre and six scenes from the New Testament are Byzantine and reached Venice in 1204 after the plundering of Constantinople. At the centre of the lower section, the enthroned Christ is surrounded by the evangelists and apostles. Below them stand the mother of Christ, the sainted Byzantine empress Irene (left) and Doge Ordelaffo Falier (right), who ordered the first enlargement of the Pala in 1105. These medallions were created in Venice in 1345, when the many individual parts were combined to make the heterogeneous items into a single piece.

❶ Viewing the altarpiece: €2

Tabernacle   In a niche of the apse stands a tabernacle with a bronze door by **Jacopo Sansovino**: its reliefs depict the resurrected Christ, surrounded by angels who present the ***Vestry door** instruments of martyrdom. The vestry door in the curve of the apse is one of the major works of Jacopo Sansovino. The door frame is of marble, and the slightly rounded door itself of bronze. Its two large rectangular reliefs represent the entombment of Christ below and the resurrection above. Prophets and saints stand in the frame panels. According to legend, the small portrait busts represent his artist's colleagues Aretino, Palladio, Francesco Sansovino (a 16th-century chronicler), himself, Titian and Veronese. He worked on the door between 1546 and 1570; his model was the paradise door by Ghiberti in the baptistery of Florence.

*Iconostasis   The iconostasis which separates the nave and the choir is by Jacobello and Pierpaolo dalle Masegne (1394). A row of eight squat columns supports the horizontal structure above. The triumphal cross stands at its centre, surrounded by the marble figures of the Virgin, St Mark and the twelve apostles. On both sides of the iconostasis stand columned pulpits which were assembled from old columns and marble panels in the 14th century: to the left, the gospel pulpit and to the right, the pulpit where the newly elected doge presented himself to the people.

*Madonna Nicopeia   The votive image of Madonna Nicopeia (the securer of victories) on the east wall of the northern transept was made in Byzantium in the

10th century. The icon, which is covered in jewels, pearls and gem-stones, was once carried by the Byzantine army and reached Venice as war booty in 1204.

The chapel of St Isidore houses the relics of the saint, which were obtained in 1125 in Chios and rest in a sarcophagus in a niche in the front wall. The recumbent figure on the sarcophagus represents the saint. The 14th-century mosaics relate various episodes from his life, partly in a highly dramatic manner.

Cappella Sant'Isidoro

The barrel-vaulted room was built in the early 15th century and has an altar with important sculptures of the Virgin between St Mark and St John, marking the transition from the late Gothic period to the early Renaissance. Note the mosaics from the first half of the 15th century and the holy water basin on the column shaft (12th century). The chapel received its name in the 17th century when it was the chapel of the mascoli (bachelors).

Cappella dei Mascoli

The name of the Altar of the Annunciation refers to its canopy-like structure: a polygonal marble pyramid roof is borne by columns which enclose a mensa. The crucifix is booty from Byzantium which was brought to Venice in 1205. The statues for the annunciation were made in the 14th century.

Altar of the Annunciation

The admission fee for the Museo Marciano is worthwhile, because of the exhibits and because of the wonderful view from the terrace. The steep steps are to the right of the main entrance. The rooms above the narthex were the workshops of the mosaic artists who worked in the church. Tapestries, sculptures and liturgical robes are exhibited in the museum. The most prominent exhibits include the former drape for the Pala d'Oro, which covered the top section of the altar. In 1345, Paolo Veneziano and his sons made the polyptych with images of Christ, the Virgin, saints and the life of St Mark.

*Galleria and Museo Marciano

The main items of interest are the famous, originally fire-gilded **bronze horses of St Mark**. They surely served as a model for Donatello's equestrian monument Gattamelata in Padua and for Verrocchio's Colleoni in Venice. Their origins are unclear. The horses were probably made in the 4th century BC in Greece. From here, they went to Rome, where they decorated the triumphal arch of Emperor Trajan. They were taken to Constantinople in the 4th century. After it was plundered in 1204, they reached Venice, where they were set up a short time later on the gallery of St Mark's Basilica. In 1797, Napoleon removed them to Paris. After his fall, the horses were brought back in 1815. The tour ends with a visit to the terrace, where the copies of the horses stand.

Admission €5

** **Burano**

✦ L/M 1/2

Population: 3130
Quay: Burano (Line 12 from Fondamenta Nuove)

Burano, the loveliest island of the lagoon, lies nearly 9km/5.5mi north-east of the main island of Venice. The boat trip takes about 40 minutes.

Lace island   The lively little fishing village has colourfully painted houses, generally with one or two storeys. According to legend, the façades are painted brightly so that the fishermen could find their way home even in dense fog. The fishing boats in the narrow canals are also brightly coloured and combine with a backdrop of houses mirrored in the water to form a magical sight. It is no surprise that the island also attracted painters. Some works can be seen in the renowned restaurant Da Romano (Via Galuppi 468). The most famous resident was the composer Baldassare Galuppi (1706–1785), after whom a street and Burano's largest piazza are named.

What to see   Art lovers find little of interest on the island except for a crucifixion by **Tiepolo** (1725) in the 16th-century San Martino church with its crooked tower. Burano is or was once famous throughout Europe for its lace. The museum of the **Scuola di Merletti**, which was founded in 1872, has an informative exhibition about the various techniques and some beautiful examples of lace (►MARCO POLO Insight p.171). And those who finish with a visit to one of the excellent fish restaurants along Via Galuppi should try a Burano ring (bussola): it tastes best when dipped in sweet wine. A wooden bridge leads to the small neighbouring island of **Mazzorbo** (population 350), where wine growing and agriculture dominate the landscape.

Campo Santa Margherita

✦ D 12

Quay: Ca' Rezzonico

The expansive, irregularly-shaped square is the heart of western Dorsoduro.

It is framed by 14th and 15th century houses and is one Venice's few squares with trees. With its many restaurants, fish and vegetable

All About Lace

According to legend, a sea captain in love left his beloved behind on the Island of Burano and soon thereafter sailed past the Island of the Sirens. While the crew, overcome by the magical song, jumped overboard, he resisted temptation in favour of his true love. Thereupon the ruler of the sirens made a whitecap rise from the ocean, which turned into the finest lace in the hands of the sailor - the bridal veil for his beloved waiting on Burano.

In fact Burano lace does have a special relationship with the sea, since it is said that its pattern was derived from the techniques used to manufacture fishing nets.

Lace was produced in Venice and on the small islands as early as the 15th century; the **Punto in aria**, the complicated airy pattern that is the trademark of Burano, was not invented until the 16th century. Soon the fine products were in demand all over Europe and adorned nobles and rich citizens with precious accessories. In France, the lace was in such high demand in the middle of the 17th century that Minister Colbert even hired knitters from Burano in order to launch domestic lace production. The dissolution of the republic in 1797 also sealed the demise of lace production. At the end of the 19th century the traditional craft was already all but forgotten when the Countess Marcello opened a new **school of lace** on Burano in 1872, where Francesca Memo, the last of the knitters who still knew the Punto in aria, passed on her skills. At the beginning of the 20th century the island had seven large lace production facilities where almost 5,000 knitters were employed. Today there are only a few masters of this art, and genuine Burano lace

has long become a luxury item. Thus most of the articles in the stores along the Via Galuppi now come from low-wage countries or are machine-made locally.

A small museum in the Galleria del Merletto Antico (Via Galuppi 215; open during business hours) displays lace art from the last two centuries, including precious fans, veils, and dresses. The **Scuola dei Merletti** also provides information about the art of the Punto in aria technique.

i Museo del Merleto, Via Galuppi 187, Tue – Sun 10am – 6pm, Nov. to Mar. until 5pm, admission €5.50, museomerletto.visitmuve.it

stands as well as numerous small shops it is one of the most lively squares in the city, a popular meeting place for students and locals. The cube-shaped building in the middle was the scuola of the furriers (varoteri). An old inscription on the façade announces the legal minimum measurements for selling fish: eels should be longer than 25cm/10in, sardines no shorter than 7cm/2.8in. The former church Santa Margherita is now the university auditorium.

*Scuola Grande dei Carmini

The Carmelite order, which was founded in the 13th century, had a monastery and a church in Venice. The brotherhood of the same name, who had one of the city's six large scuole ("S. 44), commissioned Baldessare Longhena in 1663 with building a property near the church. The scuola flourished in the 18th century and commissioned **Giambattista Tiepolo** with decorating the large assembly hall in the upper floor; between 1739 and 1744 he painted no less than nine ceiling paintings. His main work shows Mary giving St Simon Stock the scapular of the Carmelites (the scapular is part of the monk's habit, a cloth that covers the monk's robe front and back). In the corners are the personifications of the virtues and scenes from the life of St Simon Stock. Piazzetta's painting *Judith and Holofernes* (around 1743) in the passage between the dormitory and the archive is also remarkable, as well as the beautiful marble floor in the archive. From September to July there are masked concerts here on Saturdays and Tuesdays at 9pm; www.musicainmaschera.it.

MARCO POLO TIP

Nightlife alla veneziana Insider Tip

Venetian nightlife is concentrated on Campo Santa Margherita to the few clubs that stay open late (by Venetian standards), including Caffè Rosso (No. 2963), Bar Salus (No. 3112) and Margaret Duchamp (No. 3019).

Insider Tip

❶ daily 11am – 5pm, www.scuolagrandecarmini.it, admission €5

Santa Maria del Carmine (I Carmini)

The Gothic church of the Carmelites opposite (13th/14th century) was expanded in the 17th century and the tall campanile was added. Inside several paintings show scenes from the history of the order. Among the most valuable works of art are *Cima da Coneglianos*, adoration of the shepherds, (around 1504; second altar in the right-hand aisle) and Lorenzo Lottos' *St Nikolaus with John the Baptist and Lucia* (around 1523; in the left-hand aisle) as well as a Tintoretto in the right-hand aisle, *Presentation in the Temple*. The academy of art is now located in the former monastery.

❶ Mon – Sat 2.30 – 5.30pm

Palazzo Zenobio

Further to the south-west on the Fondamenta Soccorso 2596 is the Baroque Zenobio Palace, built in 1680 – 1685 by Antonio Gaspari. In its unadorned structuring the façade already shows elements of the classic style. The palace is the location of the Armenian priests' college Moorat-Raphael. The festive hall, which was painted by **Tiepolo**, can be seen upon appointment; the Collegio also rents out rooms.

❶ www.collegioarmeno.com, Tel. 04 15 22 87 70, quay San Basilio

The church that rises up to the south-west goes back to the 17th century. The story of the blind prophet Tobias can be seen in the organ balcony, a masterpiece by **Antonio Guardi** (18th century).

From here it is only a few steps towards the Guidecca Canal to the Renaissance church of San Sebastiano, which was built in 1505 – 1546 on plans by Scarpagnino. To the left in the choir is the grave of the painter **Paolo Veronese**, whose fame rests on a picture cycle from 1553. Among his most famous works are the ceiling paintings of the crowning of Mary and of the four evangelists in the sacristy as well as the story of Esther, the Jewish queen of the Persian king Xerxes, in the sancuary: *Esther is Presented to Ahasuerus, Crowning of Esther, Triumph of Mordechai.* The wall paintings in the sanctuary were created by Paolo Veronese together with his brother Benedetto. The organ case was also designed by him. His paintings *St Sebastian before Diocletian* and *The Martyrdom of St Sebastian* in the nun's choir are dated to the time around 1558. In the high altar his late work *Mother of God Enthroned with SS Sebastian, Peter, Catherine, Francis* can be seen. Part of the university is now housed in the convent of San Sebastiano. The portal to the left of the church was designed by Carlo Scarpa in 1980.

❶ Campo San Sebastiano, quay San Basilio, Mon – Sat 10am – 5pm, admission €12 (combination ticket: Chorus Pass)

✶✶ Canal Grande (Grand Canal)
✦ C–G 10–13

»Yes, I do believe that this is the most beautiful waterway in the world«, the French ambassador Philippe de Commynes enthused nearly 500 years ago.

He was speaking of the Grand Canal, Venice's main traffic artery, which extends like an inverted »S« from Santa Lucia railway station to the San Marco basin, dividing the city into two halves. The canal, actually the last segment of the river Brenta before it joins the sea, is nearly 4km/2.5mi long, 30–70m/35–80yd wide, and has a maximum depth of 5m/16ft. Only footbridges span this waterway. Venetians also refer to the waterway, which is constantly busy with gondolas, vaporetti, motorboats and rowing boats, as the »Canalazzo«, a com-

The world's most beauti-ful waterway

bination of canal and palazzo. More than 200 magnificent palazzi, 15 churches and other noble residences line its banks. They mirror Venetian architectural history from the 12th century on into the 20th century and provide a detailed illustration of the former richness and glory of the maritime republic. A **boat trip** on this unusual main street from the railway station vie the Rialto Bridge and the Volta del Canal to St Mark's Square is one of the most beautiful experiences of a stay in Venice.

FROM THE RAILWAY STATION TO THE RIALTO BRIDGE
L = left bank, R = right bank

Railway station Ferrovia S. Lucia L

Venice's railway station began operations in 1860. Today's complex dates from 1954 and lies directly on the Grand Canal right behind the **Ponte della Libertà**, the railway bridge between between the mainland and the city (1841 – 1846). In 2008 the fourth bridge over the canal was opened here: the 94m/56ft-long **Ponte della Costituzione** (Constitution Bridge) between the railway station and Piazzale Roma, where the tourists arrive by car or bus (design: Santiago Calatrava).

San Simeone Piccolo R

The domed building with the green patina is, for many visitors, the first church they see when arriving in Venice. It was built between 1718 and 1738. Its architect Giovanni Scalfurotto took the Pantheon in Rome and Palladio as his models: a wide outside stairway leads up to the columned portico adjoining the church itself.

Chiesa degli Scalzi L

The church of the »barefoot Carmelites«, actually S. Maria di Nazareth, was begun in 1670 as a monastery church to plans by Baldassare Longhena and was not consecrated until 1705. The two-storey marble façade in high Baroque style is by Giuseppe Sardi (1683–1689). The interior contains the tomb of Ludovico Manin, the last doge; there are only remnants of Tiepolo's paintings (second chapel to the right, third chapel to the left).

Ponte Scalzi

The bridge, which was built from Istrian stone, replaced an older iron construction in 1934. Every year, the boats of the Regata Storica start here – the finishing line is at Ca' Foscari (▶p.182).

Palazzo Giovanelli R

The Gothic palace with beautiful pointed-arch windows was purchased in 1755 by the Giovanelli family. They had been admitted into the class of nobles after paying 100,000 ducats.

Palazzo Flangini L

The palazzo with its rusticated ground floor, designed by G. Sardi in the 17th century, remained unfinished; one side section is missing.

San Geremia and Palazzo Labia

Shortly before the mouth of the Canale di Cannaregio, on the left bank, lies the church **San Geremia**, recognizable by its great central dome. Carlo Corbelli was the architect who, in 1753, converted the traditional layout of the church with a dome over the crossing into a modern form. In the domed area to the right of the choir hangs a painting by Palma the Younger: *Venetia Crowned by Saints*.

Slightly behind it stands the four-storey Labia palace, with the long side along **Canale di Cannaregio**, which was begun at the end of the 17th century and completed in the second quarter of the 18th century. The Labia family, merchants from Catalonia, purchased their nomination to the patrician class in 1646 for the proud sum of 300,000 ducats. Today, RAI (Italian radio and television station) has its seat here and it is used for events. The main focus is on the fine frescoes in the ballroom, which were done by **Tiepolo** in the mid-18th century. The two murals show Queen Cleopatra's Banquet in Honour of Mark Antony (Tiepolo is said to have portrayed himself in the figure dressed in blue, second from left) and Cleopatra Embarking for Rome. The ceiling painting symbolizes *Time Rejecting Beauty* (viewing currently not possible since the palace is to be sold.

*Palazzo Labia L

Two water gates lead into the 17th-century Palazzo Correr Contarini , which is also called the »House of Hearts« (Ca' dei Cuori) due to the heart-shaped family coat of arms.

Palazzo Correr Contarini L

Fondaco dei Turchi, one of Venice's oldest palaces

San Marcuola
L

Also on the left side: the uncompleted brick façade of the church S. Marcuola, built 1728–1736 by Giorgio Massari. The *Last Supper* on the left side wall of the presbytery is by Tintoretto (1547). An old copy of his *Footwashing* hangs opposite. The altars of the church are richly decorated with sculptures.

*Fondaco dei
Turchi

The crenelated Fondaco dei Turchi on the opposite side of the canal is one of Venice's oldest. It was built in the mid-13th century in the Venetian-Byzantine style. On the canal side it shows an open columned hall, to the right and left are two tower-like, three-storey side tracts, the middle part has two storeys and is divided by two rows of arcades. From the late 14th century the palace served as the residence for guests of the state. From 1621 until 1838 Turkish traders used it as their base (hence the name, from Arabic »funduk«, »warehouse, accommodation«). In the 19th century the building was reconstructed inn 13th-century style. Today it is the home of the **Museum of Natural History**. The main attractions are a dinosaur skeleton that is 7m/23ft long and almost 4m/14ft high, which was found in the Sahara desert, and the aquarium. An exhibit of plant and animal life in the lagoon is also worth seeing.

❶ Tue – Sun June – Oct 10am – 6pm, otherwise until 5pm, www.msn.ve.it, admission €8

Next to the former Turkish trading house is the Venetian republic grain and flour store also called Deposito del Megio, a compact crenelated brick building from the 15th century with small windows. On the upper floor, a relief shows the lion of St Mark (copy of an original destroyed in 1797).

Antico Granaio R

Palazzo Vendramin Calergion on the left bank is one of the the most beautiful early Renaissance palaces of Venice. It was built by Mauro Coducci around 1500 for the Loredan family. After the death of Coducci, Tullio Lombardo took over its completion. In the early 17th century, it came into the possession of the Calergi family, and in 1783 became the property of the Vendramin. Today, it houses the **casino** of Venice ("Entertainment, p.77). The backset Grimani wing was the residence of **Richard Wagner** and his family from 1882 till his death on 13 February 1883.

Palazzo Vendramin Calergi L

❶ Viewing Tue, Sat 10.30am, Thu 2.30pm by appointment, tel. 04 12 76 04 07 or 04 15 23 25 44 or arwv@libero.it.

The beautiful Baroque palace opposite with its conspicuous pointed towers was designed in 1647 by Baldassare Longhena for Bartolomeo Belloni, whose family had shortly before been admitted into the Venetian patrician class.

*Palazzo Belloni Battagia R

The Baroque church behind it, called Sant'Eustachio, was built in 1678 by Giovanni Grassi with the layout of a Greek cross. Its façade towards the Grand Canal was designed thirty years later by Domenico Rossi. The costs were met by the doge who held office from 1700 to 1709, Alvise Mocenigo II, whose tomb is here. It contains some works of the early 18th century, including works by Giovanni Battista Piazzetta, Sebastiano Ricci, Tiepolo and Pellegrini. From S. Staè there is a nice view of the four palazzi on the opposite bank: right next to the confluence of the Rio della Maddalena is **Palazzo Barbarigo** (16th cent.), followed by **Palazzo Zulian**, residence of a patron of Antonio Canova (17th cent.), **Palazzo Ruoda** (17th cent.) as well as **Palazzo Gussoni-Grimani** (16th cent.). Its façade was once adorned with frescos by Tintoretto.

*San Staè R

San Staè: Mon–Sat 10am–5pm, admission €12 (ticket Chorus Pass).

Soon after San Staè Ca' Pesaro rises up, a Baroque masterpiece that now houses two museums (▶Ca' Pesaro).

Ca' Pesaro R

The large Baroque palace Corner della Retina was built beside Ca' Pesaro and only a short time later (1724). The architect was Domenico Rossi. The preceding building was the birthplace of **Caterina Corner** (1454–1510), later queen of the Mediterranean island of Cyprus, which held strategic significance for Venice. The Corner family,

*Palazzo Corner della Regina R

old Venetian patricians, had become so rich and powerful through sugar-cane plantations on Cyprus that the Cypriot king Giacomo II di Lusignano married the eighteen-year-old Caterina in 1472. Eight months later, the king was poisoned, and one year later, their son died. At the urging of Venice, Caterina finally ceded her kingdom to the republic. As a reward, she was allowed to live in keeping with her status in Castle Asolo and later in her palace on the Grand Canal. Today, the palace is the municipal pawnshop and was sold in 2011 for €40 mil. to the fashion company Prada. Along with luxury suites the company art collection is to be housed here.

Ca' d'Oro L Diagonally opposite to the left is the most famous Gothic building on the Grand Canal, the ►Ca' d'Oro. Two smaller palazzi follow on the right: **Palazzo Giustinian Pesaro** (mid-15th century; the top floor was added in the 19th century) and **Palazzo Sagredo** (14th-cent.). While the windows in the Piano nobile still reflect the Venetian-Byzantine style, the floor above it already have Gothic pointed-arch windows.

Pescheria The pescheria, an open two-stroy hall on the opposite banks was only built in 1907 by Domenico Rupolo and Cesare Laurenti. The fish market has been held in this location for over 600 years ("Ponte di Rialto). The **Palazzo Michiel delle Colonne** opposite (L) takes its name from the unusually high and slender columns of the arcades of its lower floor.

Pescheria: the fish market has been held here for over 600 years

The Palazzo Mangili Valmarana became known primarily as the residence of the English consul Joseph Smith, who made a name for himself as an art collector and patron. The English court and the British Museum owe many of their Venetian paintings to him, particularly masterpieces by Canaletto. Smith had the palace rebuilt in the mid-18th century by Antonio Visentini in the classical style, and the rooms redecorated at great cost by Antonio Selva. Next to the palace the junction with Rio dei SS. Apostoli gives a view of the campanile of the eponymous church.

Palazzo Mangili Valmarana L

The long, three-storey Fabbriche Nuove was built 1554–1556 with loggias to a design by Sansovino. The attractive building provided storage and offices space.

Fabbriche Nuove R

Ca' da Mosto on the left bank is one of the oldest buildings on the Canal Grande. The palace with its fine marble arches on slender columns was built in the 13th century in the Venetian-Byzantine style (additional storeys were added in the 17th century). Alvise da Mosto, who in 1465 was the first European to sail around the Canary Islands and the Cape Verde islands, was born here in 1432.

Ca' da Mosto L

Right behind the Fabbriche Nuove the Fabbriche Vecchie appears, a structure with 37 window bays (Scarpagnino, 1522).

Fabbriche Vecchie (R)

The white marble palace on a corner directly before the Rialto bridge was once the seat of the highest Venetian financial authority. The imposing »palace of the finance secretaries« was built between 1525 and 1528 by Guglielmo Grigi from Bergamo. It is ornamented with semi-reliefs, a fine late flowering of Lombard Renaissance ornamentation.

*Palazzo dei Camerlenghi R

The building opposite was once the seat of the German merchants (▶ Fondaco dei Tedeschi).

Fondaco dei Tedeschi (L)

▶Ponte di Rialto

Rialto Bridge

FROM THE PONTE DI RIALTO TO PIAZZA SAN MARCO
L = left bank, R = right bank

On the left is Palazzo Dolfin Manin, one of the first works in Venice of Sansovino, a native of Florence (built 1532–1560). Two storeys rise above an open ground-floor hall; the arrangement of the columns follows the classic ideal of the Renaissance. The 120th and last doge, Ludovico Manin, lived here during his time in office 1789–1797 (today this is the seat of the Banca d'Italia). Next to it is the late Gothic Palazzo Bembo (15th century).

Palazzo Dolfin Manin L

Palazzo Loredan L Ca' Farsetti L	The next two palaces, **Loredan** and **Ca' Farsetti**, have arcades open to the canal. They are beautiful and well-preserved examples of the Romanesque-Byzantine building style of the 12th century. The upper floors were later redesigned. Since the 19th century, the city administration (**Municipio**) has been based here.

Palazzo Grimani L

»The noblest of all houses in Venice is the house of Grimani«, wrote John Ruskin (1819–1900) in his treatise on art history, *The Stones of Venice*, of the three-storey palace at the place where Rio di San Luca flows into the Grand Canal, a masterpiece of Mannerism. It was begun around 1540 by Michele Sanmicheli. The monumental façade was completed by Giangiacomo Grigi in 1559. Since 2008 the palace has been used for rotating exhibitions.

❶ Mon 9am – 2pm, Tue – Sun until 7pm; admission €4 (combined ticket with Galleria dell'Accademia €9), www.palazzogrimani.org

Riva del Vin R

Along Riva del Vin right after the Rialto Bridge there are some restaurants with tables right on the bank of the Canal Grande. Right after the ferry landing S. Silvestro **Palazzo Papadopoli** with its two roof obelisks (mid-16th cent., Giangiacomo Grigi from Bergamo) stands out. The adjacent **Palazzo Bernardo** is an example of Gothic palace architecture with beautiful, fragile tracery in the two middle storeys.

Palazzo Corner-Spinelli L

The plans for Palazzo Corner-Spinelli opposite next to the vaporetto station S. Angelo were drawn up by Mauro Coducci (1490 – 1510): two arcade storeys are built on a solid lower storey.

*Palazzo Pisani Moretta R

Palazzo Pisani Moretta on the opposite banks stands out with its apricot-coloured, perfectly symmetrical façade. It was built in the second half of the 15th century. Particularly beautiful aspects are the two gate arches which open towards the water on the ground floor, as well as the six-part loggias on the first and second piano nobile (upper floors), which are decorated with rich tracery. Tiepolo and Piazzetta were employed in 1742 for the palace interiors. Until 1857, the salon contained Veronese's work *The Family of Darius before Alexander*, which can be seen today in the London National Gallery. The palace is one of the few that are still in private ownership. Next to the right comes **Palazzo Barbarigo della Terrazza**, the seat of the German Study Centre in Venice (Centro Tedesco di Studi Veneziani, Calle Corner 2765/a, www.dszv.it).

Palazzi Mocenigo L

Palazzo Mocenigo shortly before the curve (Volta) of the canal actually combines three palaces of the Mocenigo family. Seven members of this family guided the fate of Venice between 1414 and 1778 as doges. In 1818/19 the first Palazzo Mocenigo Nero, a long double

Palazzo Pisani Moretta with two doors opening to the canal

palace (17th/18th cent.), was the residence of Lord Byron, who wrote *Don Juan* and his vision of Judgment Day here. The oldest Mocenigo palace is the adjacent Casa Vecchia, built in 1579 in the style of the late Venetian Renaissance. The Mocenigo complex is followed by **Palazzo Contarini delle Figure**, begun in 1504 by Giorgio Spavento and finished in 1546 by Antonio Abbondi, called Scarpagnino. The palace is named after the decorative details in the wall between the windows.

In the curve, where Rio Foscari flows into the Canal, Palazzo Balbi catches the eye of those who pass. It was built between 1582 and 1590 to designs by Alessandro Vittorio. The façade has some attributes of Mannerism, the transitional style between late Renaissance and early Baroque, such as double columns between the windows on the first floor, broken pediments above the windows and oval window openings. A plaque reminds us that Napoleon watched the finish of a regatta from here in 1807 (ill. p.47). Since 1973 the palace has housed the central government of Veneto.

Palazzo Balbi R

On the other side of Rio Foscari stands the palace of the same name, one of the most magnificent examples of late Venetian Gothic, which accommodates the **university** today. The site was purchased in 1452 by Francesco Foscari, who had the two Gustiniani towers which

*Ca' Foscari R

stood here remodelled into a magnificent palace. In 1574, the young king of France, Henri III, stayed here on his way from Poland to Paris, where he was to receive the French crown. The adjacent **Palazzo Giustiniani** was probably built at the same time; together, they form the largest Gothic palace complex in Venice.

*Palazzo Grassi L

The three-storey building at the S. Samuele landing, whose relatively simple façade decoration lies between Baroque and classical, was built in the mid-18th century from plans by the architect Giorgio Massari. He was also responsible for ▶Ca' Rezzonico. His patron was the mighty Grassi family, which, for the sum of 60,000 ducats, was permitted to join the Venetian patrician class in 1718, and owned the palace until the mid-19th century, when the dukes of Tornielli acquired it. Later, it was the residence of the opera tenor Poggi, and in the late 19th century, the building housed the illustrious bathhouse Degli Antoni. Restorations were made in the 1980s to plans by Gae Aulenti and in 2005 under the direction of Japanese architect Tadao Ando. François Pinault, who purchased the palace in 2004 from the Fiat group of companies, shows some of his contemporary art collection here. Temporary exhibitions also take place. The wall opposite the magnificent stairway is decorated with frescoes by Michelangelo Morlaiter. In the upper floor there are still wall paintings by Jacopo Guarana and Fabio Canal in the Rococo style. Good café in the first floor.

❶ Wed – Mon, 10am – 7pm; www.palazzograssi.it admission €15 (combination ticket with Dogana da Mar €20)

Ca' Rezzonico R

At the right is the Baroque ▶Ca' Rezzonico (museum).

Gallerie dell' Accademia R

Shortly before the wooden bridge Ponte dell'Accademia is the campo in front of the former church, followed by the Scuola della Carità, in which the **art gallery** of the Accademia is housed today (▶ p.200).

Palazzo Cavalli Franchetti (L)

Immediately behind the bridge to the left lies the beautifully restored, late Gothic Palazzo Cavalli Franchetti with its fine tracery ornamentations. Temporary exhibitions are held here (www.istitutoveneto.it).

*Palazzo Barbaro L

The adjacent Palazzo Barbaro is also from the Gothic period; it has a glorious six-arched window on the first floor. The four-arched window on the second floor already shows late Gothic style with high elongated arches. On the right is a Baroque extension by Antonio Gaspari. In 1815, the Curtis family from Boston took over the building and had the residential rooms magnificently refurbished. The palace rapidly became a favourite meeting place of artists and literary figures. Among the artists who wrote, composed and painted here were Robert Browning (1812–1889), J. McNeill Whistler (1834 –

Palazzo Cavalli Franchetti with fine tracery

1903), Claude Monet (1840 – 1926), Henry James (1843–1916), Cole Porter (1891–1964).

Today, a Renaissance palace which is worth seeing in itself (San Vio 1050) houses the private collection of mediaeval and Renaissance art of the industrialist Vittorio Cini. The following are especially worthy of note: *Double Portrait of Two Friends* by Jacopo Pontormo, Sandro Botticelli's *Judgment of Paris*, Piero della Francesca's *Madonna with Child* as well as ivory carvings.
❶ Only open for special exhibitions; www.cini.it

Palazzo Cini R

The American art collector **Peggy Guggenheim** once lived in the palace on the right-hand bank, which remained unfinished (▶Collezione Peggy Guggenheim).

Palazzo Venier dei Leoni R

On the opposite side, in spring, the eye is drawn to the red flowers of the pomegranate tree in the garden in front of the house, where sculptor Antonio Canova (1757–1821) had his first studio. From 1915 to 1919, Gabriele d'Annunzio (1863–1938) lived in the palace. In his autobiographical Venice novel *Il Fuoco* (The Fire), he described his stormy affair with the celebrated actress Eleonore Duse.

Casina delle Rose L

Sinister Secrets

As quaint and colourful as Venice appears to visitors – the city also has some obscure secrets. Thus Venetians avoid passing between the two columns in front of the doge's palace, which since 1172 depict a winged lion and St Theodore in a battle with a dragon. Murderers, thieves or swindlers used to be put to death here, and their bodies were often displayed for days as a deterrent. According to legend, anyone who passes between the columns will experience misfortune in the near future.

The **Scuola della Misericordia** on the Campo dell'Abbazzia is another magical place – an abbey from the 10th century, with all sorts of stories that revolve around its padres. It is said that a member of the order poisoned the abbot using bewitched coins; other tales tell of supernatural forces that possessed the brothers. One day God decided to send the plague as a punishment, which did in fact wipe out the entire community in one fell swoop during the Middle Ages. On the cemetery island of **San Michele** in the northern lagoon, witches are said to have assembled in order to fly to ceremonies or gatherings on the remote islands in gondolas that floated above the water.

The terrible secret of Ca' Dario

Although many spooky stories and haunting ghosts are ascribed to the **Palazzo Contarini del Zaffo** on the Fondamente Gasparo Contarini, the story surrounding the **Palazzo Dario** (also known as Ca' Dario) constructed in 1490 on the Canal Grande according to plans by Pietro Lombardo is enough to baffle even enlightened minds. It all began with the death of Mari-

etta Dario at the end of the 15th century. The daughter of the builder Giovanni Dario died of a broken heart when her fiancé Vincenzo Barbaro was entrapped in political intrigues in order to first banish him from the city and finally murder him. Other, sometimes mysterious strokes of fate resulted in the family being eliminated by the middle of the 17th century. The neighbours and new owners, the **Barbara** family, sold the Palazzo to an Armenian jeweller at the end of the 18th century but his business collapsed only a few months after he moved in. The next buyer, the Englishman **Rawdon Lubbock Brown**, overextended himself financially during renovations – and shot himself in the palace ballroom. He was followed by the poet **Henri de Regnier**, who was afflicted by a rare infection shortly after he made his purchase and died in 1936; the American **Charles Briggs** was exiled from Venice because he converted the Palazzo into a permissive gay bar; and a count from Turin, who was found slain in the palace in July 1970.

The building also proved unlucky for the next buyer **Kit Lambert** – manager of the well-known rock group **The Who**. He died of a brain aneurism at the age of only 45 after excessive consumption of alcohol and drugs. But even that is not all. Shortly after moving in during the mid-1970s, the new owner **Fabrizio Ferrari** also suffered a mysterious string of bad luck. Not only did his fortune seem to disappear into thin air - several family members also passed away in quick succession. And so the palace changed hands one final time: In 1985, it was purchased by the industrialist **Raul Gardini**. However, he became involved in numerous cases of corruption and then also failed economically; he took his own life in July of 1993 – not in the Palazzo Dario, but in Milan. Since then – no surprise here – the building has been vacant. Maybe one of the owners should have fallen into the Canal Grande – according to Venetian custom, that is supposed to bring luck.

It actually looks quite harmless: Palazzo Dario on the Canal Grande somewhat tilted with age

*Palazzo Corner Ca' Grande L	For the price of 22,000 gold ducats, Giorgio Corner, brother of the Queen of Cyprus, purchased the magnificent building called Ca' Grande in the early 16th century. In 1532, it fell victim to a major fire. His son Jacopo Corner thereupon commissioned the Florentine architect and sculptor Jacopo Sansovino to build a new, magnificent three-storey palace according to Renaissance ideas. He harmoniously composed the Venetian-style arcade with the Tuscan lower zone. In the early 19th century, the giant palace building became the property of Austria as the residence of the imperial viceroy. Today, the **government of the province of Veneto** and the **Prefecture** has its seat here.
*Palazzo Dario R	As the façades facing Rio delle Torreselle and the garden prove, Palazzo Dario was also originally Gothic until Pietro Lombardo began to redesign it in the Renaissance style in 1479 for Giovanni Dario. The palace has a reputation for bringing its owners bad luck – its story really sounds unbelievable (►MARCO POLO Insight p.184).
Palazzo Gritti L	**Palazzo Gritti** with its beautiful terrace was built in 1525 for Doge Andrea Gritti. Today, it is a well-known hotel in which such illustrious guests as John Ruskin, William Somerset Maugham and Ernest Hemingway stayed.
Palazzo Contarini Fasan L	The adjacent narrow **Palazzo Contarini Fasan** with its late Gothic flamboyant windows, which was built around 1480, is said to owe its name to its owner's enjoyment of hunting. According to legend this was the home of the beautiful Desdemona, the innocent victim of Othello's jealousy in Shakespeare's tragedy.
Santa Maria della Salute R	On the right-hand bank the familiar silhouette of the church ►Santa Maria della Salute can be seen. The adjacent seminario (around 1669, B. Longhena) houses the **Pinacoteca Manfrediniana**. The exhibits include busts by A. Vittoria (1525 to 1608) as well as paintings by A. Vivarini (15th century), Cima da Conegliano and Filippo Lippi ❶ viewing by appointment only, tel. 04 15 22 55 58
Dogana da Mar R Insider Tip	At the point, a bronze goddess of fortune offers greetings to travellers from the tower of the old customs office Dogana da Mar (17th century). In the three-sided former customs house a temple to contemporary art opened its doors 2009, the Punta della Dogana, which was reconstructed by the Japanese architect Tadao Ando. It houses part of the collection of the French businessman and patron of the arts François Pinault. Part of his collection of modern and contemporary art with works by artists like Sigmar Polke, Richard Serra, Cy Twombly, Thomas Schütte, Jeff Koons and Cindy Sherman is on display.

Behind the building is a wonderful panorama with the islands ►Giu-
decca and ►San Giorgio Maggiore. A few steps to the west at the Fondamente Zattere ai Saloni on the Giudecca Canal is the **Spazio Vedova** with works by the Venetian artist Emilio Vedova (►p. 266).
Dogana da Mar: Wed – Mon 10am – 7pm; www.palazzograssi.it, admission
€15 or €20 as combination ticket with Palazzo Grassi

Palazzo Giustinian in the Venetian-Byzantine style on the left bank
is now the centre for the Biennale. Now comes, on the same side,
Mecca for all those who enjoy famous cocktails, **Harry's Bar**, the favourite drinking haunt of Ernest Hemingway and other celebrities,
famous for its Bellini.

Palazzo
Giustinian L

The remains of a former grainery (Fontegheto della Farina, 15th
cent.) on the left bank is now the seat of the **Capitaneria del Porto**
(port authority).

Fontegheto
della Farina R

At the vaporetto station San Marco/Vallaressa the **royal gardens**
west of the Piazzetta were laid out in 1807 on the site of the former
grain stores. In a classical-style pavilion (1817) there is a tourist office. Behind the Zecca and the Biblioteca Marciana the Piazzetta and
the adjoining St Mark's Square appear (►Piazza San Marco).

Giardini Reali
L

** Ca' d'Oro ─────── ✦ F 10

Location: Grand Canal
Quay: Ca' d'Oro
🛈 Mon 8.15am – 2pm,　Tue – Sun 8.15am – 7.15pm, www.cadoro.org,
admission €8

**Ca' d'Oro is Venice's most famous former private building.
Rarely is a name as fitting as that of the »Golden House«.**

It is truly a jewel and one of the loveliest Gothic palaces in Venice. It
was commissioned by the rich noble and high state official Marino
Contarini, who employed no less than two renowned architects: Bartolomeo Bon and Mateo Raverti. The palace was built to their plans
between 1421 and 1440. The façade, which was once generously
gilded with gold leaf, is particularly famous; hence the name »Golden
House«. Even though the gold has paled by now, Ca' d'Oro is the climax of late Gothic decoration with its multi-coloured marble, balconies and the gloriously playful tracery ornamentation of the pointed
windows. The first signs of the early Renaissance are found in the
open columned hall with its central round arch on the ground floor

A beautiful
example of
Venetian
residential
culture

and the side wing (there is only one torresello) which is divided into clearly structured rectangular fields. After a long series of owners, Baron Giorgio Franchetti (died 1922), an art lover, acquired the palace in 1894 and had it carefully restored. Today, Ca' d'Oro houses his art collection **Galleria Franchetti**.

❶ Mon 8.15am – 2pm, Thu – Sun 8.15am – 7.15pm

In the small inner courtyard of the palazzo stands a well in the form of a capital, built from red Veronese marble by B. Bon. The floor of the andron (water hall) on the ground floor is also delightful. The owner of the house, impressed by the mosaics of San Marco, created it himself in 1896 from fine polychrome marble. The interior, with the wooden ceilings of its main halls, gives an impression of the residential culture of Venetian patricians in the late Middle Ages. Among the works of art, sculptures, tapestries and numerous paintings, particularly from the 15th and 16th centuries, *St Sebastian*, a late work by Andrea Mantegna, as well as two paintings by Vittore Carpaccio, *Annunciation* and *Death of the Virgin*, are noteworthy on the first floor. The fragments of frescoes by Giorgione and his colleague Titian from 1508 on the second floor once decorated the façade of the ►Fondaco dei Tedeschi. Do not miss the view from the loggia across the Grand Canal to the neo-Gothic Pescheria on the opposite bank.

> **!** MARCO POLO TIP
>
> *Ca' d'Oro or Alla Vedova* Insider Tip
>
> The Widow is the name of an osteria with genuine atmosphere where Venetians like to order a few cicheti and a glass of wine at the counter. If you prefer to sit down while eating, it is best to make a reservation (Ramo Ca' d'Oro, Cannaregio 3912, tel. 04 15 .28 53 .24; closed Thu and Sun midday).

✳ Ca' Pesaro

Location: Fondamenta Mocenigo/Grand Canal
Quay: San Staè

❶ Tue – Sun April – Oct 10am – 6pm, otherwise until 5pm (the ticket office closes one hour earlier), admission €10, **www.capesaro.visitmuve.it**

Baroque adorns modern – under this motto, after a long closure, the re-opening of Ca' Pesaro was celebrated in 2003.

The imposing Baroque palace on the Grand Canal was built 1676 – 1710 for the Pesaro family to plans by Baldassare Longhena, a master of late Baroque. His student Antonio Gaspari completed it after Longhena's death. In 1898 Felicita Bevilacqua, the widow of General La

Masa, bequeathed the palace to the city as a cultural venue. Finally, the building was sensitively restored by the Viennese architect Boris Podrecca. Today, the palace is entered through a small inner courtyard at the back with a well by Sansovino, beyond which the magnificent andron (water hall) was once open to the Canal Grande.

The extensive holdings of the Galleria Internazionale d'Arte Moderna, which was founded in 1897, include paintings, graphics and sculptures of the 19th and early 20th centuries. Main works include Gustav Klimt's erotic *Judith II* (Salome), the *Bather* by Max Klinger, Marc Chagall's *Rabbi of Vitebsk* and Rodin's *Cardinal of Calais*.

*Galleria d'Arte Moderna

The third floor houses the museum of oriental art. This unique collection came into being »on a genuine journey around the world« by Duke Enrico of Bourbon-Bardi 1887–1889 and includes outstanding Japanese pieces of the so-called Edo epoch (1614–1868), as well as smaller Chinese and Indo-Chinese sections. The Bardi Collection contains more than 30,000 objects ranging from seals, weapons and armour to porcelain, enamel work and silk paintings, which are exhibited in rotation.

*Museo d'Arte Orientale

The nearby Renaissance palace with original furnishings houses a **costume museum** with displays of exquisite fabrics (Centro Studi di Storia del Tessuto e del Costume; Salizzada San Staè).
❶ Apr–Oct Tue – Sun, 10am – 5pm, otherwise 4pm, admission €8

Palazzo Mocenigo

** Ca' Rezzonico (Museo del Settecento Veneziano)

━━━━━━━━━━━━━━━━━ ✦ E 12

Location: Rio di Santa Barnabà/Grand Canal
Quay: Ca' Rezzonico
❶ Wed – Mon 10am – 6pm Nov – Mar only until 5pm, carezzonico.visitmuve.it, admission €8

One of the most impressive palaces of the settecento (17th century) today houses the Museo del Settecento Veneziano (Venice in the 18th century) and shows the elaborate style of the venetian nobility towards the end of the Republic.

The palace was begun in 1667–1682 by Venice's most important **Baroque builder, Baldassare Longhena,** for the Bon family. A century later **Giorgio Massari** completed the family residence for the Rezzonico family. Like the Labia family they had only bought their

Mueseum of 18th cent. Venice

Venetian Palaces

About 200 palazzos from all epochs line the Canal Grande. The oldest, from the 13th century, reflect the Byzantine style; about 70 are in Gothic style, while another 130 are Renaissance. The Baroque style was used during the 17th century. One of the »youngest« palaces, the Palazzo Grassi (18th cent.) already shows signs of Classic style. A ride on the Canal Grande is a journey through Venetian palace architecture and shows that despite all of the changes the columned arcade has influenced the city on the laguna since the 13th century.

A **Palazzo Loredan**
13th cent.
(without later stories added)

©BAEDEKER

B **Palazzo Pisani-Moretta**
14th – 15th cent.

▶ **Veneto-Byzantine (13th cent.)**
The buildings have two stories and are divided horizontally. Two rows of arcades open the main façade, which faces the water. Horseshoe arches often rest on ancient or Byzantine columns.

▶ **Gothic (14th– 15th cent.)**
The three-storey façade is divided into middle section as the actual decorati zone and two narrow side tracts. The round arch of the column arcade is redesigned as a pointed arch with filigreed tracery. The capitals are elaborately decorated.

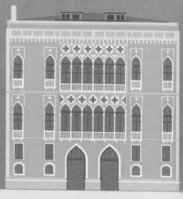

Canal Grande
The almost 4km-long (2.5 mi) s-shaped canal is Venice's most important traffic route.

Important palaces:

1 Ca' da Mosto
2 Fondaco dei Turchi
3 Pal. Ducale (Gothic: façade on the molo and piazetta; Baroque: Porta della Carta)
4 Ca' Foscari
5 Ca' d'Oro (»flamboyant Gothic«)
6 Palazzo Grimani,
7 Pal. Vendramin-Calergi
8 Ca' Rezzonico

VENEDIG

C Palazzo Contarini
15th – 16th cent.

D Ca' Pesaro
17th cent.

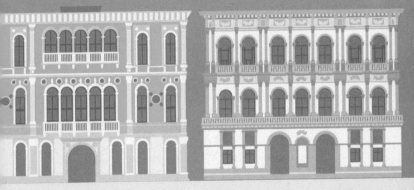

Renaissance (15th – 16th cent.)
Symmetry and harmonious proportions are emphasized more strongly again. The division of the façade shows that the side sections are enhanced compared to the middle section. Pre-Gothic style elements are grilled columns, Corinthian capitals and semicircular arches. Double columns as divisions are also typical.

▶ Baroque (17th cent.)
Venetian Baroque is an elaborately decorated Renaissance style. Columns or double columns, originally part of the outer wall, now »step out« from the wall. The façade is imaginatively decorated with garlands, cherubs and grotesque masks.

noble title in the mid-17th century. Carlo Rezzonico, later Pope Clemens XIII (1758 – 1769), was a member of this family. In the mid-19th century, the palace came into the ownership of the English poet Robert Browning, who lived there until his death in 1889. The Baroque palace has been a museum since the 1930s. Matching the grounds and the magnificent decorations, the collection provides an overview of life in Venice at the time of the Rococo, the »Settecento Veneziano«.

The approximately 40 rooms show salon art at its peak with silk wall coverings, tapestries from Flanders, playful armoires and dressers such as the precious Baroque furniture of **Andrea Brustolon** (1662–1732), who had a taste for Negroes carved from ebony and the chinoiseries and varnished furniture which were so popular in this period, as well as Venetian porcelain, ceramics and bronzes. An elegant outside stairway leads to the upper floor and into a gigantic ballroom; the ceiling paintings are by G.B. Crosato (1755). The main treasures include the wedding allegory in the adjacent hall by Giambattista Tiepolo, who immortalized the extravagant wedding of Ludovico Rezzonico to Faustina Savorgnan in 1758, and the humorous genre sketches of **Pietro Longhi** (1702–1785; second floor) about everyday life in Venice, such as *Breakfast Chocolate*, *Cruller Bakery* and *Rhinoceros*.

* Chioggia

Excursion

Location: 40km/25mi south at the end of the lagoon

Population: 54,000

Arrival: during the high season via Line 19 (Clodia, extra ticket) between S. Zaccaria and Chioggia; from the Lido (e.g. S. Maria Elisabetta stop) take the bus to Pellestrina and the ferry through the southern lagoon to Piazza Vigo (about 1.30 hrs.); the bus from Piazzale Roma is faster.

Little Venice

Chioggia (pronounced »kee-o-jah«), one of the most important fishing ports in the Adriatic, is reminiscent of Venice with its canals and narrow alleys. Of course, it cannot compete with its »big sister« in terms of artistic treasures, but on the other hand, everything is a little smaller and more intimate here. And it is a good place to go swimming.

Sightseeing

The two main axes of Chioggia are the 830m/900yd-long and 24m/26yd-wide **Corso del Popolo**, Chioggia's »board walk« with pretty old palazzi and many cafés, and the main canal with several bridges, the **Canale Vena** with the bragozzi, the colourful fishing boats typical for Chioggia. At the northern end of the Corso, at Piazzetta Vigo, the excursion boats to Venice land. Follow along the Corso past the impressive old **Granaio** (grainery) on the left; there is a fish market here every day except Monday. A few steps further the Baroque church **San Giacomo** appears on the right. In the house on the opposite side, the painter Rosalba Carriera was born in 1675 († 1757), and **Carlo Goldoni** resided here during his time in Chioggia. In his comedy *Le Baruffe Chiozzotte* (1761; Much Ado in Chiozza), Venice's celebrated poet describes the contentious peculiarities of the locals.

The **cathedral S. Maria Assunta** with its 64m/210ft-high campanile (14th century) was changed into a simple Baroque structure by Baldassare Longhena. The Gothic Oratorio San Martino beside the cathedral houses an altar by Paolo Veneziano from 1349.

Little Venice: Chioggia

At the southern city gates is the massive brick building of the former Franciscan monastery San Francesco with the Museo della Laguna Sud, which is dedicated to the history of the lagoon.

The atmosphere of the San Domenico city quarter is interesting; it lies east of Canale Vena along Chioggia's second canal. Canale San Domenico forms the backbone of the town, where fishermen repair their nets, unload boats or meet in a bar in the afternoon for caffè. To see the everyday life of Chioggia, take a walk along the canal and through one of the many narrow alleys back to the Corso del Popolo. East of Piazzetta Vigo, at the northern end of Canale S. Domenico, lies Isola San Domenico with the church of the same name, which is deocrated by an altar picture by Vittore Carpaccio (*Saint Paul*, 1520).

Isola San Domenico

Museo della Laguna Sud: Tue – Sat 9am – 1pm, Thu – Sun 9pm – 11.30pm, in Sept – June midday only 3pm – 6pm, admission €3.50

A bridge 800m/0.5mi long links the old town to the popular seaside resort of Sottomarina to the east. Behind the 11km/7mi-long sandy

Sottomarina

beach with its rows of small bathing huts and umbrellas runs a four-lane shore road. Most hotels are in rows behind the Lungomare Adriatico with a view of the beach. There are camping sites at the south and north ends of the beach.

** Collezione Peggy Guggenheim

✦ F 13

Location: Grand Canal/ Fondamenta Venier
Quays: Salute, Accademia
🕐 Wed – Mon 10am – 6pm, admission €14
www.guggenheim-venice.it

The American art collector Peggy Guggenheim moved into the incomplete palazzo in 1949. Today it is the seat of the most important museum of American and European art of the first half of the 20th century.

By comparison with the other palaces on the Grand Canal, Palazzo Venier dei Leoni almost seems like a modern building. Construction began in 1749 to plans by Lorenzo Boschetti. It is not known why only the lower floor was constructed. The name goes back to the stone lion heads which embellish the façade at the level of the water. The American art patron Peggy Guggenheim (►Famous People), lovingly and respectfully called »Venice's last doge«, lived here from 1949 to her death in 1979. While Peggy Guggenheim bequeathed the palace and the collection to the Solomon Guggenheim foundation in New York, she did it on condition that the works of art would remain in Venice and accessible to the public. The entrance is through an iron gate by Claire Falkenstein (1961) into a small garden. Here, aside from sculptures by – among others – Arp, Max Ernst and Henry Moore, are her grave and those of her dearly beloved dogs. The high-quality works in the collection represent all important artists of classical modern art: Braque, Dalí, Chagall, Duchamp, Ernst, Kandinsky, Mondrian, Picabia, Picasso, Pollock, Arp, Brancusi, Calder, Moore and others. Max Ernst, to whom Peggy Guggenheim was married for a short

---

MARCO POLO TIP

Guided tour **Insider Tip**

The audio tour of the exhibition provides a lot of interesting details on the works of art. The walls of the museum café are decorated with excellent photos from the life of Peggy Guggenheim, an extraordinary collector and patron.

time, and Jackson Pollock, whom she discovered and supported, are particularly well represented. One of the most beautiful sculptures is Constantin Brancusi's *Maiastra*, one of the most provocative Marino Marini's sculpture of a naked rider *Angel of the City* on the terrace to the Grand Canal.

Fondaco dei Tedeschi

 ✦ G 11

Location: Ponte di Rialto
Quay: Rialto

The trading rooms of 13th century German traders changed hands in late 2011 for €53 mil. The Benetton Group plans to convert the Fondaco into a luxury department store.

East of the Rialto bridge lies the Fondaco dei Tedeschi, the trading house of the German merchants (from Arabic *funduk* »storage house«, »accommodation«), first mentioned in 1228. Recently and until 2011 it was the main post office. The present structure was built in 1505 after its medieval predecessor burned down. Following Venetian tradition, the main façade to the Grand Canal has three parts. Five large gates on the canal side gave easy access to the building. The dining halls were above them in the corners. A battlement-like decorative moulding tops the façade. The architecture of the building corresponds to its purpose: four floors with 160 rooms, of which 80 are bedrooms, surround an inner courtyard. The outer rooms of the ground floor were used as sales rooms; the other rooms were stores. The upper rooms were used as living space and for administration. The customs office was on the canal. The outer façade was decorated by Giorgione and Titian, but unfortunately only fragments of the frescoes are still in existence (▶Ca' d'Oro). Both the prominent location on the Rialto and the fact that the city bore costs for rebuilding the Fondaco bespeak the economic benefit which Venice drew from the German trade: with every completed transaction, a percentage had to be given to the Venetian state. It was not for no-thing that the Fondaco was referred to as the »golden ark of the senate« in the 16th and 17th centuries. German merchants were allowed to live, store and sell their wares only here. They ate and lived together (only men were permitted) and were subject to Venetian supervision. Outside the Fondaco, they were not allowed to trade or make dealings individually, but only as a brotherhood (the associated church was ▶San Bartolomeo). In this manner, Venice kept its foreign guests firmly under control. From 1870 to 2011 the city's main post office was located here. The new owners, the Benetton Group, is converting the

Fondaco dei Tedeschi in the 18th cent. (left), followed by the Rialto Bridge, Palazzo dei Camerlenghi and Fabbriche Vecchie

complex into a shopping and exhibition centre under the direction of Dutch architect Rem Koolhaas.

AROUND FONDACO DEI TEDESCHI

San Giovanni Crisostomo

The Renaissance church in a lively neighbourhood a short distance to the north of the Fondaco is dedicated to St Chrysostom, one of the four Greek church fathers. The crossed-dome church is a masterpiece by Mauro Coducci, who built it in 1497 – 1504 on the foundations of a previous building. Giovanni Bellini's late work *SS Jerome, Christopher and Augustine* (1513) in the first side chapel on the right as well as the picture on the high altar by Sebastiano del Piombo *Madonna with Saints* (1509 – 1511; the saints include St Chrysostom). On the second altar on the left the marble top section by Tullio Lombardo is worth looking at.

Right behind the church are two small courtyards, Corte Prima and Corte Seconda del Milion, that refer to **Marco Polo** (*Il Milione* is the name of Marco Polo's book about his travels). His family probably lived here. In the **Teatro Malibran** (founded 1678), just afew steps to the south-east, concerts are held and operas are performed.

San Giovanni Crisostomo: Campo S. Giovanni Crisostomo, quay: Rialto, daily 8.15am – 12.15pm, 3pm – 7.30pm

Santa Maria dei Miracoli east of S. Giovanni Crisostomo is a master-piece of the early Renaissance, built in 1481 – 1489 on plans by Pietro and Tullio Lombardo for a miraculous picture of Mary (1408), which stands on the altar here. Outside the master builders used marble of different colours instead of sculptures as decoration; the marble was used to create rosettes, circles, octogons and crosses to decorate the façade.

*Santa Maria dei Miracoli

The hall-like interior is designed to match the exterior, which makes the golden, vaulted coffered ceiling stand out all the more effectively over the grey-red marble walls. In the ceiling coffers there are portraits of more than 50 prophets to be seen (Pier Maria Pennacchi, 1528). The elevated choir is sectioned off by a perfectly designed marble balustrade (early Renaissance) with half figures.

❶ Campo Santa Maria Nova, Mon – Sat 10am – 5pm, admission €12 (combined ticket Chorus Pass)

North of San Giovanni Crisostomo the two streets from the direction of the Rialto Bridge and the railway station (Strada Nova) meet. Here stands the outwardly unadorned Santi Apostoli church (dedicated 14th cent.), visible from far away because of its campanile, which was added in the 17th century.

Santi Apostoli

The *Cappella Corner**, which was added in the right aisle is remarkable. The square, domes room was built in the late 15th century on plans by Mauro Coducci. The beautiful example of Venetian Renaissance architecture was supposed to be the grave site of Catarina Corner, the queen of Cyprus. But her grave is in the church of San Salvador, "Mercerie while the graves of her father Marco and her brother Giorgio are located here. The richly decorated columns and the light dome create a surprising harmony. The retable by Giambattista Tiepolo, the *Communion of St Lucia* (1748), also blends in very well.

❶ Campo dei Santi Apostoli, quay Ca' d'Oro, daily 9am – 12 noon, 4pm – 7pm

★ # Fondazione Querini-Stampalia

✦ H 12

Location: Campiello Querini-Stampalia
Quay: San Zaccaria
❶ Tue – Sun 10am – 6pm, www.querinistampalia.it, admission €10

The patrician house gives a living impression of residential culture of wealthy 19th century nobility.

The beautiful 16th-century Renaissance palace near the church Santa Maria Formosa was owned by an old Venetian family that ruled the Dodecanes island of Stampalia (now Astypalaia). In 1886, the structure and its furnishings came into the possession of the city. A visit provides a beautiful impression of a patrician palace of the early 19th century. The ground floor and the gardens were carefully redesigned in the 1970s by the Venetian architect Carlo Scarpa (1906 – 1978); in 2003, extensions were made by Mario Botta. The palace houses a café-restaurant with a beautiful garden as well as an interesting bookstore. The first floor houses the richly stocked **library**.

Pinacoteca The collection, with paintings by Venetian artists of the 14th to 18th centuries, was largely assembled by Giovanni Querini-Stampalia. The cycle of paintings by **Gabriele Bella** in room 1 is especially noteworthy. It includes the famous *Women's Regatta on the Grand Canal* and *Carnival Celebration on Maundy Thursday on the Piazzetta* (mid-18th century), descriptions of everyday life in Venice. Donato Veneziano's *Coronation of the Virgin* (1372) is also well worth seeing. The most important room is room 8 with two works by **Giovanni Bellini** (*Madonna and Child*), portraits of Francesco Querini and his wife Paola by Palma the Elder, as well as Lorenzo di Credi's *Virgin with Child and St John*. The genre scenes by **Pietro Longhi** (rooms 12 and 13) provide pleasurable viewing. Bellini's *Presentation of Jesus in the Temple* in a small room right at the portego (reception or fetival hall).

Inner courtyard Scarpa turned the inner courtyard into a green space with Arabic and Japanese influences. The so-called Water Hall with its exit to the canal is also very lovely.

* SANTA MARIA FORMOSA

A short distance to the north of the Fondazione runs the **Campo Santa Maria Formosa**, bordered by beautiful palazzi. Between 1492 and 1500, Mauro Coducci built the church of the same name on the foundations of a place of worship dated from the 11th century. The façade on the Campo and the Baroque bell tower were added in the 17th century. The nearly free-standing Renaissance structure has small domes on slender columns and barrel vaults covered in outstanding Renaissance ornamentation. The main item of interest is the altar by **Bartolomeo Vivarini** with the panel *Madonna of Mercy* (1473) as well as *St Barbara* (early 16th century) by Palma the Elder on the altar in the chapel to the right of the high altar. The name »Formosa« (Venetian for »thick«) is attributed to the legend that Bishop Magnus had vision of the mother of Christ in the form of a rotund matron who told him to found the church. Until the end of

the republic, the doge visited the church every year at Candlemas.
This tradition goes back to the following occurrence: in 944, a group
of girls was abducted by Dalmatians as they were going to church.
The guild of chest-makers, who had their scuola in the church, freed
the girls. As thanks, they asked the doge to visit every year at Candlemas. »And what shall I do if it rains?« said the doge. »We will give
you a hat.« »And what if I am thirsty?« »We will give you wine.«
From then on, the doge was given a straw hat and a pitcher of wine
in Santa Maria Formosa. One of the hats is in the ▶Museo Civico
Correr.

In the church the Collegium Ducale regularly performs Baroque concerts (concert dates: www.collegiumducale.com).

❶ Campo Santa Maria Formosa, quay Rialto, Mon – Sat 10am – 5pm,
admission €12 (combination ticket Chorus Pass)

Fondazione Querini Stampalia in an early 19th cent. palace

** **Gallerie dell'Accademia**

—✦— E 13

Location: Grand Canal/ Ponte dell'Accademia
Quay: Accademia
❶ Mon 8.15 – 2pm, Tue – Sun 8.15am – 7.15pm, www.gallerieaccademia. org, admission €9 (combination ticket with Palazzo Grimani)

The gallery of paintings at the art academy, called Accademia for short, has the most significant collection of Venetian paintings worldwide from the Gothic period to Rococo.

The museum is housed in three buildings: the convent of the Lateran Canons, which was designed by Palladio in 1561, the church of Santa Maria della Carità, built 1441–1452 by Bartolomeo Bon, and the Scuola della Carità. The buildings were secularized around 1800. Shortly thereafter, art lovers turned it into a »collection site« for works of art which had become »homeless« after the dissolution of monasteries and churches as well as the clearance of nobles' palaces. This very soon resulted in a unique collection which today, housed in 24 rooms and more or less chronologically organized, offers a fascinating overview of more than 500 years of Venetian painting.

*Room 1   The tour begins on the top floor, in the former meeting room of the Scuola, which has a beautiful coffered ceiling. Altarpieces by Gothic masters of the 14th and early 15th centuries are displayed here. **Paolo Veneziano** (who worked from 1333 to 1358), Venice's first important painter, painted the altarpiece (polyptych, around 1350) from the church Santa Chiara, with the coronation of the Virgin on the central panel and four scenes from the life of Christ on each of the two side panels. Delicate colours and icon-like rigidity of the figures, particularly in the central panel, stand out in Paolo's painting, which is influenced by Byzantine forms, but becomes closer to life in the scenes of Christ.

Room 2   Room 2 exhibits altar panels from the 15th and early 16th centuries. The so-called **Pala di San Giobbe** (before 1490), one of the major works of Venetian painting in the early Renaissance by **Giovanni Bellini** (1430–1516) exemplifies the change from the small and multi-section panels of the late Gothic period to the large-format altar panel of the Renaissance. Bellini was able to compose the space within the painting as a church, with the gold mosaic of the apse arch and the marble wall coverings as a reference to the Basilica di San Marco. By showing saints around the Virgin (Sacra Conversazione), Giovanni Bellini created the Venetian prototype of a Renaissance altarpiece, which was frequently imitated, e.g. (also in this room) by Gi-

Galleria dell'Accademia

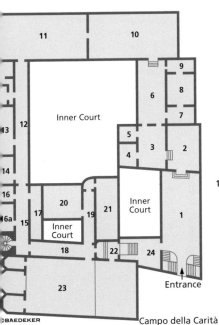

1 Early masters
2,3 Great 15th-century altar panels and Giovanni Bellini
4,5 Mantegna, Piero della Francesca, Cosmé Tura and Giorgione
6 Titian (Tiziano), Jacopo Tintoretto and Paolo Veronese
7,8 Lorenzo Lotto, Romanino and Jacopo Palma the Elder
9 Book shop
10 Titian, Jacopo Tintoretto and Paolo Veronese
11 Bonifacio Veronese, Jacopo Tintoretto, Bernado Strozzi and Giambattista Tiepolo
12,13 Marco Ricci, Francesco Zuccarelli, Giuseppe Zais, Jacopo Bassano and portraits by Jacopo Tintoretto
14 17th-century works
15 Giovanni Antonio Pellegrini, Tiepolo and Giannantonio Guardi
16,16a Works of the young Tiepolo, Alessandro Longhi, Giambattista Piazzetta and Fra'Galgario
17,18 Canaletto, Francesco Guardi, Tiepolo, Pietro Longhi, Rosalba Carriera and works of academicians
19,20 Bartolomeo Montagna, Giovanni Agostino da Lodi, Boccacio Boccaccino and the »Miracle of the Relic of the Cross«, Vittore Carpaccio
21,22 »Miracle of St Ursula«, Vittore Carpaccio and room in classical style
23 Former church Santa Maria della Carità Works of 15th-century Venetian school and murals of Scuola di San Marco
24 Sala dell'Albergo; Titian, Antonio Vivarini and Giovanni d'Alemagna

ambattista Cima da Conegliano (about 1459 – 1517) with his *Enthroned Virgin with Child* or by Vittore Carpaccio (about 1465 – 1526) with his *Presentation of Jesus in the Temple*.

Masterpieces by Giambattista Cima da Conegliano, Piero della Francesca (1416/1417 – 1492), Bellini's brother-in-law Andrea Mantegna (1431 – 1506) as well as Jacopo (1424 – 1470/71) and Giovanni Bellini are exhibited in the following rooms.

Room 5 contains numerous Madonna images, mostly half-length figures, by **Giovanni Bellini**, which prove the wide range of expression of this important Venetian Renaissance painter, including the *Madonna of the Trees* (1487) with great atmospheric effect and human dignity, as well as the *Virgin and Child between St John the Baptist and a Saint* (about 1505) before the backdrop of a charming mountain landscape. Bellini's *Pietà* (about 1505) shows his interest

Giovanni Bellini: *Pala di San Giobbe*

in the man-made environment and late Gothic piety. The grieving Virgin with Christ's body in her lap appears before a wide landscape background, a combination of views of Vicenza (cathedral, basilica of the council) and Cividale (Nasone bridge). Aside from Titian, **Giorgione** (1476/1477 – 1510) was the most important pupil of Giovanni Bellini. His famous painting *The Tempest* (La Tempesta; ▶p.57) was done shortly after 1505 and shows the mood just before a thunderstorm breaks. Using layers of colour which flow into each other, Giorgione produces a new synthesis of colours and space. On the other hand, stark realism marks Giorgione's portrait of a woman with the inscription »This is what time made of me.«

Mannerist works in **room 6** include the legendary *Handing of the Ring to the Doge* (1545 – 1550) by a fisherman at the prompting of the evangelist Mark, which **Paris Bordone** (1500 – 1571) from Treviso set at the centre of a fantastic architectural prospect in exquisitely cool colours.

Similar narrative qualities are found in the *Rich Man's Banquet* (1543 – 1545) by **Bonifacio de´ Pitati**, an allegory comparing the rich waster with musicians in joyous company under the portico of his villa with the ragged Lazarus who waits for alms in vain. The falcon hunt and the lovers in the garden refer to the pleasures of life, while the burning buildings in the background probably represent the fires of hell.

Titian's Mannerist depiction of the powerful figure of St John the Baptist, on the other hand, probably alludes to the sculpture of Michelangelo.

Room 7 The portrait of a young noble in his study by **Lorenzo Lotto** (1480 – 1556) in room 7 is a masterpiece of Mannerist portraiture.

Room 8 Among the impressive works of the 16th century are Bonifacio de' Pitati's *Massacre of the Innocents, Holy Family with Saint Catherine and St John the Baptist*, a late work in an extended triangular composition with diffuse light and perfect colour harmony by Palma il Vecchio (also known as Palma the Elder; 1480–1528), as well as *Christ Mourned with Saints* (1510), the first known work of the Lombard artist Girolamo Romani (Romanino).

A comparison between Paolo Caliari (1528–1588), known as Veronese, and Jacopo Robusti (1514 – 1594), known as Tintoretto, illuminates various currents of painting during the Counter-Reformation. On the end wall of the room hangs a giant painting by **Veronese**, *Banquet in the House of Levi,* a commission for the refectory of the Dominican church Santi Giovanni e Paolo completed in April 1573. Barely three months later, Veronese was ordered to the Holy Office of the Inquisition under suspicion of heresy, since his depiction of the Last Supper with figures such as a jester with a parrot, German lansquenets and dogs had been too free. Despite Veronese's defence on the grounds of artistic licence, he was ordered to alter the painting within three months at his own expense. The only thing he changed was the title, probably in agreement with the Dominicans who commissioned him, making reference to the fifth chapter of the gospel of St Luke: »And Levi prepared a feast for him

**Room 10

Lorenzo Lotto: *Portrait of a Young Man*

in his house.« So the Last Supper became a feast for guests, a theme which Veronese often depicted as a magnificent celebration.

By contrast, drama and unreality are the hallmarks of the art of **Tintoretto**. The work that he painted for the chapter house of the Scuola Grande di San Marco in 1548, *Saint Mark Frees a Slave* shows one of the miracles of St Mark, according to which the evangelist protected a pious slave, who had defied the orders of his master by going away to worship the relics of St Mark, from the punishment of being blinded and having his legs shattered. No less spectacular are the unusual suites of rooms in Tintoretto's depiction of the *Abduction of the Body of Saint Mark from Alexandria* (1563/1564). His *Saint Mark Saves a Pious Saracen at Sea* was probably done in the same year – another example of his ability to depict an exciting event using intense red, blue and yellow colouring.

The devastating *Pietà*, the last, uncompleted work by **Titian** (1488/90 – 1576), uses muted colours to show the fall from life into death, the group of mourners with the body of Christ before an architecture of niches with the statues of Moses and a sibyl. By comparison to the

Carpaccio's *Healing of a Possessed Man by the Relic of the Cross*

infectious joy of life in his early works, e.g. in the Assunta in the Frari church, the work of Titian's old age shows the relentlessness of death. The picture was originally intended for the Frari church, where Titan wanted to be buried.

The *Mystic Marriage of Saint Catherine* (1575) at the front of the room   **Room 11**
is a late work by **Veronese** with an almost Baroque pathos. Further works by Veronese, usually former ceiling paintings which were meant to be viewed from below, include *Ceres and Hercules Pay Homage to Venezia* (1575 – 1577) and the *Arrival of Saint Nicholas as Bishop of Myra*. Veronese's enthroned Virgin with Christ and the infant St John as well as Joseph, St Jerome, St Francis and St Justina is a ground-breaking Baroque altarpicture. **Tintoretto**'s early works (about 1550) include the two paintings *Adam and Eve* and *Cain and Abel*, each of whom is shown naked from the front and rear, the former resting in harmony, the latter engaged in conflict, within a landscape. Venetian painting reached new heights with the light world of colour and joyous compositions of the Rococo painter Giovanni Battista **Tiepolo** (1696 – 1770), who rendered the large ceiling painting *Saint Helena Finds the True Cross* (the mother of the emperor Constantine).

Significant works in the following rooms include the portrait of the   **Room 13 and**
procurator Jacopo Soranzo by **Tintoretto**, *St Jerome in Meditation* by   **16**
Jacopo da Ponte, also known as **Bassano** (1517 – 1592), both in room 13, as well as the four mythological scenes *The Rape of Europa, Diana and Actaeon, Diana Discovers Calypso* and *Apollo and Marsyas*, early works from the years 1720 – 1722 by Giambattista **Tiepolo** in **room 16**.

Fantasy architecture, capricci of ruins and vedute with strong con-   **Room 17**
trasts of light and shade are characteristics of Antonio Canal, also known as **Canaletto** (1697 – 1768), who combined observation of life with imagination in an entertaining manner. **Rosalba Carriera** (1675 – 1758) gained great fame with her pastel portraits. Few artists proved to be such keen-eyed chroniclers of Venetian everyday life in the 18th century as **Pietro Longhi** (1702 – 1785).

The cycle of paintings on the **miracles of the relic of the True Cross**   ****Room 20**
is unique. Renowned Venetian artists painted it between 1494 and 1502 for the Sala dell'Albergo of the Scuola di San Giovanni Evangelista, in which a relic of the cross of Christ was kept from 1369. **Gentile Bellini** (1429 – 1507) painted the procession on Piazza San Marco with a detailed reproduction of the piazza from the time around 1500. The 13th-century medieval mosaics, which were later replaced, can still be seen above the five portals of St Mark's Basilica. The exhi-

bition continues with **Gentile's** depiction of the miracle of the True Cross relic at the Ponte San Lorenzo, where the relic had fallen into the water during the annual procession. It reappeared in the hand of the searching grand master of the Scuola and pulled him ashore. Witnesses to this event shown on the left of the painting include Catarina Cornaro, Queen of Cyprus, with her court and members of the Scuola to the right. Gentile sets the miraculous healing of Pietro de Ludovici in a church, most likely San Giovanni Evangelista. Vittore **Carpaccio** (1465–1526) has the miracle of the healing take place at the Rialto bridge and draws a precise picture of the buildings in the busy merchant quarter.

** Room 21 The **cycle on the life of Saint Ursula** in room 21, which was painted for the Scuola di Sant'Orsola, is the work of Vittore **Carpaccio** (about 1465 to 1526). According to legend, Ursula, a Christian princess from Brittany, consented to marry Aetherius, the son of a heathen English ruler, on condition that he would be baptized and make a pilgrimage to Rome with her. On the return journey, Ursula and her companions suffered martyrdom, as had been predicted to her in a dream, before the gates of Cologne, which was besieged by the Huns.

Room 23
Room 24 The former church contains works of the early Venetian Renaissance, including altarpieces from the 1460s by Giovanni **Bellini** and his assistants. The last room (room 24), the guest house of the Carità brotherhood, houses **Titian's** *Mary in the Temple* (1534 – 1538). The only painting which he created for the brotherhood still hangs in its original place.

Ponte dell'- Accademia For centuries, the Ponte di Rialto was the only bridge across the Grand Canal. It was only in 1854 that the Austrian occupying power – Venice was part of the Habsburg kingdom of Lombardo-Venetia from 1815 – decided to build a second pedestrian crossing. This resulted in the iron academy bridge, which was replaced with a higher wooden bridge in 1932.

* I Gesuiti

✦ G/H 9/10

Location: Campo dei Gesuiti
Quay: Fondamente Nuove
❶ April – Oct Thu – Sat 10am – 12 noon, otherwise on appointment, tel. 04 12 70 24 64

The Jesuits were not tolerated in Venice due to their closeness to the pope. Only in 1657 were they allowed into Venice.

In 1715, the order decided to build a large monastery. In 1729, the church was completed to plans by Domenico Rossi. Its richly decorated protruding façade in the Baroque style, following the pattern of the mother church Il Gesù in Rome, impressively reflects the self-confidence of the order. The barrel-vaulted hall with its side chapels, transept and choir is impressively furnished: wall coverings of green and white marble, mighty columns, pilasters, gilding and a high altar with an altar canopy and sculptural decoration. The main item of interest, one of the paintings in the first chapel on the left, is ****Titian's Martyrdom of Saint Lawrence** (1558–1560): beside the tortured saint, a light shimmering in the dark night announces the heavenly message, the soul's hope of eternal life. The Assumption of the Virgin by Tintoretto in the left transept, and the wall and ceiling paintings by Palma the Younger in the sacristy are also worthy of note.

In the adjacent Oratorio, the remains of a hospice founded in the 13th century for crusaders, an cycle by Palma the Elder (1583 – 1591) relates the story of the order of the Templars.

Oratorio dei Crociferi

❶ Tours only on appointment at info@ scalabovolo.org, admissions €60

* Ghetto

✦ E 9/10

Location: Ghetto Vecchio and Ghetto Nuovo
Quays: San Marcuola, Ponte Guglie

In Cannaregio, not far from Santa Lucia railway station, lies the world's oldest ghetto.

Today, only a few of the approximately 150 Venetian Jews live in this city quarter, including pensioners in the old people's home Casa Israelitica de Riposo, and in other ways, too, the ghetto scarcely differs from its surroundings. Nevertheless, a special atmosphere has remained here. It is revealed during a stroll through the quarter, when visiting the little museum and in a tour of a synagogue.

Oldest ghetto of the world

The Venetian republic was always home to people of varied nationalities and religions, who were all subject to strict control. This particularly applied to the Jews (►MARCO POLO Insight p.209), who only had limited residence rights. When anti-Semitic feeling intensified in the early 16th century, the Serenissima thought of a solution which was later adopted by nearly all cities: in 1516, the approximately 700 Jews were resettled to a city quarter in Cannaregio which had once been part of a cannon works, was surrounded by water and was called the »ghetto« in the Venetian dialect. This expression soon came into use for the Jewish quarters in all of Italy. The Jews were al-

MARCO POLO TIP

! *Mouth-watering* Insider Tip

Volpe, a bakery in the Old Ghetto, makes traditional Jewish delicacies including empade (almond pastries) and unleavened bread (pane azzimo; Paneficio Volpe, Calle del Ghetto Vecchio, tel. 0 41 71 51 78.
Gam-Gam, the only kosher restaurant in Venice, is situated at the entrance to the ghetto and has a wide range of traditional dishes (Sottoportego del Ghetto Vecchio, Cannaregio 1122; tel. 04 12 75 92 56, gamgamkosher. com, closed Fri evening and Sat.

lowed to move about freely in the daytime, but at dusk, they had to return to the ghetto. The entrances were closed at night and guarded by armed men. The Jews lived their own life in the ghetto. There were three communities of differing origins: Ashkenazim, Levantines and Sepahrdic Jews. The Jewish population increased greatly. In 1541, the ghetto was expanded to include the Ghetto Vecchio (old ghetto), and in 1633, the Ghetto Nuovissimo (newest ghetto). At times in the 17th century 5,000 people lived here, and the shortage of space forced the residents to build upwards. In this way, up to eight-storey »skyscrapers« were constructed. Behind simple house façades, the ghetto contains the five best-preserved synagogues of the Middle Ages, a unique documentation of Jewish customs.

Sightseeing
The so-called schools and synagogues in the ghetto **can only be viewed with guides** (in Italian and English); the meeting and information point is at the Jewish museum, beginning hourly from 10.30 am, June – Sept until 5.30pm, otherwise until 4.30pm, Fri usually only until 3.30pm, www.ghetto.it.

The best way to reach the ghetto is from Fondamenta di Cannaregio and through a narrow access passage (Sottoportego, next to the kosher restaurant Gam-Gam, ▶Tip above), which was once closed at night. Only a few steps away, above on the left in the wall, a stone tablet from 1704 can be seen with the catalogue of punishments for Jews who secretly adhered to their religious customs despite converting to Christianity. The narrow alley leads to Campiello delle Scuole, on which there are two synagogues. The **Scuola Spagnola** from the second half of the 16th century was redesigned in 1635 by the Baroque architect Baldassare Longhena. Brass chandeliers, gilded wood, multi-coloured marble and an elaborately ornamented balustrade decorate the interior. The **Scuola Levantina**, probably Venice's most magnificent synagogue, impresses with a richly carved lectern (teva) on spiral columns by Andrea Brustolon from Belluno.

Campo di Ghetto Nuovo
A narrow bridge leads to Campo di Ghetto Nuovo. Narrow, high buildings line the piazza. A memorial by sculptor Arbit Blatas tells of Rabbi Ottolenghi and 200 Venetian Jews who were deported with him between 1943 and 1944. At the house number 2912, a faded in-

The Oldest Ghetto in the World

The most famous Jew in Venice, Shylock, may be an invention by William Shakespeare (The Merchant of Venice, 1596/1597), but the city's ghetto actually exists. It is even the oldest in the world.

There were probably small Jewish communities in Venice around the year 1000, when it was one of the most important reloading points between Europe and the Levant, the orient. In 1152, 100 Jews are mentioned in a census. As successful businessmen, they maintained trade relationships across all oceans. This was beneficial to the republic, since – using Jewish intermediaries – it was even able to sell goods to those countries with which it was feuding. This was one of the reasons that Jews settled in northern Italy and especially in Venice during a period when their fellow believers were being persecuted in Europe. However, their freedom was restricted. They were not permitted to own real estate, nor could they pursue a trade other than becoming a doctor (they were barred from the Christian guilds); they also had to pay taxes »for their protection«. However, they were very successful in the business of loaning money (in which Christians could not engage since the New Testament forbade charging interest).

Scuola Tedesca, the ghetto's oldest synagogue

Fear of Foreign Infiltration

When ever more Jews streamed to the city after the infamous decree by Ferdinand the Catholic in 1492, which banished all Jews from Spain and Portugal, even the Venetians began to have misgivings. To make it easier to monitor them, the republic assigned the Jews a specific residential area in March of 1516: »All Jews must live together in the complex of houses located in the ghetto near San Girolamo; to ensure that they are not out and about all night, two gates shall be erected on the side of the Ghetto Vecchio where there is a small bridge, and also on the other side of the bridge; that is, one gate for each of the locations mentioned. Each gate must be opened in the morning at the sound of the Marangona bell and must be locked in the evening at 12.00 midnight by four Christian guards, who are hired and paid for their services by their Jews at a price our council deems appropriate.« The name of the site where a foundry used to be located, **Getto** in Venetian, soon became the accepted term for the Jewish quarters in Italy and then all over the world. In 1516 the population of the ghetto was 700; by 1536 the number had more than doubled, and by 1630 it peaked at 5,000 residents. Thus Jews represented between 2.5 and 3.3 % of the total population of Venice in the 17th century. Soon the ghetto was overcrowded. At times, 897 persons per hectare lived here (236 in the remainder of the city). Due to the lack of space, the houses grew upwards; some of them had up to eight storeys.

Three Nations

Three communities, called nations, existed side by side: Ashkenazim (Jews from Germany, Poland and other parts of eastern Europe); Levantines from the orient; and Sephardim, fugitives of the inquisition in Spain and Portugal. They had their own synagogues, called **Scuole** – which now provide a unique point of reference regarding Jewish customs and culture during the renaissance – as well as their own teachers and judges, rabbis and social institutions. The group that represented their interests, **Università**, which was a panel with twelve and later six members with far-reaching social, religious and economic authority, was the negotiation partner for the Venetian government and regulated the distribution of the financial burdens that were imposed on them by the community in the form of taxes and forced loans. In short, the ghetto was a city within the city. This multicultural Jewish community produced eminent rabbis, scholars and poets, including

Leone da Modena (1571-1648), **Simone Lazzatto** (1583-1663), **Simone Calimani** (1699-1784), and **Sara Coppia Sullam** (1590-1641), whose correspondence with the Genoese clergyman Ansaldo Céba represents an important contribution to the understanding between Christians and Jews. Hebrew printing, for which Venice was the most important centre, was essential in order to spread all of these ideas.

The End of the Ghetto

Although the Jewish community in Venice was frequently subjected to hostilities, the Jews lived in relative safety by and large. When the situation of the republic continued to worsen during the 18th century, even Jewish capital was unable to stem the decline of Venice. Since the forced loans continued to increase in the face of the Turkish wars – the Jewish community paid the enormous sum of 800,000 gold ducats between 1669 and 1700 – the financial means of the Jewish lenders were finally exhausted; by 1737, the banks actually went bankrupt. The population shrank. Towards the end of the 18th century, only 1,620 Jews lived in the ghetto; approximately one third of them was well off, while the rest lived on the edge of poverty. In the end, outside forces were required to change their fate. On July 7, 1797, French soldiers tore down the ghetto gates; the residents became free citizens. The Jewish population gradually settled in other parts of the city. The ghetto degenerated. This did not change until Italy capitulated and the country

was occupied in September 1943. 200 Jews were deported in August 1944. There are two monuments in their memory. Only a few Jews live in the ghetto today. There are only about 200 in the entire city, since young Jews are also moving to the mainland. And so the oldest ghetto in the world is kept alive by tourism alone. The synagogues are scarcely recognizable from the outside, since they were actually built right into the residences. They can only be viewed as part of a guided tour (meeting place and information in the Jewish Museum, ►p. 213).

A Levantine Jew in Venice

scription marks the site of the »banco rosso«, one of the Jewish pawn houses, which were called »verde«, »negro« or »rosso« depending on the colour of their receipts, and lent money to all classes of Venetian society. Behind high, inconspicuous façades, three ****synagogues** are concealed on the upper storeys. Five windows, a Baroque dome and a cartouche with the inscription »Santa Communità Italiana» identify the **Scuola Italiana**, the most modest of the Venetian synagogues, which was built in 1575. The adjacent **Scuola Ganton** – the name may go back to the donor family or the location on a corner – was founded in 1531. The building is not recognizable from the outside, except for a small wooden cupola. Inside it is similar to a church, with a prayer pulpit (bima) in a small domed apse. The **Scuola Tedesca** is in the same building as the museum. The oldest synagogue in Venice can be recognized by its five large arched windows in the façade (three have been bricked up). It was built into the exist-

Campo di Ghetto Nuovo

ing houses in 1528, which produced its slightly asymmetric layout. In the 18th century, it acquired a worldly character, and was rebuilt in the manner of a theatre. At that time it received its oval, gilded women's gallery.

The little museum of the Jewish community exhibits liturgical items, manuscripts and documents about the history of the Venetian Jews, including oil lamps, crowns and cases for the law scrolls as well as a protective covering for the Esther scroll, which has been dated to the 5th century BC. This scroll tells of the rescue of the Persian Jews by Queen Esther. The museum has a bookstore and a café. **Museo Ebraico**

Museo Ebraico: Sun – Fri June – Sept 10am – 7pm, otherwise until 5.30pm, admission €4, with guided tour of the synagogue €10, www.museo ebraico. it; further information: www.jewishvenice.org and moked.it/veneziaebraica

Old Jewish Cemetery on the ►Lido: tours Sun 2.30pm, after registering in the museum, tel. 0 41 71 53 59, also on other days; meeting point Lido, Riviera San Nicolò, opposite the boat landing

The church dedicated to Job of the Old Testament, San Giobbe, is an excellent example of Venetian early Renaissance sacred architecture. ***San Giobbe' Elena**
Its builders were from 1450 Antonio Gambello, who began building the church with the Late Gothic campanile, and Pietro Lombardo, who continued with the beautiful doors, the choir dome and the Cappella Martini from 1471 in the Renaissance style. The Cappella Martini (second side chapel) with its colourfully glazed terracotta tiles   from the school of the Florentine Luca della Robbia, at the fourth side altar on the right a St Peter by Paris Bordone (16th cent.) and the grave marker for the doge and church benefactor Cristoforo Moro (in office: 1462 – 1471) in front of the high al-

> **Insider Tip**
>
> **MARCO POLO TIP**
>
> ! **Dalla Marisa**
>
> The little trattoria at the Ponte dei Tre Archi cooks only according to traditional (mainland) recipes, e.g. sguazzetti alla bechera, stewed beef innards, or tasty venison ragout. Generous portions and very reasonable for Venice. When ordered in advance, there are also fish lasagna or stuffed clams. Make sure to make reservations! Dalla Marisa, Cannaregio, Fondamenta S. Giobbe 652/b, tel. 041720211.

tar all deserve special attention. In the sacristy is a portrait of Moro and a triptych by Antonio Vivarini (around 1445).

❶ Campo San Giobbe, quay Stazione Santa Lucia, Mon – Sat 10am – 1pm, admission €12 (combination ticket Chorus Pass)

It is only a few steps from here to the end of the Cannaregio Canal, which offers a nice view of the lagoon. In the Ex-Macelli, the former slaughterhouse from the 19th century, part of the university of Venice is housed today. **Fondamente di S. Giobbe**

Giardini Pubblici

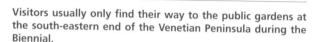

✦ **L-M 14**

Location: Riva dei Sette Martiri
Quay: Giardini

Visitors usually only find their way to the public gardens at the south-eastern end of the Venetian Peninsula during the Biennial.

Modern art in the public gardens

The public gardens at the south end of the Venetian peninsula were built in 1807 at the command of Napoleon I. Since the founding of the **Biennial**, the exhibition pavilions of the various nations have stood here, including interesting examples of modern architecture. Nonetheless, there is enough space for Rococo and 19th-century statues and for a stroll under palm trees, acacias and plane trees. The most impressive buildings – which, however, are accessible only during the Biennial – include, to the right of the main entrance (by Antonio Selva, 1810) the Venetian pavilion (1954 – 1956) by Carlo Scarpa and beside it, the Russian pavilion in *Gründerzeit* style (1914). Turn left at the main entrance to get to the Italian pavilion in the classical style. Other renowned architects represented here are Josef Hoffmann (Austrian pavilion, 1934), Gerrit Thomas Rietveld (pavilion of the Netherlands, 1954) and Alvar Aalto (Finnish pavilion, 1956). The book pavilion, built of glass, was designed by the Glaswegian James Stirling (with Michael Wilford, 1991), the Australian pavilion (1988) by Peter Cox.

Sant' Elena

Sant' Elena, the south-easternmost residential quarter in Castello, was not reclaimed from the lagoon until the 19th century. In addition to a naval school, the football stadium of the city is situated here.

San Pietro di Castello

A little to the north, on the island of San Pietro di Castello was once the oldest settlement of the lagoon, namely **Olivolo**. According to a 7th cent. legend St Peter is supposed to have appeared to Bishop Magnus of Altinum and commanded him to build a church on that spot. San Pietro was the seat of the spiritual leader of the city in 775 – 1807, until the office was passed to St Mark's cathedral (until then it was »only« the Doge's palace chapel). The present building was constructed in the 17th cent.; the façade is supposed to go back to Andrea Palladio. The impressive campanile was created by Mauro Coducci 1482 – 1488, the tower canopy is from the 17th cent. Next to the Baroque high altar (1649) the choir frescos (1735) by Girolamo Pellegrini, the altar picture of SS John Evangelista, Peter and Paul, which is ascribed to Veronese, as well as the Cattedra di San Pietro, the seat of St Peter, are important. Peter is supposed to have sat on

Contemporary International Culture

The oldest international forum for contemporary culture, the biennial of Venice, goes back to the initiative of the Venetian mayor, man of letters and artist Riccardo Selvatico in the year 1895.

When the gates opened for the first biennial on 30 April 1895 on the site of the Giardini in the Castello district, 516 works by 285 artists were on display in a single pavilion, which attracted almost 225,000 visitors. Success with the public was sustained during subsequent biennials; in 1909, a full 457,960 art connoisseurs came to Venice, a record that was not broken until 1976. Initially, the art show was organized by topics instead of nationalities, and the works were selected through consultation with domestic and foreign art associations. The 1907 biennial was the first to feature **national pavilions**. Today, the biennial site is home to approximately 30 pavilions administered by national commissioners, including some architecturally very interesting buildings. Critics of the art show allege that little new material is being displayed and that the biennial is serving the art market and tourism. However, the art show has defended its place in the international art scene. It takes place in odd-numbered years and runs for almost six months (June to November).

It has also claimed additional exhibition spaces all over the city in addition to the Giardini, including the **arsenal** which is not accessible except during the art show, and former scuole and deconsecrated churches. Tickets are available at Hellovenezia (▶p. 301).There is a varied music, dance and film supporting program parallel to the biennial. The next art biennials will take place in 2015, 2017 and 2019. In even-numbered years, the **architecture biennial** which is also very prestigious, provides information on current trends. More information is available at www.labiennale.com.

this marble throne in Antioch; the back is an Arab gravestone with Qur'an texts carved into it. Cappella Vendramin owes its rich sculpturing to Baldassare Longhena.

❶ Mon – Sat 10am – 5pm, admission €12 (combination ticket Chorus Pass)

La Giudecca

✷ C-H 14/15

Population: 4700
Quays: Zitelle, Redentore, Palanca, Sant'Eufemia (Vaporetto 2, 41, 42)

The island off the coast of Venice's old city, about 2km/1.2mi long and at the most 300m/1000ft wide, actually consists of eight connected islands.

Largest island of the lagoon
From the Zattere quay the Isola della Giudecca, to the south of the Canale della Giudecca, looks like a 2km/1.25-mi-long stage set. Three buildings dominate it: at the two ends, the church Le Zitelle and the massive former pasta factory Stucky, and at its centre, Palladio's Il Redentore church. La Giudecca actually consists of eight islands separated by canals (rii) and linked by bridges. Its original name was **Spina Lunga** (long fishbone); it probably owes its present name to the Giudicati, people who were banished here from Venice in the 9th century for minor offenses. Then well-off patricians discovered the island as a summer retreat. From the 14th century to the early 19th century, they built beautiful villas with extensive parks on the side towards the city centre, tucked away behind walls. The side towards the lagoon was occupied by seven monasteries and small palazzi of the literary academy, whose most brilliant member was Carlo Goldoni. In the 19th and 20th centuries, several industrial operations moved here, and the island became a workers' quarter. Aside from housing and a women's prison, there are still some workshops here, as well as the legendary Hotel Cipriani, the youth hostel and a few artists' studios. The com-

MARCO ⊕ POLO TIP

Insider Tip

Cheap sleep and Harry's Dolci

For budget accommodation in a wonderful location: Ostello Venezia, the youth hostel on the island of Giudecca. It is necessary to book well in advance (Zitelle quay, bed and breakfast €21, www.hos telvenice.org, tel. 04 18 77 82 88). For a break from sightseeing, go to Harry's Dolci at Fondamenta S. Biagio 773. Harry's Dolci is cheaper than its famous »big brother« Harry's Bar and has a magnificent view of Dorsoduro and San Marco from the terrace (wide selection of sweet delights as well as main courses; closed Tue and mid-Nov to mid-March, tel. 04 15 22 48 44.

poser Luigi Nono, born in 1924 opposite on the Zattere, lived the end of his life (until 1990) on Giudecca; the **Nono archive** (www.luigi-nono.it) is housed in the monastery SS Cosma e Damiano.

The brilliant white Capucine church is regarded as one of the main works of Andrea Palladio. He was guided by models from antiquity, particularly the ten books of architecture by Vitruvius from the time of the Emperor Augustus. Consequently, Palladio composed the front of I Redentore from three temple façades placed one inside the other. Palladio adopted the double pediment and attic storeys from the Pantheon in Rome, while the dominant dome between the nave and the monks' choir forms the centre of the aisle-less hall church. The **Festival of the Redeemer** (Festa del Redentore) and the church have their origins in a plague epidemic of 1576, which claimed the lives of 50,000 people, one third of the population of the city. At that time, the senate vowed to build the church and hold a celebration for the Redeemer (Redentore). The Capucine order took responsibility for pastoral functions. Construction began in July 1577. After Palladio's death, the building was completed by Antonio da Ponte, the architect of the Rialto bridge, in 1592. Three oval chapels lie on each side of the nave, whose design is reminiscent of a hall in Roman baths. Their altarpieces depict scenes from the life of Christ. The *Baptism of Christ* originates from the workshop of Veronese, while the two altarpieces *Flagellation* and *Transfiguration of Jesus* are from the school of Tintoretto. While the late Baroque main altar was built only in 1680, the bronze crucifixion group dates from the late 16th century. Like the high altar, it is by Girolamo Campagna (1550 – 1623).

M II
Redentore

❶ Mon – Sat, 10am – 5pm, admission €3, quay: Redentore

Il Redentore

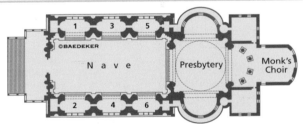

Altar Paintings
1 »Ascension of Christ«, school of Tintoretto
2 »Nativity« by Francesco Bassano
3 »Resurrection« by Francesco Bassano
4 »Baptism of Christ«, school of Veronese
5 »Entombment of Christ« by Palma il Giovane
6 »Flagellation of Christ«, school of Tintoretto

Il Redentore by Andrea Palladio

Festa del Redentore

After the church was consecrated, the doge made a procession here over a floating bridge of boats every year with the leading persons of the state to attend the mass of thanksgiving. This **Festival of the Redeemer** is still held. On the third Sunday in June, the Venetians take part in a procession, now across a pontoon bridge, from Zattere across the Canale della Giudecca to the Redentore church. The festival ends in the evening with magnificent fireworks and a parade of illuminated boats.

Le Zitelle

The church 500m/550yd east, Le Zitelle, whose official name is Santa Maria della Presentazione, also derives from Andrea Palladio. However, it was only built after his death, from 1582–1586, by Jacopo Bozzetto. The church itself is largely a structure of the 18th century. The monastery that was once associated with it was a foundation for girls from poor families (zitelle = virgins), who produced famous lace here; today it houses a conference centre. The adjacent Art nouveau palace **Casa dei Tre Oci** is used for rotating exhibits. At the point of the island is the luxury hotel Cipriani (www.hotelcipriani.com).

The church dedicated to the Roman martyr Euphemia, about 600m/650yd to the west, was founded in the 9th century. It received its classical colonnade in the 18th cent. from Tommaso Temanza. At that time, its interior was also painted by Giambattista Canal, following the example of ▶Il Gesuiti. Bartolomeo Vivarini painted the triptych *San Rocco and the Angel* as well as the scene in the lunette above it, *Virgin with Child* (1480; first altar in the right aisle).

Sant'Eufemia

The giant brick complex Mulino Stucky occupies the west end of the island. Despite vigorous protests, the well-off Swiss pasta manufacturer Giovanni Stucky had it built in 1895, with a mill, grain silos and warehouses, by the architect Ernst Wullekopf in the neo-Gothic style. It was in operation until 1954. Since 2007 it is the **Hilton Molino Stucky**, a gigantic 380-bed hotel and conference centre (▶p. 78).

Mulino
Stucky

On the plot Giudecca 484, where the German company Junghans once manufactured clocks and detonators for bombs, Judeca Nova was built to plans by Cino Zucchi (Milan) and Boris Podrecca (Vienna/Stuttgart) in Bauhaus style out of and between sections of the Junghans buildings worth saving, with luxury apartments, stores and a cultural centre.

Judeca Nova

Islands in the Lagoon

 Excursion

Many small islands lie like enchanted oases in the shallow waters of the Venetian lagoon. Emilio Casteler described them as »floating gardens«, and Lord Byron saw the islands »rising from the waters as if invoked by fairies«.

The archipela-
go of Venice

Except for ▶Burano, ▶Murano and ▶Torcello, few islands are inhabited today, and it is hard to imagine that Venice's history began here 1500 years ago. In the course of time, the islands served a variety of purposes. Some had monasteries, accommodation for pilgrims on their way to the Holy Land, or hospices and quarantine stations. Others had forts or powder stores built on them for Venice's defence system. Nearly all these structures have been abandoned. The buildings fell into ruin, though the building material often found new uses, and nature took over. In recent years, the city authorities have leased or sold some islands to private investors or environmental organizations. Other islands were rediscovered by Venetians as places for excursions – especially in summer, when Venice is »flooded« by tourists. The larger islands are served by the vaporetto network. Out- of-the-way islands can be explored individually or on guided tours.

Venice's
archipelago

The Venetian Lagoon

Pravè
Vécchia

Portegrandi

Altino

Ca' Montiran

F. Zero

ale

arello

Valle

Cason
di Val Dogà

V. di Cà Zane

Can. Silonetto

Silone

Can. Cenesa

Paluda del Bombagio

Palude Maggiore

Cason
Grassabo

Grassabo

Vallesina

Palude di Cona

Monte
dell'Oro

I. S. Cristina

Cason Vecchio
di Grassabo

Palude
della Rosa

la Cura

ex Saline di S. Felice

Ca' Lio Maggiore

Tarcello

Ossario di
S. Ariano

Can. d. Ancora

Palude
della Centrega

Can. d. Bàri

Liona

Laguna
del Cavallino

Porte
Falconera

Porte
del Cavallino

rto
Polo

*I. Buèl
el Lovo*

Mazzorbo

Palude del Traìo

Lio Piccolo

Ca'Zóia

Can. di Burano

Burano

Valle Paleazza

ra

Monte

Scomenzera S. Giacomo

*I. Madonna
del Monte*

**S. Francesco
d. Deserto**

Can. S. Felice

V. Sacchetta

Le Mesole

Cavallino

Il Ghetto

Can. Pordelio

*Porto di
Paive Vécchia*

ra

Can.
Bisatto

*I. San Giacomo
in Palude*

Sant' Erasmo

Treporti

Te Due
Sorelle

Cason
di Valle

Ca' di Valle

Can. di S. Nicolò

Michele

Le Vignole

Litorale di S. Erasmo

Can. d. Orfano

Can. d. Crevan

Ca' Pasquali

Ca' Vio

Ca' Ballarin

Can. Pordelio

Punta Sabbioni

Ca' Savio

Litorale del Cavallino

èrvolo

Lido

*I. S. Làzzaro
degli Armeni*

Canale di Treporti

Porto di
Lido

Città
ardino

a' Bianca

Bizio Lido

M a r e   A d r i á t i c o

2 km

1,74 mi

©BAEDEKER

NORTHERN LAGOON

*San Michele

The cypress-covered cemetery island, halfway between Fondamente Nuove and ▶Murano, was used in the 13th century by Camaldolese monks. It has been the cemetery island of Venice since 1870. Among others, the Russian ballet impresario Sergei Diaghilev (1872 – 1929), his countryman and composer Igor Stravinsky (1882 – 1971) and the American poet Ezra Pound (1885 – 1972) rest here. Of the monastery, the 15th-century Gothic cloister and the lovely Renaissance church San Michele by Mauro Coducci (1469 – 1478) remain. A connecting door gives access to the hexagonal Cappella Emiliana, which is decorated with red and green marble and was added in 1530 by Guglielmo Bergamasco. Currently the cemetery island is being expanded by 60,000m2/72,000sq ft and a terrace on plans by the architect David Chipperfield. So far the impressive Corte dei Quattro Evangelisti has been completed.

❶ Church of San Michele daily 7.30am – 12.15pm, 3pm – 4pm
Vaporetto 4.1, 4.2 from Fondamente Nuove

Sant'Erasmo and Le Vignole

For centuries, Le Vignole and particularly Sant'Erasmo have been Venice's vegetable gardens and popular places for excursions: miles of wet, fertile land with large fields on which asparagus, artichokes (castraure), onions, potatoes and grapevines grow – all of which are sold in the Rialto market. Both islands were fortified in the 19th century. Reminders of this include the Forte di Sant' Andrea on Le Vignole, which was built in 1543 by Michele Sanmichele and expanded in 1571 after the Battle of Lepanto, and the Torre Massimiliana on Sant'Erasmo. The ferry first stops at **Le Vignole**. The island used to be named Isola delle Sette Vigne, island of the seven vineyards. Wine is still grown here, and is known for its slightly salty taste (wine festival, Festa del Mosto on the first Sunday in October). **Sant'Erasmo** (www.santerasmovenezia.com) is the largest island in the lagoon and suitable for a long hike. About 800 people still live here, mainly engaged in agriculture (there are three quays as well as private automobile traffic). It is best to disembark at the first stop (Capannone) and walk in the direction of Torre Massimiliana. There is a small beach at the fortification tower in the south-east of the island, where Ai Tedeschi has simple, good food (open daily). From here, the road leads through fields and meadows around the island. At its centre, there is a second bar, Ca' Vignotto.

Insider Tip

❶ Vaporetto 13 from Fondamente Nuove; A❶ Tedeschi: open daily; Ca' Vignotto: only midday, Thu – Sat also evenings, tel. 04 12 44 40 00

*San Francesco del Deserto

Legend tells that St Francis stopped on this tiny island between Burano and Sant'Erasmo on his way home from the Holy Land in 1220. Franciscan monks lived on the island from the 13th century to the

secularisation in 1806 by Napoleon. From that time, it remained abandoned until the 19th century. Today, nothing reminds visitors of the times of decay. The few monks who live here offer guided tours for a small donation. The monastery buildings are grouped at the centre of the island. The small church dating from 1228 is situated amongst cypress trees and has an enchanting atmosphere.

San Francesco del Deserto

❶ Vaporetto 12 from Fondamente Nuove to Burano, continue with a water taxi; tours Tue – Sun 9am –11am, 3pm – 5pm. With accommodations after prior reservations, tel. 04 15 28 68 63

The first residents of this island south-west of Sant'Erasmo were hermits. From 1846, a quarantine station for people and goods was located here. In 1576, during the plague epidemic, up to 10,000 are said to have been housed here. Today, nature has largely reclaimed the island.

Lazzaretto Nuovo

❶ Vaporetto 13 from Fondamente Nuove at 9.25am and 4.05pm. Tours by the Archeoclub d'Italia: April – Oct Sat, Sun 9.45am and 4.30pm, otherwise on appointment, tel. 04 12 44 40 11, www.lazzarettonuovo.com

SOUTH LAGOON

The ferry to San Lazzaro (▶below) first stops on the island of San Servolo (4.8ha/12ac), where monks already lived in the seventh century. From the 12th cent. until 1716 it was the home of Benedictine nuns; their convent later became a psychiatric institution. Since 2003 the Provincia di Venezia has run a modern seminar centre with guest house here (www.sanservolo.provincia.venezia.it). The tour includes the church and the Museo del Manicomio (museum of the insane asylum). The Venice International University, a joint project of Venice, Barcelona, Munich and Durham universities for students and lecturers (information tel. 04 12 71 95 11 and www.univiu.org) is also located on the island.

San Servolo

❶ Tours on appointment: tel. 04 15 24 01 19; information Venice International University: tel. 04 12 71 95 11, www.univiu.org

San Lazzaro, the island before the Lido, is only 3 hectares (7 acres) in size – space enough for a monastery, a garden and a little cemetery.

**San Lazzaro degli Armeni

Today, about 30 Mechitarist monks live here. In 1717 Mechitar, the Armenian founder of the order (born 1676 in Sivas, Anatolia; Armenian: Sebaste) fled to Venice from Ottoman forces with 19 brothers of the order. The doge granted them the use of the little island. The monastery museum exhibits documents on Armenian history and a 3,000-year-old Egyptian mummy, below a ceiling painting by Tiepolo. Its most precious treasure is the Armenian library with about 150,000 books and writings from the years 862 to 1700, among them the Armenian translation of a lost Greek biography of Alexander the Great as well as a medical book from 1281. In the monastery's own publishing house, the monks published the main works of Armenian literature, translations of important works of Italian literature, and a series of dictionaries. One exhibition commemorates Lord Byron. The romantic poet and traveller lived on the island in 1816 to learn the language of the monks. The monastery can be viewed daily on a guided tour by the monks between 3.30pm and 5.30pm.

About 300,000 of the eight million Armenians belong to the Armenian Catholic church. It recognizes the pope, but celebrates its mass with old Armenian liturgy. The patriarch is based in Lebanon.

❶ Monastery tour daily 3.30pm (timed to the arrival of vaporetto 20 from San Zaccaria, departs 3.10pm), admission €6

La Grazia and Lazzaretto Vecchio

The many pilgrims who sailed from Venice to the Holy Land in the Middle Ages had their own accommodation on the islands La Grazia and Lazzaretto Vecchio. Later, epidemics and infectious diseases were treated here. Lazzaretto Vecchio has recently found use as an animal shelter.

Lido di Jesolo

✴ **Excursion**

Population: 25 600 (mit Jesolo)
Arrival: Bus from Piazzale Roma to Lido di Jesolo (1.15 hrs.; www.atvo.it)

Almost 6 mil. visitors are attracted to the 15km/9mi-long Jesolo beach every year.

Beach of superlatives

Lido di Jesolo, that means about 15km/9mi -long rows of beach lounges on fine sand, more than 400 hotels, several campgrounds, cpuntless restaurants, cafés, bars and discos as well as a colourful selection of sports. The main shopping street Via Andrea Bafile, which runs parallel to the beach, is the place to meet in the evenings; it is closed off to vehicles at 8pm during the high season and so it turns into a 10km/6mi-long promenade. Busses go to Venice from Piazza Drago and via Cavallino to Punta Sabbioni. The town of Jesolo, where the beach gets its name, is located a good 3km/2mi away from the coast. Three monasteries and 40 churches show that it actually used to be a centre of Christian culture.

The 15km/9mi-long and very narrow spit of land Litorale del Cavallino north-east of Venice is an excellent camping and beach area with its sand beaches and pine forests. Line 12 (from Fondamente Nuove via Burano and Treporti) and 15 (from San Marco/San Zaccaria) boats run regularly to Punta Sabbioni opposite Venice (pay parking lots).

Litorale del Cavallino, Punta Sabbioni

Lido di Venezia

✦ A–M 16/17

Population: 16,000
Quay: Santa Maria Elisabetta (Vaporetti 1, 5.1,5.2, 6; car ferry 17 from Tronchetto to San Nicolò)

In the 19th century, writers such as Lord Byron, Shelley and Musset »discovered« the uninhabited flat strip of sand that separates the lagoon of Venice from the open sea.

The island, which is 12km/7.5mi long and no more than 4km/2.5mi wide, with its flat sandy beaches was an inviting place for a stroll, swimming or riding – a seaside holiday. In the early 20th century, the Lido was an elegant seaside resort with luxurious hotels and international guests. Today, it is a suburb of Venice, and the luxury hotels have gotten a bit dusty. But its beaches still attract Venetians and holiday-makers. However, with the exception of one small strip, the beaches are mainly private. Glitter and glamour only appear in late August during the world's oldest film festival.

Faded charm

Venice has always been a favourite backdrop for cinematic history. The first Venetian **film festival** took place in 1932 in the Hotel Excelsior, with great success. Three years later, the Palazzo del Cinema, designed by

> **MARCO ⏺ POLO TIP**
>
> ❗ *Hire a bike – noleggio cicli* **Insider Tip**
>
> The best way to explore the Lido is by bicycle. Hire one at Gardin (Piazzale Santa Maria Elisabetta 2/A, tel. 04 12 76 00 05, www.biciclettegar din.com) and Lido on Bike (Gran Viale Santa Maria Elisabetta 21/B, tel. 04 15 26 80 19, www.venicebi kerental.com). But remember: after a few days in car-free Venice, on the Lido you will have to get used to traffic again.

Luigi Quagliata, was opened on the Lido. Every year at the end of August and in early September, the famous Premio Leone d'Oro di San Marco, the Italian variant of the American Oscar, is awarded to the best films and actors here. Films are shown in the Palazzo del Cinema and in some smaller cinemas (www.labiennale.org). Major directors such as John Ford, Louis Malle, John Cassavetes, Vittorio De Sica, Fellini and Visconti enjoyed major triumphs here. And even today, the Golden Lion is one of the most coveted awards in the art of film.

What to see on the Lido

Today, only a few 19th-century buildings, villas in the Liberty style (the Italian variant of Art Nouveau) and hotel complexes serve as reminders of the imposing past, particularly the neo-Moorish Grand Hotel Excelsior and the exclusive Des Bains; now a residence it was once the illustrious setting of Thomas Mann's *Death in Venice*, which was filmed by Luchino Visconti. To reach it, start at S. Maria Elisabetta quay and follow the Gran Viale to the beach on the other side of the island.

San Nicolo

Until 1797, the church of San Nicolò at the north end of the Lido (quay San Nicolò) was the goal of the **Sposalizio col Mare** (the marriage of the doge with the sea). According to a custom first documented in 998, the doge went out onto the sea once a year from the Porto di Lido and tossed a ring into the waves as a symbolic marriage of Venezia to the sea. In the 17th century, the church was remodelled in the Baroque style. This was the resting place of the bones of St

High class address on the Lido: Grand Hotel Excelsior

Nicholas, which Venetian sailors had stolen from the cathedral of Myra on the south coast of Asia Minor – or so it was thought. However, the Venetians then discovered that the residents of Bari in Apulia had got there first. The choir stalls (1635) by Giovanni da Crema tell the legend.

Nearby there is, apart from the Jewish cemetary (see below), the small **airport Aeroporto Nicelli**. There is a beautiful view from here across the lagoon to the fortifications of Sant'Andrea on the island of Le Vignole (▶p.222).

Insider Tip
Cimitero Israelitico

Jews have been buried in the cemetery since the 14th century. The old section is especially picturesque. Here, a simple stone slab over a mass grave is a reminder of the plague epidemic of 1630 to 1631, which claimed the lives of nearly 2,000 Jews. The Jewish museum offers guided tours from April to October (▶Ghetto).

Malamocco, Alberoni

The quiet villages of Malamocco and Alberoni lie in the south of the island. There is a gold course and a public beach near Alberoni. From here, a car ferry operates across the busiest opening in the lagoon to **Pellestrina**, a narrow island protected since the mid-18th century by the **murazzi**, embankments of Istrian stone. At the outermost end of Pellestrina, the ferry crosses to ▶Chioggia.

✷ Madonna dell'Orto · Santa Maria dell'Orto
————————————————— ✦ **F 8/9**

Location: Fondamenta della Madonna dell'Orto
Quay: Madonna dell'Orto
❶ Mon–Sat 10am –5pm, admission €12 (combination ticket Chorus Pass)
www.madonnadellorto.org

A sidetrip to the north is worthwhile: to see the enchanting Madonna dell'Orto church, one of the city's most beautiful Gothic sacred structures.

The garden madonna

The fact that this church was originally dedicated to St Christopher , the patron saint of travellers, is commemorated in a statue by Bartolomeo Bon above the entrance. According to legend, its present-day name derives from the discovery of a Madonna statue in a nearby vegetable garden (»orto« in Italian). The conspicuous brick façade of the church, which was completed in 1462, is adorned by figures of the twelve apostles which are ascribed to Jacobello dalle Masegne and his workshop.

Tintoretto's »home church« Madonna dell'Orto

The interior contains the tomb of Jacopo Rubusti, also known as **Tintoretto**, who was buried in the chapel to the right of the presbytery. His son Domenico rests at his side. The artist, who lived nearby, created several works for this church, among them *The Last Judgment* (on the right in the choir), *Worship of the Golden Calf* (on the left in the choir), *St Agnes Revives Licinius* (fourth chapel to the left) and *Presentation of Mary in the Temple* (about 1552) above the entrance to St Mark's chapel in the right aisle. Another item of interest is a panel depicting St John the Baptist with Saints (1493) by Cima da Conegliano (first altar to the right) — a Madonna (1480) by Giovanni Bellini was stolen in 1993, a reminder is the empty place in the last chapel in the left aisle.

Campo dei Mori   On the other side of the canal lies Campo dei Mori. Its name probably comes from the Mastelli merchant dynasty, who originally came from the Morea – the Venetian name for the Peloponnese – who had a palace built for themselves here in the 12th cent. The merchants are immortalized in strange statues, identifiable by their turbans, in the façade of a corner house. The painter Tintoretto died on 31 May 1594 in the house next to the fourth Negro figure (Casa del Tintoretto; Cannaregio 3399).

The church with the impressive brick façade to the north-west of Madonna dell'Orto was built in the late 14th century. It is dedicated to St Louis of Toulouse (Alvise is the Venetian form of Louis). Inside, the column-borne nuns' choir above the entrance as well as the *Ascent to Calvary* on the right wall of the choir, by **Tiepolo**, are of interest. He also painted the *Flagellation* and the *Crowning with Thorns* (1740).

Sant'Alvise

❶ Mon – Sat 10am–5pm, admission €12 (combination ticket Chorus Pass)

✳ Mercerie

✈ **G/H 11/12**

Location: Between the Rialto bridge and Piazza S. Marco
Quays: Rialto, Vallaresso San Marco

The Mercerie, a chain of several streets, is the oldest and most important link between the political-religious and economic centres of the Serenissima: San Marco and Rialto.

Merchants have always offered their wares here (»mercerie« means dry goods). Today, it is the shopping quarter of Venice. Anything can be found here – unusual jewellery stores, shops with an assortment of kitsch, elegant fashions, artistic carnival masks and costumes. However, bargain-hunters will quickly be disappointed: Venice is expensive.

The classic shopping street

Keep right from the Ponte di Rialto to reach the small **Campo San Bartolomeo**. This piazza – where a monument to Carlo Goldoni stands – is the meeting place of Venetian youth in the evenings. Past the church San Bartolomeo and across Marzaria 2 Aprile is Merceria San Salvador, named after its church (▶below). In its further course, the Mercerie change their names and join the large Piazza San Marco below the clock tower (Torre dell'Orologio) as Merceria dell'Orologio.

Campo San Bartolomeo

The church at the centre of the Mercerie was built between 1507 and 1534 by Tullio Lombardo and Sansovino in the Renaissance style. In the 17th century, Giuseppe Sardi designed its Baroque façade. The interior, which is covered by three domes, contains some precious art treasures, among them the magnificent tomb of Doge Francesco Venier by Sansovino (1556, after the second altar on the left), as well as the wall tombs of the Corner family on the end walls of the transept arms, including the tomb of Caterina Corner (1454–1510), Queen of Cyprus. Titian painted the *Annunciation* (last altar to the right before the crossing; the marble frame is by Sansovino) and the *Transfiguration of Christ* (above the high altar). Further items of note

✳ San Salvador

are the *Martyrdom of St Theodore* by Paris Bordone (to the right of the choir) and *Christ in Emmaus* by Vittore Carpaccio (in the Cappella del Santissimo to the left of the high altar).

❶ Mon–Fri 9am–12 noon, 4 – 6.30pm, www.chiesasansalvador.it

OTHER SHOPPING STREETS

Even more exclusive (and expensive) shopping is found below the arcades of Piazza San Marco, **Calle Vallaresso** to the west, which meets Salizzada San Moisè at right angles and its extension, **Calle Larga XXII Marzo**, which is unusually wide for Venice. Top designers, high-class leather shops, jewellers and exquisite antique shops have settled here. For a pleasant break after a long shopping tour only has fastfood shops and (in the nearby side streets) expensive restaurants.

San Moisè   Even though the Baroque façade, done in 1668 by Alessandro Remignon, seems excessive to some connoisseurs, Venetians love their church of San Moisè, which was dedicated to Moses in the 9th century and lies on Campo San Moisè , at the beginning of Calle Larga

Shopping paradise Calle Larga Marzo XXII

XXII Marzo. Inside is a *Footwashing* by Tintoretto and a *Last Supper* by Palma the Younger. The stone-sculpted altar by Heinrich Meyring shows Moses receiving the Ten Commandments on Mount Sinai. The concrete-grey façade next to San Moisè is part of the **luxury hotel Bauer**.

❶ Mon – Sat 9.30am – 12.30pm, 3.30 – 7pm, Sun 9.30 – 11.30am, 2.30 – 6.30pm

The donor of the church at the west end of Calle Larga XXII Marzo with its unusual Baroque façade, also called **Santa Maria Zobenigo** (1680, Giuseppe Sardi) was Antonio Barbaro. In return, the successful capitano da mar had himself immortalized on the façade: he stands carved in stone above the main portal, with some of his ancestors below him. The lower zones are decorated with reliefs showing panoramas of the cities which played a role in his career: Padua, Chania (Crete), Zadar (left), Rome, Corfu and Split (right). Inside are two early works by Tintoretto (about 1550) and one by Peter Paul Rubens (17th century) in the Molin chapel.

Santa Maria del Giglio

❶ Mon–Sat 10am–5pm, admission €12 (combination ticket Chorus Pass)

✴✴ Murano

✦ J/M 4-7

Population: 4930
Quay: Murano (Vaporetti 4.1, 4.2 from Fondamente Nuove)

The »island of glass blowers« is reminiscent of Venice itself, with its main canal and numerous small side canals.

▶MARCO POLO Insight p.232

From the Colonna quay, follow the two main streets Fondamenta dei Vetrai and Fondamenta Cavour past workshops where the glass-blowers can be watched at work and stores are filled with glass souvenirs. The island makes its living from glass production even today.

Murano was one of the first islands to be settled. Until 1291, the residents lived from fishing and the salt trade. The decision to move glass production from Venice to Murano brought prosperity to the island. In the 16th century, when Murano had about 30,000 residents, the island became a popular summer residence

MARCO POLO TIP

! *Glass art* *Insider Tip*

Remember: free transfers to Murano always include a sales pitch. The following ateliers are recommended: Cenedese, Fondamenta Venier 48, Mazzega, Fondamenta da Mula 147, Venini, Fondamenta Vetrai 47–50 Ferro & Lazzarini, Fondamenta Navagero 75. In the summer the ateliers and shops are mostly open at weekends.

Blown Jewels

Glass manufacturing was known in Venice as early as the end of the 10th century. It received a significant boost after the fourth crusade in 1204 when oriental techniques were adopted. From then on, the glass industry was guarded like a state secret. Venice had a glass monopoly for centuries.

At the time, the workshops were still located at the centre of the city on the lagoon. After repeated catastrophic fires, the last one of which took place in 1291, the senate ordered them to be moved to Murano – the official reason was to reduce the risk of fires, but the unofficial reason that probably comes closer to the truth was to prevent espionage. The first known guild rules also came from this period; the »**Mariegola**« from 1441, framed with velvet and silver, can be admired in the Museo Correr. Murano glass was a coveted **luxury item** as early as the middle of the 14th century; pearls, lenses for glasses, chandeliers and filigree drinking glasses were exported all the way to China. Starting in the 15th century, the list of pro-ducts also included magnificently framed mirrors after Muzio da Murano discovered that applying a solution of tin and quicksilver creates a lasting reflective surface.

Discoveries

In the middle of the 15th century, Angelo Barovier invented **Cristallo**, a glass reminiscent of rock crystal that is free of bubbles and tints. Around the same time another master created **Calcedonio**, a multi-coloured glass similar to agate. **Rubino**, tinted pink by the addition of a gold solution, was an inven-

tion from the 16th century; **Aventurin**, sprinkled with copper particles and exuding a mysterious shimmer, was invented by Briani in the 17th century. The most sophisticated techniques include the **filigree** net and Reticella glass known since the 16th century, with fine white and coloured threads applied to the surface of the blown glass. In the old technique known as Murrine or **Millefiori**, coloured rods are incorporated in transparent glass. **Lattimo** is a milky white glass, which was usually decorated with lacquer in the 15th century and then looked like porcelain.

The most important raw materials – quartz sand (mostly pebbles from the Tessin river up until the 17th century), limestone and soda – are brought to the melting point in an oven at 1,400°C. After cooling to between 1,000 and 500° C the glass is formed; afterwards, the item is allowed to fully cool slowly. Various colours are created by adding metal oxides.

Privileges and Threats

Glass production was the best-kept secret until the 17th century. The guild of the Vetrai, the glass blowers, was held in high esteem and enjoyed numerous privileges. Murano had its own government and a **Libro d'Oro** that listed the long-

Glassblowers at work on Murano

established families. However, they were prohibited from leaving the lagoon **under pain of death** since this meant a betrayal of secrets. An edict from 1454 said: »A glass blower who brings a skill to another country to the detriment of the republic shall be asked to return home; if he refuses, his nearest relatives shall be thrown into prison… if he persists in his disobedience, clandestine measures are to be taken in order to eliminate him wherever he may be.« In spite of these threats, some fled to northern Europe in the 16th century. In the 17th and 18th centuries, flourishing manufactures were set up with glass blowers lured away from the city on the lagoon, mainly in France and Bohemia. Foreign competition and the end of the republic in 1797 ultimately led to the demise of glass manufacturing on

Murano; it was finally revived in the middle of the 19th century through the engagement of traditional glass blower families such as the Barovier, Seguso, Salviati and Teso.

Today there are almost 100 glassworks employing around 6,000 people on the island, with most of the products destined for the export market. But now it is no longer a secret; instead, one can watch the glassmakers ply their trade in many of the facilities. But the existence of many glassblowers is currently threatened by the financial crisis and increasing imports from China (and fakes). The city of Venice is already working on compensaion plans for out-of-work glassblowers …

Exciting reading: Donna Leon, *Through a Glass Darkly*.

for rich Venetian patricians, who had palaces and pleasure gardens here – and finally, Italy's first botanical gardens were laid out here. Even today, the island is one of the main attractions during a visit to Venice and easy to reach.

San Pietro Martire

The church, which was rebuilt in 1511 after a fire, has valuable art treasures: the *Enthroned Madonna* (1488) in the right aisle is by Giovanni Bellini, likewise the *Assumption of the Virgin* (1505–1513). The left aisle contains Veronese's paintings *St Jerome in the Desert* and *St Agatha in the Dungeon*. There is also the beautiful Palazzo Da Mula, a Renaissance villa.

*Museo del Vetro

Insider Tip

The glass museum in Palazzo Giustinian (17th century; Fondamenta Giustinian 8) has one of the largest collections of Venetian glass. Exhibits from Roman times as well as from Bohemian and Moorish glass-blowers are also on display. One of the most famed exhibits is the **Coppa Barovier** (room 1), a unique wedding chalice from the 15th century. It is made of dark blue glass decorated with enamelled medallions showing pictures of the couple and allegorical scenes. This work is probably by the daughter of Angelo Barovier, from Murano's most famous family of glass-blowers. The department for modern glass blowing is also interesting.

❶ ❶ Fondamenta Giustinian 8, Apr – Oct daily 10am – 6pm, otherwise only until 5pm, admission €8; museovetro.visitmuve.it

Arches, niches and columns: Santi Maria e Donato

Murano's most beautiful church was initially dedicated only to the
Virgin. From the 12th century, it was also dedicated to St Donatus. It
was built between the 7th and 12th centuries and is one of the oldest
places of worship in the lagoon. The east façade is especially beautiful.
The choir consisting of two rows of arcades combines Venetian-Byzantine and early Romanesque elements. Inside, columns of Greek
marble with Venetian-Byzantine capitals separate the two aisles from
the nave. The lovely 12th-century mosaic floor with its lively animal
figures and fine ornamentation is like an oriental carpet. The tall figure of the Mother of God in a mosaic with gold background in the
choir niche (around 1450). Above the altar is the reliquary of St Donatus. The painted relief icon of St Donatus above the side altar to the
left is one of the earliest works of Venetian painting (1310). On the
wall on the left side is the altarpiece *Death of the Virgin* (late 14th century), *Madonna with Saints* at the entrance to the baptistery (1484) by
Lazzaro Bastiani. On the right in front of the choir is a sarcophagus
from Altinum, which was formerly used as the basin of a fountain.

**Santi Maria
e Donato*

❶ daily 9am – 12 noon, 3.30pm – 6pm, Sun open only at midday

★★ Palazzo Ducale ·
Doge's Palace

— ✦ H 12

Location: Piazza San Marco
Quay: Vallaresso San Marco, San Zaccaria
❶ April – Oct daily 8.30am – 7pm otherwise until 5.30pm, ticket office closes
one hour earlier, admission €16 (combination ticket with Museo Correr,
Museo Archeologico Nazionale and Biblioteca Nazionale Marciana), www.
palazzoducale.visitmuve.it.
Itinerari segreti tour on appointment, €20, tel. 0 41 42 73 08 92 or online
(daily, Ital. 9.30am and 11.10am, Engl. 9.55am and 11.35am)

**The Doge's Palace, Palazzo Ducale, was the seat of power of
the republic for more than 1000 years – both the residence of
the doge and the state prison. Today, it is one of the most important secular buildings in the world.**

The first Doge's Palace on this site was built in 814. It was a dark wood-
en structure with massive fortified towers, protected by canals on three
sides and by the lagoon to the south. In the 12th century, it was replaced by a new structure in the Byzantine style with loggias and arcades. Around the mid-14th century, the membership of the Grand
Council had risen to more than 1,000. Since a new, more spacious
meeting hall was needed, it was decided to build today's Doge's Palace.

OUTSIDE VIEW

The palace is 71x75m/233x246ft in size and consists of three wings around an inner courtyard that is roughly trapezium-shaped. From 1340 to 1400, the south wing facing the Molo was built. Between 1424 and 1438, the west wing on the Piazzetta followed, and finally, in 1483, the east wing, which took until the 17th century to build. The ▶Basilica di San Marco forms the northern boundary. Fires in the palace repeatedly caused great damage, but mainly affected the interior furnishings. The façade of the Doge's Palace is derived from those of Venetian nobles' palaces of the 12th and 13th centuries: on the ground floor, open arcades rest on low columns without bases, which are sunk nearly 40cm/16in into the pavement (the level of the piazza has been raised several times). Above this is a loggia with slender, more closely spaced columned arches. The pointed arches and quatrefoil openings in the gaps served as a model for Venetian ornamentation of the entire late Gothic period. The upper part of the façade is clad in white and red marble, with pointed-arch windows as openings in the wall surface. Pierced crenellations crown the building.

MARCO POLO TIP

! *Don't miss* *Insider Tip*

- Scala dei Giganti in the inner courtyard
- Collegio and Anticollegio
- Sala del Maggior Consiglio with the world's largest painting on canvas
- Itinerari Segreti, a guided tour to the mysterious inner workings of the Doge's Palace
- Hieronymus Bosch in the Sala del Magistrato

Ponte dei Sospiri The east façade toward Rio di Palazzo was designed by Mauro Coducci. Here, the elegant »Bridge of Sighs« catches the eye (▶photo p.16). It links the Doge's Palace to the **Prigioni Nuove** (the new prisons, 1589–1614) on the other side of the canal. They were built of Istrian stone to plans by Antonio Contin, and already herald the Baroque style in Venice.

**South façade The south façade – the main view from the lagoon – is one of the oldest parts of the exterior. Only the balcony of the central window breaks through the uniform surface of the upper structure. According to an inscription, Doge Michele Steno was the donor in 1404. The Gothic window framing was produced in the workshop of Pierpaolo dalle Masegne. The crowning balcony was renewed after the fire in 1577. The statue of Justice is by Alessandro Vittoria, the statue of St George by Giovanni Battista Pellegrini (18th century). The sculptural decoration on the corners of the building dates from the 14th century; the statues on the side to the Ponte della Paglia show the archangel Raphael and Tobias (top) and the drunken Noah. In the

Palazzo Ducale and Campanile, landmarks of the maritime republic

direction of the Piazzetta, they show the archangel Michael as well as Adam and Eve. Both here and on the façade towards the Piazzetta, there are 14th-century **capitals** (many have been replaced by copies; the originals are exhibited in the Museo dell'Opera). Various motifs – leaf capitals, busts of emperors, mythical beasts, animals, allegories of virtues and vices, seasons and the ages of man – are freely combined here.

The façade towards the Piazzetta, which was carried out between 1424 and 1438, is a mirror image of the older south wing. The balcony followed in the 16th century. A lion of St Mark is enthroned above it, and above the lion, Justice. It was from here, between the two pink columns, that the doge observed the executions that were carried out on the Piazzetta. The sculptures at the corner towards the Porta della Carta – the archangel Gabriel with the judgement of Solomon below – are ascribed to Bartolomeo Bon.

**West façade

The Porta della Carta forms the architectural link between St Mark's Basilica and the Doge's Palace. Aside from Ca' d'Oro, it is regarded as the most important work of the Gothic period in Venice. Giovanni and Bartolomeo Bon worked on the design from 1438 to 1442.

Porta della Carta

MARCO ⊕ POLO TIP

!

Secrets of the Doge's Palace Insider Tip

The tour reveals the historic centre of power of the Serenissima: the headquarters of the secret police was in the middle of the Palazzo Ducale, invisible to the world outside. The tour (several times daily in English, French or Italian lasting about 75 min.) has to be booked at least two days in advance (▶Info p. 235).

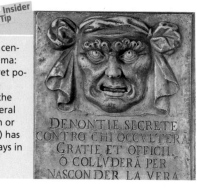

Two large supporting pillars frame the entrance and the window above it. Above the gate, Doge Francesco Foscari kneels before the lion of St Mark, demonstrating the subordination of the individual to state power ("ill. p.38). Above the window, St Mark is shown, and above him, the allegory of Justice, accompanied by two lions. Its name, »Gate of Paper«, comes from the supplicants who were not allowed to enter the palace. At this gate, the council and government officials received written requests and petitions. Due to the gilding, which has faded today, the door was also called the »Porta aurea«. The laws of the republic were announced at this gate.

INNER COURTYARD

*Scala dei Giganti

Today, the palace is entered through the Porta del Frumento on the lagoon side. In the courtyard, two bronze wells (mid-16th century) and the Scala dei Giganti are visible before the east wing. The »giants' stairway«, designed by Antonio Rizzo from 1483, was the scene for major events. Newly elected doges swore loyalty on the top step. Every Easter Monday after the mass in San Zaccaria the »corno ducale« in the form of a stylized Phrygian fisherman's cap, which was embroidered by the nuns of Zaccaria, was placed on the doge's head. The name of the stairway comes from the two colossal statues of Mars and Neptune (1550) by Jacopo Sansovino, representing the rule of Venice on water and on land. The fine relief decoration of the stair balustrade and the pedestal of floral Renaissance ornamentation are noteworthy.

*Arco Foscari

The richly decorated triumphal arch, Arco Foscari, lies opposite the stairway. The niches of the lower floor contain the figures of Adam and Eve by Antonio Rizzo (replicas stand here today; the originals are in the Andito del Maggior Consiglio). On the second floor above the door, allegories of virtues and vices stand on turrets and pedestals.

Above the gate, St Mark gives blessing. The arch was completed under Cristoforo Moro between 1462 and 1471. The side towards the courtyard was covered in the early 17th century.

To the left of the main courtyard lies the Cortile dei Senatori with a late Renaissance front: arcades on the ground floor, windows crowned with pediments on the upper floor, and the crowning balustrade, behind which there was originally a small roof terrace. The senators gathered in this small courtyard before receptions. The small adjacent chapel was the private chapel of the doge.

Cortile dei
Senatori

More can be learned about the workings of the lagoon republic on the guided tour **Itinerari Segreti** (»secret pathways«). The tour concentrates on the hidden part of the Palazzo Ducale, including the offices of the secret police, the torture chamber and the (old) prison below the roof. It was from one of these cells that **Casanova** succeeded in making his spectacular escape in 1755 with the aid of a monk. The tour ends on the top floor above the Sala del Maggior Consiglio. Here, the system of the Venetian **soffitto** (flat ceiling with paintings) is presented. It is found in all palazzi, but can normally only be seen from the painted – that is, the lower – side.

On secret
pathways

HALLS OF THE DOGE'S PALACE

As the official seat of government and the highest judges, as well as the election and meeting place of the representatives of the people, the Doge's Palace contained, in addition to the doge's residence, meeting halls, courts, torture chambers and prison cells. Today's decoration was newly carried out after several fires in the 16th century. Leading artists participated in the work, particularly Tintoretto, Titian and Paolo Veronese. The paintings describe the most important events in the city's history, from the myths of the founding period to the greatest military successes. From the inner courtyard, the route first leads via the Scala dei Censori (censors' stairway) up to the loggia (first floor). The **Bocca di leone**, the so-called lion's mouth (▶ill. p.238) set into the wall, was a letterbox for secret (not anonymous!) reports.

From the loggia, the **Golden Stairway** leads up to the former apartments of the doge (second floor) and then to the rooms of office on the third floor. The staircase was designed by Sansovino (1538), but only completed after 1577. It is named after the gilded stucco ornamentations of its coffered ceiling (Alessandro Vittoria). The frescoes (Battista Franco) describe the defence of Cyprus and Crete and the *Virtues of Good Government*. The beautiful floor is noteworthy (it creates a three-dimensional impression to those looking back).

*Scala d'Oro

Atrio Quadrato

The Scala d'Oro ends in the **square anteroom**. As is the custom in Venice, the ceiling (soffito) is divided into fields in magnificent frames. The main painting by Jacopo Tintoretto (1561–1564) shows the sword of justice being handed to Doge Girolamo Priuli.

Sala delle Quattro Porte

The four doors, which are framed by marble columns, give the large waiting hall, which may have been designed by Palladio, its name. The ceiling paintings are by Tintoretto (1578–1581): at the centre, Jupiter symbolically gives Venice rule over the Adriatic; the eight oval paintings represent the Venetian cities and regions on the mainland. The most important wall painting, a votive image of Doge Antonio Grimani on the north wall, was begun by Titian and completed by his nephew. The painting *Neptune Offers Venice the Treasures of the Sea* is by Tiepolo.

*Sala dell' Anticollegio

The paintings in the »**waiting room**« for foreign representatives deal with mythological themes. The central ceiling fresco *Venice Awards Recognition and Honours* is by Veronese. Tintoretto painted the four works on the sides of the doors: *Minerva Separates War and Peace*, *Vulcan's Forge*, *Mercury and the Three Graces* and *Venus Marries Bacchus to Ariadne* (1577/1578). On the wall opposite the windows hangs Paolo Veronese's *Rape of Europa* (1580) and the *Return of Jacob from Canaan* by Jacopo Bassano (1574).

*Sala del Collegio

The highest-ranking visitors were received in the **conference hall of the state council**. The ceiling paintings by Veronese celebrate the power and glory of Venice, showing *Mars and Neptune*, *Faith as the Strength of the Republic* and *Venetia Enthroned with Justice and Peace*. The fields around the edges show the virtues: the dog stands for loyalty, the cornucopia for growth and success, the crane for alertness, the spider's web for industry, the eagle for moderation, the sceptre for generosity, the ermine for purity and the lamb for gentleness. On the wall painting above the doge's throne, Veronese immortalized Doge Sebastiano Venier, the supreme commander in the battle of Lepanto (1571). On the wide-format painting opposite, Doge Andrea Gritti kneels before the Virgin. Both this composition and the three votive images on the side opposite the windows are ascribed to Tintoretto and his workshop.

*Sala del Senato

The **senate hall** was the meeting place of the senate, which met twice weekly and had 40, then 60 and later 100 members. The doge and his committee used the seats at the end, while the senators in red robes sat at the sides. The ceiling paintings by Tintoretto and his workshop again serve to represent Venice. At the centre, Venetia is made the ruler of the seas by the Olympian gods. Other scenes are devoted to the right of coinage, the veneration of the eucharist, while

Palazzo Ducale Second Floor

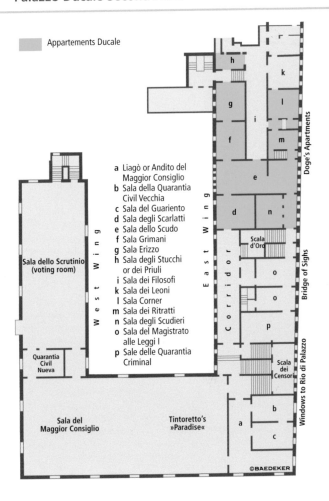

Appartements Ducale

a Liagò or Andito del
  Maggior Consiglio
b Sala della Quarantia
  Civil Vecchia
c Sala del Guariento
d Sala degli Scarlatti
e Sala dello Scudo
f Sala Grimani
g Sala Erizzo
h Sala degli Stucchi
  or dei Priuli
i Sala dei Filosofi
k Sala dei Leoni
l Sala Corner
m Sala dei Ritratti
n Sala degli Scudieri
o Sala del Magistrato
  alle Leggi I
p Sale delle Quarantia
  Criminal

Sala dello Scrutinio
(voting room)

Quarantia
Civil
Nueva

Sala del
Maggior Consiglio

Tintoretto's
»Paradise«

West Wing

East Wing

Corridor

Scala
d'Oro

Scala
dei
Censori

Doge's Apartments

Bridge of Sighs

Windows to Rio di Palazzo

©BAEDEKER

military power and the protection of thought and literature are depicted in the smaller paintings. On the wall above the tribunal hangs another painting by Tintoretto, *The Dead Christ Supported by Angels*. On the opposite wall, Doge Pietro Lando and Doge Marcantonio Trevisan pray to the body of Christ which is borne by angels

** *Seat of the Serenissima*

In the early 9th century the administrative seat of the city of Venice was moved to the Canal Grande and the first doge's seat was built. The Palazzo Ducale today stands on the same site. It was the doge's residence and ruling seat of the Serenissima. The assembly room of the Grand Council was here, the government offices, the law courts, the prison and the arsenal.

❶ Balcony facing Piazzetta
From the 15th century balcony on the west side the doge watched executions, which took place on the Piazzetta between the columns.

❷ South façade
The oldest part and the display side of the doge's palace is the south façade. At both corners there are figure groups from the 14th century.

❸ Cortile
The doge's palace used to be netered through the Porta della Carta, but today the entrance is the Porta del Frumento on the sea side.

❹ Scala dei Giganti, Arco Foscari
On the Scala dei Giganti in front of the east wing the coronation ceremony for the doge took place. Opposite is the richly decorated triumphal arch Arco Foscari.

❺ Sala del Maggior Consiglio
In this room the assemblies of the Grand Council took place, the doges were elected and the members of government and high officials were installed into their offices. The paintings were added after a fire in 1577. Under the ceiling is a frieze with (mostly invented) portraits of the first 76 doges. A black curtain represents the picture of Doge Marino Falier, who was executed as traitor in 1335. The throne wall is decorated by Tintoretto's *Paradise*.

❻ Appartamento Ducale
In the east wing were the residential rooms of the doge. They had to bring their own furniture along when they moved in and had to arrange to have them removed after they died.

❼ Sala dello Scrutinio
The elections for various government offices took place here.

❽ Museo dell'Opera
In the museum some 14th century capitals are exhibited, which used to be part of the palace's façade (replaced outside with copies).

❾ Ponte della Paglia
From the Bridge of Straw across the Rio di Palazzo (mid-14th century) the Bridge of Sighs can be seen (Ponte dei Sospiri). Prisoners would cross the bridge from the palace to get to the cells in the New Prison.

❿ Drunk Noah
The relief on the south-east corner of the palace represents the drunk Noah (14th cent.), maybe as a symbol of human weakness; on the corner facing the Piazzetta are statues of Adam and Eve to be seen (p. 244).

In the second side room of the Andito, remnants of the *Coronation of the Virgin* painted by the Paduan Guariento for the Sala del Maggior Consiglio in the 14th century can be seen. After the fire in 1577, the painting was covered by Tintoretto's *Paradise*.

Sala del Guariento

The largest hall in the palace is the impressive Sala del Maggior Consiglio (54 x 25 m / 177 x 82 ft). Here, the up to 1,800 members of the **Grand Council** elected the members of government and high state officials, debated and made all important decisions of the republic, including that of its dissolution in 1797. The eye is drawn to the mural *Paradise* behind the doge's throne, the largest painting in the world at the time of its unveiling at 7x22m/23x72ft. It was begun by Veronese. After his death in 1588, the commission passed to Tin-

Sala del Maggior Consiglio

Tintoretto's *Paradise* in the Sala del Maggior Consiglio (detail)

toretto, who was nearly 70 years of age at the time. He worked on *Paradise* for four years. Christ is enthroned at the centre. Before him kneels Mary, surrounded by seven stars as reminders of her seven joys and pains, as well as more than 500 other figures, of which only the heads are visible in most cases. The ceiling paintings celebrate the Serenissima. Veronese's *Triumph of Venice* is above the dais, while the work at the centre, *Venetia gives Doge da Ponte an Olive Branch* is by Tintoretto. At the end of the hall *The Provinces Pay Tribute to Venezia* is by Palma the Younger. The two side ceiling paintings represent heroic deeds by individual army commanders, while the large murals show events from the history of the city. Below the ceiling is a frieze with 76 portraits of doges by Domenico Tintoretto. One painting is covered by a black cloth. The inscription refers to Doge Marino Falier, who was beheaded for high treason (and therefore not shown).

Insider Tip

Sala dello Scrutinio

The small **Sala della Quarantia Civil Nuova**, where a court was responsible for affairs of provinces that were subject to Venice (decorations relating to the legal system in the 17th century), leads to the Sala dello Scrutinio. Public election procedures were carried out here. The murals and ceiling paintings show sea and land battles, among them Tintoretto's *Victory of the Venetians over the Hungarians before the Gates of Zara in 1346. The Last Judgment* is by Palma the Younger, while the marble triumphal arch (1694) honours the army commander and Doge Francesco Morosini.

*Hieronymus Bosch

The seating of the **Sala del Magistrato alle Leggi** in the **Sala della Quarantia Criminal** dates from the 17th century. The walls are ornamented with paintings by Flemish artists; the altarpieces by Hieronymus Bosch are particularly impressive.

Appartamento Ducale

The private chambers of the doge are on the second floor. They are empty, since every newly elected doge had to bring his own furniture when he took office and arrange for it to be removed after his death. The **Sala degli Scarlatti**, a kind of anteroom for the doge's advisors, has a beautiful wood ceiling and ornamented fireplace (1507) by Antonio and Tullio Lombardo. The hall of maps, **Sala dello Scudo**, documents the regions ruled by Venice. The **Sala Grimani**, named after Doge Marino Grimani, has a lovely ceiling (15th century) and a fireplace by Lombardo. The **Sala Erizzo**, named after Doge Francesco Erizzo, is graced by a frieze of cherubs and symbols of war. The stucco decorations in the **Sala degli Stucchi** were newly created in the 18th century. The *Portrait of Henri III* is ascribed to Tintoretto. The **Sala dei Filosofi** was a room giving access to the doge's chambers. Once twelve paintings of philosophers from the 18th century decorated the walls. The **Chiesetta** (chapel, currently not accessible) was designed in 1593 by Scamozzi. On the altar stands a Madonna statue by Sansovino. Today, two paintings by D. Tintoretto hang in the **Sala degli Scudieri**, a passageway.

The prison consist of the »old« prison (**Prigioni Vecchie**) in the Dohe's Palace and the »new« prison (Prigioni Nuove) on the other side of the Rio di Palazzo. They are connected by the **Bridge of Sighs** (▶ill. p. 12). Major criminals landed in the so-called pozzi (wells), the rooms of the lower prison floors, which were regarded as cold and damp. The political prisoners were sent to the piombi (lead chambers) on the higher floors, which were feared due to the unbearable heat of summer. **Casanova** managed to escape from one of these cells in 1755 with the help of a monk. The larger and better ventilated rooms of the **Prigioni Nuove** are now used for the occasional exhibition as well as for Baroque concerts of the Collegium Ducale (www.collegiumducale.com).

Prigioni

Back in the palazzo, enter the Sala Censori. Civil cases were heard here; a frieze shows the portraits of several judges (17th century).

Sala Censori

The exit is reached via the Avogaria, once the seat of the state attorneys in the republic. The Avogaria – three patricians with an office term of one year – monitored compliance with the laws. On the wall at the entrance is a *Resurrection with Three Avogadri* (D. Tintoretto); opposite the windows hang three more paintings by Tintoretto. The tour ends via the Sala dello Scrigno, where the Golden Book (Libro d'Oro, list of noble families) was kept, and the Sala della Milizia da Mar.

Avogaria

SAN ZACCARIA

Cross the two bridges Ponte della Pagalia and Ponte del Vin to get to the church San Zaccaria, not far from the Riva degli Schiavoni. It was built in honour of St Zacharias, the father of St John the Baptist. Today's church was built between 1460 and 1500 to plans by the two great architects Antonio Gambello and Mauro Coducci. The massive façade is an astonishing example of a fundamentally Gothic building altered in the forms of the early Renaissance. The campanile is still Byzantine, the choir Gothic, and the nave embodies the style of the early Renaissance. The altar painting in the left aisle is particularly noteworthy – an *Enthroned Madonna with Saints Peter, Catherine, Lucia and Jerome* (1505), a late work by **Giovanni Bellini** (the figures are outstanding examples of Venetian craftsmanship). Pass through the right-hand transept to reach the chapel of Athanasius

Around Palazzo Ducale

– the choir stalls are by **Francesco** and **Marco Cozzi** (1455 to 1460) – and the Tarasius Chapel. The mosaic floor around the altar is from a previous church (12th century). Paintings by Antonio Vivarini and frescoes by Andrea del Castagno on the vault (1442) can be seen here. The crypt of the church is usually flooded.

San Zaccaria was regarded as the most worldly monastery of hedonistic 18th-century Venice. The monastery balls and amours of the pious women were the talk of the town. There was probably one main reason: it was San Zaccaria, in particular, which received the unfortunate daughters of patrician families who were put into a monastery for dynastic or financial reasons, and the ladies, whose lives had been stolen from them, avenged themselves in this way.

❶ Campo S. Zaccaria, quay San Zaccaria, Mon – Sat 10am – 12 noon, 4pm – 6pm, Sun 4pm – 6pm

San Zaccaria

** Piazza San Marco

✦ G/H 12

Quays: San Zaccaria, Vallaresso San Marco

Heart of the lagoon city

The centre of Venetian life is Piazza San Marco, which Napoleon called »the finest drawing-room in Europe«, and is also known as la piazza (since all other squares are called Campo, there is no danger of confusion).

It is unlikely that any other city in the world can greet visitors with a comparable entrée. This is the site of the most famous buildings, proof of a glorious past, and the very first look leaves an unforgettable impression. To the east, the ▶Basilica di San Marco dominates the piazza. On its other three sides, it is bordered by the clock tower, the Procuratie Vecchie (in the north), the Ala Napoleonica and the Procuratie Nuove (in the south). The transition to the Piazzetta with the library is formed by the high Campanile and elegant Loggetta. The piazza narrows from Basilica di San Marco to the Ala Napoleonica, which gives it greater depth (on average it is 175m/190yd long, 82m/90yd at the church, and 56.6m/66yd wide at the Ala Napoleonica). There is nothing to distract from the closed architectural feeling of the piazza, which is paved in slabs of brown trachyte and

MARCO POLO INSIGHT

? *Do not feed*

Since 2008 feeding the famous pigeons of St Mark's Square is not allowed. Even rice throwing rice after a wedding is subject to a fine. Up to then around 100,000 pigeons left around 4 tons of droppings every day, which not only defaced the buildings and squares, it also created enormous cleaning bills!

white marble. In the course of the centuries, Piazza San Marco has always been the religious, political and social heart of Venice and has lost nothing of its effect to the present day, when it is the preserve of onlookers.

The piazza has a long history. It was originally an island through which the canal flowed, and on which the nuns of the Zaccaria monastery grew fruit and vegetables. In 1174, the canal was filled in, and in 1267 paved with bricks. Of today's buildings only St Mark's Basilica and the Campanile are the only ones that already existed then. The Procuratie Nuove were built in the 16th century. Shortly before this, the clock tower, the Procuratie Vecchie, the Biblioteca Marciana and the mint (zecca) had been built. The piazza acquired its present paving in 1735, when the characteristic lines of white marble were set to show the position of the vendors' stands which occupied the piazza for various markets. Piazza San Marco was primarily a market place until the end of the republic – except when it served as the stage for celebratory parades and processions. The Ala Napoleonica was not added until the early 19th century. Today, Piazza San Marco is a place for strolling and a venue for open-air concerts and theatrical productions. Every visitor should enjoy the pleasure of sitting over a coffee or a glass of wine in one of the surrounding concert cafés and listening to the waltzes and evergreen melodies. The pigeons of San Marco are also part of it all, regardless of whether they are descended from the doves which the Venetian founding fathers brought to the lagoon in the 5th century on their flight from the Huns, or from those released into freedom by the doges every year on Palm Sunday, or from those that brought to the lagoon the message of the conquest of Constantinople in 1204.

History of the piazza

The two three-storey lengthwise wings with their arcades, the Procuratie Vecchie and Procuratie Nuove, bound Piazza San Marco to the north and south. The Procuratie Vecchie (from 1500, Bartolomeo

*Procuratie

Bon) were the seat of the procurators, the most important officials in the city after the doge. They managed St Mark's Basilica and the great fortune of the church, which derived from public and private donations as well as ongoing income. Later, when their tasks were extended to cover all communal government and their numbers increased, the new Procuratie Nuove building was erected on the other side (1583–1640, Vincenzo Scamozzi und Baldassare Longhena). Scamozzi used the library by his teacher Sansovino as a model, added a third floor and finished with a cornice instead of a balustrade Today, it houses the Fondazione Bevilacqua La Masa, whihc organizes exhibitions and cultural events (www.bevilacqualamasa.it), also the Archaeological Museum (entrance on the Piazzetta, ▶p. 252, 253). As well as exclusive stores, the arcades are home to Venice's most famous cafés.

Ala Napoleonica The piazza is closed off at the west end by the Ala Napoleonica, a connecting building added by Giuseppe Soli in 1810 at Napoleon's wish. Soli simply continued the first two floors of the Procuratie Nuove, left out the third floor to avoid disturbing the Procuratie Vecchie, and added a wide band of stone relief at the top to maintain the height. Between 1805 and 1814, it formed the entrance to the residence of Napoleon, which he had installed for himself as »King of Italy« in the library and in the Procuratie Nuove.

Museo Correr The core of this municipal museum is the art and city history collection of Teodoro Correr (1750–1830). The first neo-classical halls are devoted to statues by Antonio Canova (1757–1822). In the other rooms, much local history is revealed by coins, weapons and official garments, and a city view by Jacopo de' Barberi dated to 1500 is also on display. Right at the very beginning, the highlights of the gallery of paintings on the second floor include the Venetian-Byzantine panels by Paolo and Lorenzo Veneziano (*Handing over the Key*, 1369) and a Gothic *Madonna with Child* by Jacobello del Fiore. The early Renaissance is represented in the expressive *Pietà* by Cosmé Tura and the *Portrait of a Young Man* by Baldassare Estense. A separate hall is devoted to the three Bellinis. Vittore Carpaccio's idiosyncratic painting *Two Venetian Patrician Ladies* is also noteworthy (around 1510).

Insider Tip Since 2012 after many years of restoration the so-called Stanze di Sissi are open again, nine rooms in which the Austrian empress lived when she stayed in the city between 1854 and 1862.

The adjacent **Risorgimento Museum** provides information about the political development of Venice from the end of the republic (1797) to the time when it joined the kingdom of Italy (1866).

❶ Ala Napoleonica, April–Oct.daily 9am–7pm, otherwise until 5pm, admission €16 (combination ticket for the museums on St Mark's Square), correr.visitmuve.it

Piazza San Marco, the heart of the maritime republic

The great clock tower on the north side of the piazza, above the passage to the ▶Mercerie, was built by Mauro Coducci in the Renaissance style in 1496–1499 to complete the Procuratie Vecchie. The top floor with the star-covered blue mosaic and the lion of St Mark were added by Giorgio Massari in 1755. On his platform, two bronze negroes with hammers strike the hour. The large decorated clock, a work of Gian Paolo and Gian Carlo Ranieri (father and son), shows the months, zodiac signs and phases of the moon in addition to the time. In Ascension week as well as on the day of the Epiphany, the Three Magi, led by an angel, move around the Madonna and Child at every full hour.

ⓘ Viewing on appointment, admission €12, torreorologio.visitmuve.it

*Torre dell' Orologio

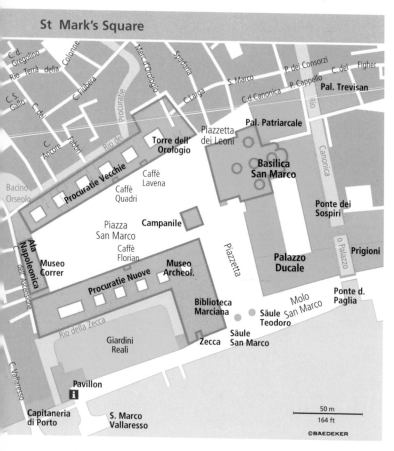

St Mark's Square

Lavena, Quadri and Florian

The three legendary cafés under the arcades of the Procuratie are the classic places to meet in Venice. In summer, each café has its own band, which adds to the atmosphere of Piazza San Marco with operetta melodies.

The first coffee house to open, in 1720, was Caffè **Florian**, which is now a protected monument. It was known as »Venezia Trionfante« before it took the name of its owner Floriano Francesconi. The thematically decorated interiors such as the Chinese, Turkish and Senate rooms have long been assured of their place in world literature. Among others, Ernest Hemingway, Mark Twain, Goethe, Honoré de Balzac, Marcel Proust and Thomas Mann drank their coffee here. The choice of café reflected political divisions in the 19th century, when the Venetian patriots Manin and Tommaseo preferred Florian while the Austrian officers went to **Quadri**. Quadri, which is only half a century younger and known for its irresistible pastries, is thus also a historic site. The coffee house owes its name to its former owner Giorgio Quadri, a Levantine from Corfu, who, in his day, made the best »coffee in the Turkish style«. Founded in 1750 and lovingly restored in 1990, Café **Lave-na** with its nostalgic furnishings is reminiscent of the period of Austrian imperial rule, when it was still called »Ungheria«. Giuseppe Verdi was often a guest here, as was Richard Wagner with his wife Cosima and his father-in-law Franz Liszt.

> **? MARCO ⊕ POLO INSIGHT**
>
> *Reusable statuary*
>
> The marble statue of St Theodore was probably originally the second century statue of a Roman emperor which was remodelled. The bronze lion of St Mark was originally an Assyrian or Persian chimera; wings were added and a book placed between its paws.

▶Basilica di San Marco

St Mark's
Basilica
*Campanile

The square Campanile, 98.6m/325ft high, is the link between Piazza San Marco and the Piazzetta. It was begun in the 10th century. However, the work took until the 12th century; finally, in the 15th century, the pointed spire of the tower which greets approaching ships from afar was also added. The tower collapsed on 14 July 1902 without injuring anyone. It buried the small Baroque hall at its base, the **Loggetta**, which had been built in 1540 to plans by Sansovino. The careful rebuilding was completed after ten years. Today, an elevator ascends the Campanile to the bell chamber, which presents a wonderful panoramic view over the city and lagoon. Since longer piles were rammed into the mud when the tower was rebuilt the foundation has shifted again. Now two ring-anchors made of titanium by Thyssen-Krupp will act as a corset for the foundation when they are attached at 40 cm (16 in) and 2.5 m (8.25 ft) under street level.
❶ Apr. – June, Oct. 9am – 7pm, July – Sept. until 9pm, Nov. – Mar 9.30am until 3.45pm, ticket office closes 1 hr. earlier, admission €8

**Piazzetta

The Piazzetta is bordered towards the sea by two immense granite columns, the **Colonne di Marco e Teodoro**, which mark the original mainentrance to Venice. Originally three columns were brought from Tyre (Lebanon) by Doge Michieli in 1125. However, one fell into the sea during unloading. The eastern column is crowned with the lion of St Mark, the symbol of the evangelist Mark. On the top of the western column stands the statue of St Theodore. He was a Greek and the head of a monastery in Constantinople, until he was banished to Venice. He was the first patron of the city until St Mark took

View from the Piazzetta to Santa Maria della Salute

his place. Public executions formerly took place between the columns and the bodies were left exposed. For this reason, superstitious Venetians do not walk between them.

*Libreria
Sansoviniana

The venerable library opposite the ▶Palazzo Ducale is the principal work of architect and sculptor Sansovino. The foundation was laid in 1537. After Sansovino's death, Vincenzo Scamozzi completed the work (to 1588). The façade is regarded as one of the most perfect works of the Italian Renaissance. Palladio praised the structure, which is also referred to as the Biblioteca Marciana or the Libreria Vecchia, as the most magnificent building since ancient times.
The **Biblioteca Marciana** (St Mark's Library) originated in Cardinal Bessarion's collection of manuscripts, donated in 1468. However, the magnificent stairway (Alessandro Vittoria), the equally grand vestibule (ceiling painting *Wisdom* by Titian, 1560) and the Great Hall (salone) are accessible in tours. The exhibition rooms contain astonishing treasures, cameos, manuscripts, calligraphy and book illustrations, including the Breviarium Grimani (1510–1520), 831 pages long with numerous Flemish miniatures. The actual Biblioteca Mar-

ciana with more than 750,000 volumes is housed in the adjacent **Zecca**, a structure with a façade towards the lagoon which was built in 1545 – also to plans by Sansovino – and housed the mint until 1870.

❶ Entrance Piazzetta, tours: Sun 10.30am, 12 noon, 2.30pm, otherwise on appointment, tel. 04 12 40 72 38, marciana.venezia.sbn.it (combination ticket "below)

The entrance to the Museo Archeologico is approximately at the centre of the Biblioteca Marciana with Greek and Roman exhibits as well as the library of Domenico Grimani, the founder of the collection.

Museo Archeologico

❶ Entrance Ala Napoleonica: Apr – Oct 9am – 7pm, otherwise until 5pm, admission €16 (combination ticket for all museums on St Mark's Square).

✳ Ponte di Rialto

✛ G 11

Location: Grand Canal
Quay: Rialto

The Rialto bridge is one of the best-known symbols of Venice. Until the mid-19th century it was the only bridge across the Grand Canal.

The Academy bridge was only built in 1854, and the Ponte dei Scalzi followed in 1858 (today's bridge was built 1934 – 1938) and in 2008 the Ponte della Costituzione was built, both near the railway station. The name is derived from Rivus Altus (high bank); the first Venetians settled on this island in the early 9th century. As early as 1180, the first wooden bridge was built across the canal on this site. It was replaced by a drawbridge which collapsed in 1444 under the weight of onlookers who were watching a procession of boats from the bridge. On the painting in the Accademia, The Miracle of the Cross by Vittore Carpaccio, a wooden bridge from this time is recorded (▶p.204). Many renowned architects participated in the competition for today's bridge. In 1588, Antonio da Ponte was chosen for his single-arch solution. Three years later, the 28m/92ft-long bridge of Is-

Where Venice began

MARCO ⊕ POLO TIP

Insider
For gourmets Tip

Dreams come true for keen cooks in Drogheria Mascari (Ruga dei Spezieri 381; closed on Sundays and Wednesdays). After shopping, there are inviting places to enjoy a drink around Rialto: for instance Bancogiro in the arcade of the Fabbriche Vecchie (Campo S. Giacometto 122, tel. 04 15 23 20 61). Small snacks are served on the ground floor, warm dishes on the first floor, and there are even a few tables with a view of the canal in front of the house.

trian marble was inaugurated. It rests on 6,000 oak piles at each end, which were driven into the muddy underground. Its span is 48m/157ft, and the clearance height beneath it is 7.50m/25ft. Three pathways lead across the great bridge arch; they are separated by two rows of stores selling leather, jewellery and souvenirs. From the upper bridge platform, there is a magnificent view of the life and activities on and around the Grand Canal.

Rialto market

Rialto was the **business centre** of Venice for many centuries just as St Mark's Square was the political centre and the Arsenale was the industrial centre; not only did the long-distance traders unload their wares at the docks (as the names still show today), but the largest banking and merchant houses also had their headquarters here. The central market of Venice still takes place here today. The range of products is enormous – fruit and vegetables from the surrounding islands, seafood from the lagoon – and an atmosphere unlike any other, as long as you come early!

Insider Tip

❶Mon– Sat until noon

Fish market in the Pescheria: Tue – Sat 5am – 11am.

San Giovanni Elemosinario

At the end of Ruga degli Orefici, where the goldsmiths traditionally had their workshops, the little church of S. Giovanni Elemosinario

Fruit and vegetables have always been sold here

(1539, Scarpagnino) stands on the left between houses. Items of interest include an altar painting by Titian and in the right side chapel, a painting by Pordenone.

❶ Mo. – Sa. 10am – 5pm, admission €12 (combination ticket Chorus Pass)

The church **San Silvestro**, at the end of Fondamenta del Vin, where   San Silvestro
the boats of wine traders used to dock, contains a noteworthy work
by Tintoretto, *The Baptism of Christ* (c. 1580; first side altar on the
right). Unlike the depiction of the same theme in the ▶Scuola Grande
di San Rocco, this painting is limited to a personal meeting between
St John the Baptist and Christ, with the dove of the Holy Spirit radiating light above him.

⋆ San Giorgio Maggiore

⟶ H 14

Location: Canale di San Marco
Quay: San Giorgio (Vaporetto 2)
❶ Mon – Sat 9.30am – 6.30pm, Sun 8.30am – 11am, 2.30pm – 6.30pm,
Oct – April weekday evenings only until sunset, admission: church is free,
campanile €5, tel. 04 15 22 78 27

There is a wonderful view of the Isola di San Giorgio Maggiore, especially of the church, from the Piazzetta and the Riva degli Schiavoni.

The picturesque ensemble of campanile, dome and façade form a wonderful accent in the lagoon of Venice. A Benedictine monastery was founded here already in the late 10th century, with the church as part of it. Today's structure goes back to a design by Andrea Palladio from 1563. However, the great architect did not witness its completion in 1610. As in Palladio's other Venetian churches, ▶San Francesco della Vigna ("Santi Giovanni e Paolo) and Il Redentore (▶La Giudecca), the façade is reminiscent of an ancient temple with colossal columns, niches and pediments; however, it seems slightly disproportional when viewed up close.

With reference to Roman and ancient architectural ideas, Palladio   Interior
designed the white-grey interior like a relief, using columns, pillars,
pilasters and entablature, as a basilica with semicircular ends to the
transepts and a central dome over the crossing, leading east into a
square presbytery and an apsidal monks' choir. The gaze is drawn to
the high altar (1591–1593) in the presbytery, a masterpiece by Girolamo Compagna, a student of Sansovino. The side walls of the altar
space are adorned by two large-format works which Tintoretto com-

San Giorgio Maggiore

pleted late in life: *Rain of Manna* and *The Last Supper*, both done in 1594, the year of his death. The monks' choir has magnificent choir stalls (1594–1598) of walnut wood decorated with scenes from the life of St Benedict.

Campanile

Insider Tip

To the left of the monks' choir, a hallway leads to the elevator of the campanile. The 60m/197ft-high tower was originally part of the previous buildings from 1470. It collapsed later and was rebuilt in 1791, using the Campanile of San Marco as a model. The view from the belfry across the lagoon is overwhelming.

Monastery

The monastery was in an advanced state of decay when the banker Vittorio Cini (1885–1977) purchased it. Today, it is the seat of a cultural foundation, **Fondazione Cini**. The complex includes two cloisters: the rear cloister was built between 1520 and 1540, while the front cloister was begun in 1579 by Andrea Palladio and completed by Baldassare Longhena, who also designed the early Baroque stairway and the library (1641). The 128m/420ft-long dormitory was built in 1488 – 1521. The head wall of the refectory was taken up by a 9.90 × 6.69 m (32 × 22 ft (!)) ***Wedding in Cana*** by Veronese, which Napoleon stole in 1797 (to be seen in the Louvre in Paris); since 2007 there is a perfect copy in the original place to be admired. The modern Teatro Verde, an amphitheatre at the centre of the beautiful monastery park, occasionally stages shows and concerts (information at the tourist office and under www.cini.it).

❶ Tours usually on Sat, Sun except holidays 10am–4pm, info: www.cini.it click on Calendario, admission €10

★ San Polo

✦ E/F 11

Location: Campo San Polo
Quays: San Silvestro, San Tomà
❶ Mon–Sat 10am–5pm, admission €12 (combination ticket Chorus Pass)

The first church on this site dedicated to the apostle Paul, after whom this city quarter is named, was built in 837. Later the quarter developed into Venice's business centre and continues to be one of the liveliest parts of the city.

Today's structure is largely from the 15th century; the campanile opposite the entrance (14th century) and its two lions at the base (12th century) are older. The church interior was altered in the 19th century. The beautiful 15th-century wooden ceiling, a feature surviving in Venice only in Santo Stefano and San Giacomo dell'Orio, contrasts with the classical colonnades of bright marble. Initially, the *Last Supper* by **Tintoretto** (1568/69) to the left of the entrance draws the eye. This is his third version of this subject (the first, from 1547, is in the church San Marculoa; a second version is in San Trovaso; in his old age, he painted a further version for San Giorgio Maggiore.) The second altarpiece on the left, *Mary Appears to St John Nepomuk* (1751) by Giovanni Battista is a masterpiece of composition in light. **Tiepolo**'s son **Giovanni Domenico**, who was only 22 years old at the time, painted the 14 stations of the cross in the Oratorio del Crocefisso (1749; the entrance is below the organ). It is a fine depiction of Venetian nobles in all their magnificence.

Tiepolo's masterpiece

Campo San Polo

Until 1750, a canal led along the east side of the **city's second largest plaza**: Campo San Paolo. Its course can be traced by the winding line of the late Gothic Palazzo Soranzo. Palazzo Corner Mocenigo on the opposite side is a late work of Michele Sanmicheli from the mid-16th century. The piazza, where festivals and bull fights took place into the 19th century and which invites guests to linger in its shade in cafés, is an **open-air cinema** from the end of July to the end of August (information from the tourist office or from daily newspapers).

Casa Goldoni

Take Calle Saoneri to reach the Gothic Palazzo Centani, the house in which the comic poet Carlo Goldoni (1707 to 1793) was born. Today it houses a theatre museum that commemorates the famous author.
❶ Palazzo Centani, Campo San Tomà; Mon – Sat 10am – 5pm, Thu – Tue 10am – 5pm, Nov – March only until 4pm, admission €5, carlogoldoni. visitmuve.it

✳ San Trovaso

✦ E 13

Location: Campo San Trovaso
Quay: Accademia, Zattere
❶ Tue – Sun 3pm – 5.30pm

The church, which was built in 1590, is actually dedicated to the saints Gervasius and Protasius, but its name was shortened to San Trovaso.

The church has has two beautiful façades: according to legend, these were the entrances of two feuding families. The church has some paintings by well-known masters, including **Tintoretto:** in the left transept, a *Last Supper*, the second of four versions of this theme, and in the left choir chapel, the *Temptation of St Anthony* (around 1557) as well as **Michele Giambono's** altarpiece *St Chrysogonus* (about 1440) in the right choir chapel. The altar reliefs in the right transept, marble works by an unknown master which were probably done around 1470, are also of interest.

On Rio di San Trovaso is one of the last **gondola shipyards** in Venice, Squero di San Trovaso, where the gleaming black symbols of the city are built to this day according to the

! MARCO ⊕ POLO TIP

Ombra and cicheti Insider Tip

Not far from the Zattere vaporetto quay are several popular addresses which sell »liquid shadows« and small sandwiches (▶MARCO POLO Insight p.116): Cantine del Vino già Schiavi (next to the Ponte S. Trovaso), Cantinone (San Trovaso 992) and Al Bottegon (Fondamenta Nani 992).

One of the last gondola shipyards on Rio di San Trovaso

ancient tradition (►p.262; www.squerosantrovaso.com). The low wooden houses with pretty flower balconies are a reminder that many shipbuilders originate from the Dolomite valleys near Cortina d'Ampezzo.

From here it is not far to the popular shore promenade **Zattere**, which was built in 1519, stretches along the Giudecca Canal from the former Stazione Marittima to the Punta della Dogana ("p.186). This is where the giant rafts (Ital.: zattere) of tree trunks arrived from the forests of the Alps or Dalmatia; they were needed to build Venice. They were processed in the nearby workshops.

Zattere

The wooden ceiling of the Renaissance church (1494–1524) southeast of San Trovaso was painted with 58 portraits of prophets and saints in the 16th century by Umbrian artists. The façade of the adjacent former monastery includes a so-called **Bocca di leone** (lion's mouth), a letterbox for letters containing denunciations from the time of the republic.

Santa Maria della Visitazione

The name of the nearby church is a reminder of the Jesuate order, which had a monastery here until its dissolution in 1668 (it was subsequently taken over by the Dominicans). The church is in elaborate Baroque style and was built between 1726 and 1736 to designs by Giorgio Massari. The sculptural decorations are by Giovanni Maria Morlaiter (1699–1781). The ceiling frescoes by **Giambattista Tiepolo** show *The Life of St Dominic* (1738). Tiepolo also painted the *Virgin Enthroned with Saints* (first side chapel on the right; 1738).

*Santa Maria del Rosario ai Gesuati

Queen of the Canals

According to legend, the gondola was created when the half moon fell from the heavens to give refuge to a pair of young lovers. A beautiful image – but the long, narrow watercraft which can navigate even the shallowest canals has been around for about 1,000 years.

The gondolas used to be magnificently decorated and some were even equipped with **felze**, roofed cabins, until the doge Girolamo Priuli prohibited the display of wealth in 1562. Since then, all gondolas are black. Making them is a special art in which only very few are still proficient. One of the last and oldest workshops is the **Squero di San Trovaso**.

The Gondola

Eight types of wood are required to build a gondola: The flat bottom is made of fir which expands in water and creates a tight seal; the rounded planks are made from hard oak. Basswood is used for the bow and stern, the cross members are made from flexible elm, lightweight birch is used for the interior floor, the curved parts of the superstructure are made from cherry, and the sheathing from mahogany and larch. In about two months, a 10.87m/35.66ft long and 1.42m/4.66ft wide, 350kg/772lb boat impregnated with linseed oil and four layers of luscious black paint is created out of **280 components**. The gondola owes its wilful form partly to its **asymmetry**: Around 1880, the ingenious designer Tramontin came up with the idea of shortening the boat by 24cm/9in on the right-hand side: The result of this slight curvature is that the gondola can travel straight and not just in circles, even though the gondolier always stands and rows only on one side (to the rear and on the left). The up to 80kg/176lb **forcola**, the cradle for the oar installed astern on the starboard side, is a wood craft masterpiece. It is customized to the stature of the gondolier, permits eight different oar positions, and has become a popular collector's item. Another typical element is the 20kg/44lb **ferro**, which is attached to the rear of the bow and makes the gondola more stable. Its points represent the six quarters of Venice, the seventh the Island of Giudecca.

The Trade of the Gondoliers

When gondolas were for Venetians only, being a gondolier was a job for starvelings. Today, this Venetian tradition comes at a price. Such a black lacquered beauty costs around €20,000. Training takes a long time. Maintaining the boats is expensive, they usually require repairs after twelve years and their life expectancy is no more than 45 years. Moorings and licenses also have to be paid for – the latter are usually passed on from father to son, or else sold for €300,000 and more. And in spite of all efforts to make the boats more elaborate, they have no chance of survival against the motorized competition on the canals. Of the formerly more than ten thousand gondolas in Venice, less than four hundred remain today. This is in spite of the fact that they are the ecologically superior alternative since they cause little undertow and wash. Those who have retained a sense of romance should take a trip in the elegant watercraft, which is then carefully guided through the postcard backdrop by a (hopefully singing) gondolier. No need to mention that such a pleasure comes at a price: A gondola currently costs around €120 for 60 minutes. A cheaper (and shorter) alternative is a trip in a **traghetto**. These boats, which are somewhat wider and longer than classic gondolas, offer standing room for 19 persons. Traghetti take locals and visitors across the Canal Grande at several locations (for a subsidized price). Meanwhile the first **gondoliera** has begun working. The Italian Giorgia Boscolo passed the difficult exam in 2010, something which her German predecessor Alexandra Hai could not do in 2007 – due in part to the massive male opposition. She now works as a »private« gondoliera for a hotel.

Elegantly shaped forcole have become popular collector's items

O sole mio

There are still around 470 traditionally built gondolas, but they are in danger of being replaced by plywood copies. Constructors, next to the carpenter, include: forcole carpenters, mechanics and ornamental blacksmiths, engravers, gilders and upholsterers. Even the black paint is a local specialty. The Museo Storico Navale he an impressive collection of gondolas.

▶ **Traditional gondolas are made of eight different kinds of wood:**

1. WALNUT
»Forcola« (rowlock)
The forcola, which is mounted on the starboard side, makes eight rowing positions possible, from fast to various kinds of docking to rowing backwards

Gondola builder's guild
www.elfelze.org

»Ferro di prua«
The »ferro« balances out the weight of the gondolier. The six metal teeth symbolize the six neighborhoods of Venice; the seventh tooth, which points to the stern, stands for the island Giudecca. They are crowned by the doge's cap.

3. BIR
light wood f
the inner flo

4. PINE
stretchable and
especially dense,
ideal for gondola bottoms

5. OAK
hardwood for the
outer walls,
which protects
during collisions

6. CHERRY
soft and easy
to work,
ideal for décor

7. MAHOGANY
fine wood
for the covers

8. ELM
flexible
wood
for the ribs

⑧

⑥

⑦

②

⑤

▶ **History**

1483
first depiction
of a gondola

16. cent.
means of transportati
no. 1 in Venice
(10,000 gondolas)

15th cent.
The form changed,
the »felze« (roof) was added,
entgondolas are decorated with gold

AD 697
first
mentioned

1094
mentioned as »godulana«:
low boat with rowing crew

| 1000 ◀ Jahr | 1100 | 1200 | 1300 | 1400 | 1500 | 1600 |

The »gondoliere«
There are currently about 400 gondoliers, who earn as much as €5,000 monthly during the high season. Training takes 1.5 years. A gondola licence costs up to €350,000.

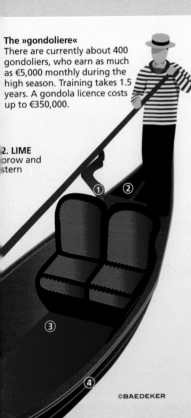

2. LIME
prow and stern

① ② ③ ④

©BAEDEKER

A gondola is asymmetrical, i.e. 24cm/10in shorter on the right than the left. This slight curve prevents it from going in circles as the gondolier stands on the left and rows on the right.

▶ The straw hat
It has been in use since the middle of the 20th century. The colours of the bands traditionally show which part of Venice the wearer is from.

»Nicolotti«
San Polo,
Santa Croce,
Cannaregio

»Castellani«
San Marco,
Castello,
Dorsoduro

▶ The gloss
Seven layers of black varnish give the gondola its shiny finish.

▶ The construction
Building a »real« gondola is time-consuming and complicated. Built completely by hand, it takes about two months to build a unique boat that will last for 35 years.

- 500 hours of work
- 280 parts
- 400 – 500 kg (900 – 1100 lbs)
- 10,87 m (35ft 8in) long
  1,42 m (4ft 8in) wide
- 13,000 – 25,000 Euro

▶ Gondolieri and their language

Oi!	Careful!
Sià stali!	To the right!
Sià premi!	To the left!
Sià de longo!	Straight ahead!
Gondola, gondola!	Call

▶ The prices
40-minute ride without singing, about:

80 € daytime   100 € evenings

1562
Black is prescribed as the colour of gondolas in order to restrict the elaborate decorations

1880
Domenico Tramontini designed the first asymmetrical gondola

2007
first woman, a foreigner, becomes »gondola driver«

2010
first woman becomes »gondoliera«

| 1700 | 1800 | 1900 | 2000 |

Piazzetta painted the panel *St Dominic* (around 1743; second altar to the right) and the painting with the Dominican saints Vincenzo Ferrer, Ludovico Bertrando and Giacinto (third altar to the right). The altarpiece *The Three Saints* (c. 1733) is by Sebastiano Ricci, the *Crucifixion* by **Tintoretto** (c. 1560; first and third altars to the left).

❶ Mon – Sat 10am – 5pm, admission €12 (combination ticket Chorus Pass)

Spazio Vedova

In the old salt warehouses (Magazzini del Sale) along the Zattere di Saloni towards Dogana da Mar the Venetian painter Emilio Vedova (1919 – 2006) had his studio. After being remodelled by Renzo Piano many of the paintings of the main representative of Italian Informalism can be seen here.

❶ Wed – Mon 10.30am – 6pm, www.fondazionevedova.org, admission €8

** Santa Maria Gloriosa dei Frari – Frari

✦ E 11

Location: Campo dei Frari
Quay: San Tomà
ℹ Mon – Sat 9am – 6pm, Sun from 1pm, admission €12 (combination ticket Chorus Pass)

Since the San Marco and Rialto quarters offered little space to build large new churches, the doges provided the two main mendicant orders, the Franciscans and the Dominicans, with properties in the thinly populated west and north regions of the city in the mid-13th century.

Building history

Today the church that is simply called Frari domantes the eastern part of San Polo. Together with San Zanipolo, the church of the Dominicans ("Santi Giovanni e Paolo), it is one of the largest Gothic churches in Venice. The first church that was built on this site between 1250 and 1338 by the Franciscans (frari = fratres, brothers) soon seemed inadequate, and they began new construction in the choir and in the transept around 1340. The nave did not follow until the 15th century, and with the consecration of the high altar in 1469, the simple Gothic brick structure, which reflects the Franciscans' ideal of poverty, was completed. Today, the church is usually entered through a side entrance under the campanile (at 83m/272ft the second-highest building in Venice). The hall-like interior is divided into a rather dark nave with aisles, an aisle-less transept and a straight choir at the end with the well-lit wall of the main choir chapel, which

Santa Maria Gloriosa dei Frari

is framed on both sides by three narrow, low chapels. The magnificent furnishings, particularly the tomb monuments and the altar painting with their donors, are like a pantheon of Venetian history and include the graves of four dogi and five high-ranking military officers.

Above the main portal on the inside of the façade is the wall tomb in black-and-white marble of Senator and General (»proveditor d'armata«) Girolamo Garzoni, who fell in the Turkish war in 1688. The deceased, who is crowned by a genius, is flanked by the personifications of religion (left) and Venezia (right). The tomb to its right honours the procurator Pietro Bernardo († 1538), to the left rests the procurator Alvise Pasqualino († 1528). The second arch of the left aisle contains the tomb pyramid of **Antonio Canova** (1757–1822), in which the heart of the most important classical sculptor was entombed. His body rests in the mausoleum in his birthplace of Possagno. The design for the tomb pyramid is by Canova himself (it was originally intended for **Titian**, who died of plague in 1576; the tomb of the latter on the opposite side was built by pupils of Canova more than 250 years after his death). The following tomb for Doge Gio-

Nave

Santa Maria Gloriosa dei Frari

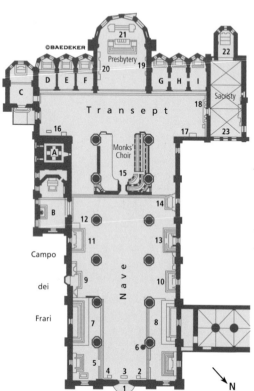

G. Campagna (1593)
7 Tomb of A. Canova († 1822)
8 Monument to Titian († 1576)
9 Tomb of Doge Giovanni Pesaro
   († 1659) at side door
10 Altar of Purification
11 »Madonna di Ca' Pesaro«
   (Titian)
12 Tomb of Bishop Jacopo Pesaro
   († 1547)
13 Altar of St Joseph of Copertino
14 Altar of St Catherine
15 Choir stalls (1468)
16 Monuments to Genero Orsini
17 Tomb of General I. Marcello
   († 1484)
18 Tomb of Admiral Benedetto Pesaro
   († 1503)
19 Tomb of Doge Francesco Foscari
   († 1457)
20 Tomb of Doge Niccolò Tron
   († 1473)
21 High altar with Titian's »Assumption
   of the Virgin« (»Assunta«, 1516–1518)
22 »Madonna Enthroned with Saints«
   by G. Bellini (1488)
23 »Madonna and Child with St Francis
   and St Elizabeth, who accompany the
   doge and his wife«
   by Paolo Veneziano
A Bell tower

CHAPELS
B Emiliani
C Corner: marble statue of John
   the Baptist (1554); altarpiece
   by Bart. Vivarini (1474)
D Milanesi: tomb of Claudio Monteverdi
   († 1643); altarpiece by Al. Vivarini
E Trevisan (Melchiore Trevisan, † 1500)
F San Francesco
G Fiorentini: wooden statue of John
   the Baptist by Donatello (1451)
H Sacramento: wall tomb of
   the Florentine envoy Duccio degli
   Alberti († 1336)
I Bernardo: altarpiece by Bart. Vivarini
   (1488)

1 Main entrance
2 Tomb of Alvise Pasqualino
   († 1528)
3 Tomb of Girolamo Garzoni
   († 1688)
4 Tomb of Pietro Bernado
   († 1538)
5 Crucifix, altar
6 Holy water basin with
   statuettes by

vanni Pesaro († 1659) derives from a design by Baldassare Longhena. The next altar has a famous painting by Titian, the so-called **Pesaro Madonna** (1519/1526), a religious image and a secular group portrait rolled into one: framed by an ensign bearer and a captured Turk, the donor Jacopo Pesaro, who fought against the Turks in the pope's service, kneels to the left; his brother Francesco and younger members of his family appear on the opposite side.

A magnificent *rood screen (1468–1475, Bartolomeo Bon and Pietro Lombardo) separates the nave from the monks' choir. The wonderfully carved and inlaid *Choir stalls were created by Marco Cozzi in 1468; the marble reliefs of the outer sides are from the workshop of the Lombardo brothers.

In the main choir chapel, red flames radiate from Titian's monumental altar painting of the *Assumption of the Virgin* (1518). At the centre of the image, the lovely mother of God floats heavenwards in a sunlike gloriole on an arc formed by numerous winged cherubs, and is received by God the Father.

Assumption of the Virgin

Among the doges' tombs in the main choir chapel, the late Gothic monument by Antonio and Paolo Bregno for Francesco Foscari († 1457) on the right wall is of particular interest. This doge extended Venice's rule to the mainland (terra ferma). Two knights with shields have drawn the curtain aside and give a view of the recumbent figure of the deceased, which is surrounded by the virtues of rulers. The tomb for Doge Niccolò Tron († 1473) on the left wall was done by Antonio Rizzo in the early Renaissance style with niche figures which hark back to antiquity.

The left transept contains the impressive altar painting of the enthroned Madonna with saints (first half of the 16th century), which was created by Bernardino Licinio under the influence of Titian, in the **Capella San Francesco**. The adjacent Capella Trevisan contains the tomb (early 16th century) of Melchiore Trevisan by Lorenzo Bregno. In the Cappella Milanesi, the tombstone commemorates the composer **Claudio Monteverdi** (1567–1634), the first director of music at San Marco and founder of Venetian opera with works such as *Orfeo* (1607) and *L'Incoronazione di Poppea* (1642). On the altar is a panel entitled *St Ambrose with Saints* and a *Coronation of the Virgin* (around 1503) by Alvise Vivarini. The Cappella Corner is ornamented by a holy water basin with the figure of St John the Baptist (around 1554) by Jacopo Sansovino as well as the triptych *St Mark Amongst Saints* (c. 1474) by Bartolomeo Vivarini.

Left transept

The right-hand transept, inside the Cappella Fiorentini, shows the expressive, coloured wooden statue of St John the Baptist (1451), the city patron of Florence, by **Donatello**, which depicts the ascetic saint in an urgent posture of preaching. The adjacent Cappella del Sacramento contains the wall tomb of the Florentine envoy Duccio degli Alberti († 1336), and in the adjacent Cappella Bernardo there is a surprising multiple-section altar panel (1488) with the Virgin and saints in a beautiful Renaissance frame by Bartolomeo Vivarini. Above the passage to the sacristy is the triumphal arch-like funerary monument for Admiral Benedetto Pesaro († 1503) and to its right,

Right transept

Titian's *Assumption of the Virgin*

on the wall, the monuments to General Jacopo Marcello († 1484) in the early Renaissance style as well as the equestrian monument, the first in Venice, for General Paolo Savelli († 1405).

The apse of the sacristy contains a masterpiece by **Giovanni Bellini**. In 1488, the Pesaro family commissioned Bellini's triptych for its family burial vault. The central section shows the enthroned Virgin with the Christ child, while the wings represent St Nicholas and St Peter on the left as well as St Benedict and St Mark on the right, the name patrons for Pietro Pesaro, the father, and for his sons Nicolò, Marco and Benedetto. The harmony and tranquillity radiated by this altarpiece with its rich colours also fascinated Albrecht Dürer, who saw the panel in Venice in 1495 and later used it as a model for his famous *Four Apostles* (1526; in the Alte Pinakothek, Munich). The *Madonna with Child, St Francis and St Elizabeth Accompanying the Doge and his Wife* (1339) is by Paolo Veneziano.

AROUND THE FRARI CHURCH

Archivio di Stato
The Franciscan monastery, which is built around two cloisters, is the seat of the Venetian state archive. After the archives of the Vatican and Vienna, it is the third-largest archive in Europe with more than 15 million books and manuscripts.

Campo di San Rocco
There are more sights waiting at Campo di S. Rocco, the church San Rocco and above all ►**Scuola Grande di San Rocco.

South of Campo di S. Rocco, on the other side of Rio di Ca' Foscari, it is worth taking a look inside the church San Pantalon (1686). For more than 20 years, from 1680 to 1704, Giovanni A. Fumiani worked on »the largest ceiling painting in the world«, a Baroque composition with figures from the life and death of the name-giving saint. The chapels of the church also contain a late work by Paolo Veronese (*The Miracle of St Pantaleon*, 1587) as well as a painting by Antonio Vivarini and Giovanni d'Alemagna (*The Coronation of the Virgin*, 1444). **Pasticceria Tonolo**, on the corner of Calle San Pantalon and Calle Crosera, sells truly delicious cakes and sweets.

San Pantalon

San Pantalon: Campo S. Pantalon, Mon – Sat 10am – 12 noon, 1pm – 3pm

The monastery church of the Theatine order near Piazzale Roma was built between 1591 and 1601 by Vincenzo Scamozzi – probably using plans by Andrea Palladio. The open portico in front of the church building by A. Tirali dates from the 18th century. The paintings to the left of the entrance, *St Lawrence* by Bernardo Strozzi (1581–1644) and to the left of the choir arch *The Inspiration of St Jerome*, a significant late work by Johann Liss (1597–1630) from Oldenburg, Germany, are noteworthy. While Liss painted the altar picture in 1629 he became ill with the plague and died shortly afterwards at the age of only 32. Today, the Theatine monastery houses part of the architectural faculty. One of the entrance portals is by Carlo Scarpa, who taught at this institution. It is also worth looking at the cloister (1600). Cross a bridge to reach **Papadopuli Park**, site of lavish festivals in the 19th century.

San Nicolò da Tolentino

> **MARCO ⊕ POLO TIP**
>
> ❗ *For nautical fans* Insider Tip
>
> The bookstore Mare di Carta between the church and the Grand Canal has (nearly) everything about the sea and navigation: Italian and foreign-language ocean charts, books, magazines, CD ROMs etc. (Fondamenta dei Tolentini 222, www.maredicarta.it).

❶ Campo dei Tolentini, quay Piazzale Roma, Mon – Fri 8.30am – 12 noon, 4.30pm – 6.30pm, Sun only midday

The name of the church north of the Frari church probably came from »lauro« (laurel). Its foundation stone was laid in the 9th or 10th century. The massive Veneto-Byzantine Campanile and the transept were built around 1225, the nave received its present form in the 15th century, and the three-section presbytery followed in the mid-16th century. In the interior, a richly carved wooden ceiling in the form of a ship's hull is noteworthy. Among the exhibits, the following are of particular interest: in the choir, a *Sacra Conversazione* by Lorenzo Lotto (1546); in the old sacristy (beside the left choir chapel) two works by Palma the Younger, in the new sacristy (beside the right choir chapel) – among other things – a lovely ceiling painting by Paolo Veronese. The pulpit in the unique chalice form dates from the

* San Giacomo dell'Orio

16th century; the column of green marble in the south transept is a spolia from the 6th century.

❶ Campo San Giacomo dell'Orio, quay San Staè, Mon – Sat 10am – 5pm, €12 (combination ticket Chorus Pass

Campo San Giacomo dell'Orio
The pretty campo, the heart of San Croce, benches or cafés invite guests to linger. In the summer months Réfolo on the tiny Campiello dei Morti behind the church has very good pizza.

❶ Tel. 04 15 24 00 16, closed Mon, Tue

** Santa Maria della Salute

✦ F 13

Location: Fondamenta della Salute
Quay: Salute
❶ daily 9am – 12 noon, 3pm – 5.30pm, admission sacristy: €3

Santa Maria della Salute seen from the sea – the most beautiful view of Venice – the perfect counterpiece to ▸Basilica di San Marco, the ▸Palazzo Ducale and the Campanile.

Building history
The Baroque church with its massive dome dominates, along with the Dogana da Mar (▸p. 186), the mouth of the Grand Canal. It was built as a token of thanks for the deliverance of the city from the plague of 1630, which had claimed 40,000 lives, nearly one third of the population, in Venice. the 33-year-old Baldassare Longhena was commissioned to build the church. In 1631, he began work over a foundation of about 100,000 wooden piles. The building was completed in 1687 – five years after the death of the builder. With its stairway, monumental portal and two mighty domes, the church not only reaches an astonishing width and but it also enhances the whole appearance of the city. The church of Mary shows the Virgin as the »Ruler of the Seas« (Capitana del Mar): her statue on the 55m/181ft-high dome bears the staff of a Venetian high admiral.

Interior
Santa Maria della Salute is an octagonal central structure. The interior still pays its due to the Renaissance. Eight massive pillars support the tambour dome; there are six side chapels each on the right and left. The floor is also very beautiful. Of the numerous sculptures – there are said to be more than 120 figures on the entire building – the group by the Flemish Giusto Le Court (before 1674) on the **high altar** is probably the most significant work: the Virgin fulfils the plea of Venetia and drives away the pestilence. The Greek-Byzantine icon

It would not be Venice without the domes of Santa Maria della Salute

from the 13th century on the high altar, the *Madonna della Salute* or *Mesopanditissa*, was brought here from Crete in 1672 by Francesco Morosini.

The three outer chapels on the west side are decorated with works by Luca Giordano (1674) on subjects from the life of Mary: *Presentation in the Temple*, *Assumption of Mary* (1667), *Birth of Mary*. In the eastern chapels are pictures by Pietro Liberi: *Annunciation* and *St Anthony* (1665) as well as *Miracle of Pentecost* by **Titian** (1546).

In the sacristy (left of the high altar) are the most outstanding paintings in the church, most of which come from various deconsecrated churches in Venice: *Wedding of Cana* on the long wall was painted by **Tintoretto** in 1551. **Titian** painted *St Mark with SS Cosmos, Damian, Roch and Sebastian* (1511) as well as the ceiling painting *Cain and Abel*, *Abraham's Sacrifice* and *David and Goliath* (1542 – 1544).

Every year on 21 November, Venice celebrates the **Salute Festival** by building a bridge across the Grand Canal to the church, and commemorates the end of the plague.

** Santi Giovanni e Paolo · San Zanipolo

✦ H 11

Location: Campo Santi Giovanni e Paolo
Quays: Fondamenta Nuove, Ospedale
❶ Mon – Sat 9am – 6pm, Sun only from 12 noon, admission €3
www.basilicasantigiovanniepaolo.it

In the 13th cent. San Marco and Rialto had become too crowded to build large churches. So Doge Jacopo Tiepolo gave the Dominicans the grounds north of the city. Today San Zanipolo along with Frari (▶p. 266) are among the largest churches in Venice.

**Building
history**

The imposing brick church, together with the adjacent Scuola Grande di San Marco, which is still used as a hospital, and the Colleoni equestrian statue in the courtyard, form an outstanding ensemble from the Gothic period and the Renaissance. Its façade adheres to the Dominican ideal of poverty: there is no belltower and the tabernacles on the gable were added later. Financing problems were probably the reason for the 200-year construction period: the nave was completed in 1369, the choir and the dome over the crossing only in 1450. In accordance with the Dominican ideal of poverty, the exterior of San Zanipolo, as the church is named in the Venetian dialect, is plain. The marble portal is a work by Bartolomeo Bon (1460), while the framing columns are from an earlier church on Torcello.

Interior

Its size already is impressive. With a length of 101.5m/333ft and a height of 35m/115ft, it is **Venice's largest church**. Its interior space, which is subdivided by tall columns, is proportioned with more vertical emphasis than the Frari church. Due to the absence of a choir screen, there is an unobstructed view all the way into the light-flooded apse. The church is also referred to as the pantheon of Venice, since 27 doges were entombed here. Its funerary monuments were created by renowned artists and reflect the development of sculpture from the late Gothic period via the High Renaissance to Baroque. The tombs of doges Pietro, Giovanni and Alvise Mocenigo lie at the west wall. The Renaissance funerary monument for Pietro Mocenigo (c. 1481, left) which extends down to the floor, with Hercules statues as pedestal reliefs, no longer shows the doge as a recumbent figure, but as a hero. The tomb completed around 1500 by Tullio Lombardo for Giovanni Mocenigo (right) is classically austere, the triumphal arch motif being replaced by an arrangement of columns. In the middle of the inner wall of the entry the colossal tomb of Alvise Moceni-

*Insider
Tip*

go, who passed away in 1577, was built between 1580 and 1646 and bears the marks of early Baroque-Classicistic decorative design.

The marble statue of the kneeling St Jerome on the first aisle altar was designed by Alessandro Vittoria (1525–1608). The tomb for Doge Nicolò Marcello with its base, columns, pilasters and entablature, which was created in 1481 by Pietro Lombardo, is next to the second round pillar. Beside it is the tomb monument for Doge Tommaso Mocenigo in the transitional style from late Gothic to Renaissance, using a fabric canopy for the first time, with shell niches and the portrait-like recumbent figure of the deceased. Not far away is the wall tomb of Doge Pasquale Malipiero in the early Renaissance style by Pietro Lombardo, decorated with a pietà relief, griffins and a fabric canopy.

Left aisle

The adjacent **sacristy** (16th century) has beautifully carved wall panelling of walnut wood and a ceiling painting by Marco Vecellio with *St Dominic and St Francis Praying to the Virgin* as well as an altar painting with a *Crucifixion* by Palma the Younger.

In the left transept, on the facing wall are three tombs for the doges of the Venier family: Antonio (dogat 1382–1400), Francesco (1554–1556) and Sebastiano (1577–1578). Set into the left wall of the Cap-

Scuola Grande di San Marco and San Zanipolo

pella Cavalli is one of the oldest tombs in the church, for Giovanni Dolfin (1356–1361), a simple sarcophagus with reliefs of the doge and his wife before the enthroned Christ, the adoration of the magi and the death of the Virgin. The *Cappella del Rosario, the votive chapel built in 1582 to commemorate the sea victory at Lepanto (1571), had ceiling paintings by Paolo Veronese (1528–1588) added to its new carved ceiling after the fire of 1867, among them *Adoration of the Magi, Assumption of the Virgin* and *Annunciation and Adoration of the Shepherds.* The rear wall of the chapel is ornamented by the *Nativity.*

Presbytery   In the presbytery (main apse), the impressive high altar in the form of a triumphal arch (around 1619) from designs by Baldassare Longhena has figures of St John and St Paul, the patron saints of the church (about 1660). On the left side wall, the eye first meets a Gothic tomb with the recumbent figure of Doge Marco Corner who died in 1368. The five-section retable above it with a Madonna figure was created by the Tuscan sculptor Nino Pisano. The adjacent Renaissance tomb (around 1492) for Doge Andrea Vendramin (doge 1476–1478), one of the main works of **Tullio Lombardo**, elevates the Roman triumphal arch motif out of the wall surface into a monumental sculpture. The recumbent figure, which is guarded by servants, rests on a sarcophagus surrounded by personifications of the virtues, above them in an arch relief the enthroned Virgin, while young warriors in poses from antiquity stand in the side niches. The opposite wall is graced by the funerary monument (1572), framed by colossal columns, of Leonardo Loredan (dogat 1501–1521) who appears as a state official and peacemaker between the personifications of Venezia (left) and the League of Cambrai (right). The adjacent Gothic tomb for Doge Michele Morosini, who died in 1382 – the year of his election – shows the combination of architecture, painting and sculpture which was typical for the 14th century. The end wall of the right transept is adorned by *Christ Bearing the Cross* (15th century) by Alvise Vivarini, the *Coronation of the Virgin* (16th century) by Giovanni da Udine and the altar painting (1542) by Lorenzo Lotto – showing the influence of Titian – *Alms-Giving of St Anthony Pierozzi* (an archbishop of Florence who died in 1459 and was canonized in 1523) as well as a large, glowing glass window (after 1470) from the workshops of Murano with the saints George, John, Paul and Theodore in the lancet segments.

Right aisle   The **Cappella di San Domenico** from the early 18th century contains a fascinating major work of the Rococo period, a ceiling fresco full of movement and immersed in surreal light by Giovanni Battista Piazzetta (1682–1754), the *Apotheosis of St Dominic* (1727). The right aisle in the direction of the exit leads to the tomb of Silvestro Valier, the doge who died in 1700 and was the last to be entombed in Zanipolo. The design is theatrical Baroque. The adjacent Cappella della Pace contains a Byzantine icon given to the Dominicans in 1349. The adjacent chapel of the *Suffering Mother of God* is basically a late Gothic room with paintings from the 17th century and an altar painting showing the cross being taken from Christ (19th century). A few steps farther is a triptych ascribed to Giovanni Bellini, in the early Renaissance style (around 1475–1480) with a beautiful original frame. The central panel shows St Vincenzo Ferrer, a Spanish Dominican, while St Sebastian and St Christopher are shown on the side panels and the predella depicts scenes from the life of St Vincent (1346–1419).

Santi Giovanni e Paolo · San Zanipolo

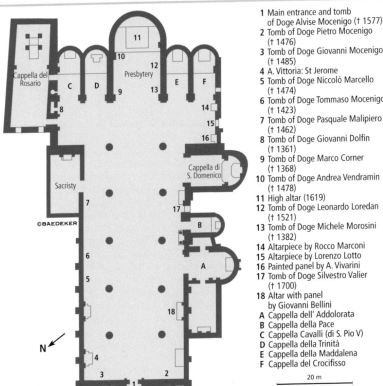

1 Main entrance and tomb
   of Doge Alvise Mocenigo († 1577)
2 Tomb of Doge Pietro Mocenigo
   († 1476)
3 Tomb of Doge Giovanni Mocenigo
   († 1485)
4 A. Vittoria: St Jerome
5 Tomb of Doge Niccolò Marcello
   († 1474)
6 Tomb of Doge Tommaso Mocenigo
   († 1423)
7 Tomb of Doge Pasquale Malipiero
   († 1462)
8 Tomb of Doge Giovanni Dolfin
   († 1361)
9 Tomb of Doge Marco Corner
   († 1368)
10 Tomb of Doge Andrea Vendramin
   († 1478)
11 High altar (1619)
12 Tomb of Doge Leonardo Loredan
   († 1521)
13 Tomb of Doge Michele Morosini
   († 1382)
14 Altarpiece by Rocco Marconi
15 Altarpiece by Lorenzo Lotto
16 Painted panel by A. Vivarini
17 Tomb of Doge Silvestro Valier
   († 1700)
18 Altar with panel
   by Giovanni Bellini
A Cappella dell' Addolorata
B Cappella della Pace
C Cappella Cavalli (di S. Pio V)
D Cappella della Trinità
E Cappella della Maddalena
F Cappella del Crocifisso

20 m

Colleoni monument on the square in front of San Zanipolo

AROUND SAN ZANIPOLO

*Monumento di Colleoni

The Colleoni monument in the courtyard, the second epoch-making equestrian monument of modern times after Donatello's *Gattamelata* statue in Padua, was modelled between 1481 and 1488 by the Florentine sculptor Andrea del Verrocchio and cast in 1496 by Alessandro Leopardi (ill. p.41). Horse and rider – and this is new – are shown in the moment when they start to move. The figure itself has little in common with the army commander Bartolomeo Colleoni (1400–1475). Rather, it represents the ideal of a proud and power-conscious condottiere. Colleoni fought for Venice on the terra ferma (mainland) from 1448, accumulating a huge fortune in the process. On his deathbed, he bequeathed his possessions to the state on the condition that he would receive a monument »in front of San Marco". The state did not want to fulfil the condition that was linked to the payment, but it did not want to lose the money either. Finally, it had the monument erected in front of the house of the brotherhood of San Marco – after all, the dying man had not explicitly stated that it had to be the *church* of San Marco!

Scuola Grande di San Marco

The scuola immediately next to San Zanipolo church was the house of the rich brotherhood of the goldsmiths and silk traders. Today, it serves as the main entrance to the city hospital. Its beautiful Renaissance façade was begun around 1490 by Pietro Lombardo (lower section); his son Tullio created the reliefs and the two lions. Mauro Coducci finally completed the upper section around 1500. The illusionistic wall design of the ground floor, the sculpted arches and the figure decoration of the gable are highly effective. There is also a remarkable relief over the entrance gate, *St Mark Giving a Blessing* by Bartolomeo Bon, one of the masters of the Porta della Carta at the ▶Palazzo Ducale.

As the name says, there were numerous vineyards (vigne) on east of San Zanipolo before it passed to the Franciscans in 1253, who built their first monastery here. Sansovino began the construction of the large church in 1543, but it was only completed 30 years later by Andrea Palladio. He designed the façade (1568–1572) in the style of an ancient temple, a central design element in his churches ▶San Giorgio Maggiore and Il Redentore (▶La Giudecca as well). The hall-like interior has numerous side chapels with tombs of important Venetian families. The high-class works of art include the panel *Enthroned Madonna* in the right aisle (c. 1470) by Antonio da Negroponte. The Cappella Santa (access from the left aisle) is adorned by a *Madonna with Saints* (1507) by Giovanni Bellini. The sacristy contains a triptych by Antonio Vivarini (15th century). A *Madonna with Saints* (1551) by Paolo Veronese hangs in the fifth chapel. The cycle of sculptures (c. 1500) in the Cappella Giustiniani to the left of the high altar is ascribed to Pietro Lombardo.

*San Francesco della Vigna

❶ Campo San Francesco della Vigna, quay Celestia, daily 8am – 12.30pm, 3pm – 6pm

Santo Stefano

✦ **F 12**

Location: Campo Santo Stefano
Quay: Accademia
❶ Mon – Sat 10am – 5pm, admission €12 (combination ticket Chorus Pass)

After the Frari chruch and SS Giovanni e Paolo, Santo Stefano is the third largest church in Venice the belongs to a religious order. It is also one of the city's most important Late Gothic churches.

At the upper end of the long **Campo S. Stefano**, which is lined by bars, restaurants and cafes, stands the 15th-century Augustine brick church with its crooked bell tower. But only the south side faces the square; its beautiful main façade faces a narrow sidestreet.

It has a beautiful coffered wooden ceiling in the form of an inverted ship's hull. Two important Venetians are entombed in the richly decorated interior: in the nave is the tomb of Doge Francesco Morosoni (doge 1688–1694), who re-conquered the Peloponnese for Venice, destroying the Parthenon on the Acropolis in Athens at the same time – since the Turkish powder magazine was housed there. Before the first altar to the left lies **Giovanni Gabrieli** (1557–1612). The composer was active at the Basilica di San Marco from 1586 and a pioneer of early Baroque music.

The sacristy is a small pinacoteca of Venetian painting. The greatest treasure is three paintings by **Tintoretto:** *Last Supper*, *Washing of Feet* and *Christ on the Mount of Olives*. Furthermore, there is **Bartolomeo Vivarini's** *St Nicholas of Bari* (c. 1475).

❶ Mon–Sat 10am–5pm, Sun from 1pm

* Campo Santo Stefano

The elongated Campo S. Stefano together with **Campo San Vidal** forms one of the largest squares in Venice. While bullfights were held here until 1802 the many restaurants and cafés invite people to linger now. In the east, it is bounded by the long **Palazzo Loredan** (16th century; seat of the Istituto Veneto di Scienze, Lettere ed Arti); in

Campo Santo Stefano, one of Venice's largest places

front of the palazzo there is a monument to the author Niccolò Tommaseo (1802–1874). On the opposite side stands the **Palazzo Morosini Gatterburg**, built for Doge Francesco Morosini who held office from 1688 to 1694, and whose victories over the Turks are retold on the portal ornamentation at the main and side entrances. A few steps farther south stands the magnificent Baroque palace of the **Pisani** family with a beautiful inner courtyard, begun by Bartolomeo Monopola around 1614. Today it is the seat of the Benedetto Marcello music conservatory.

The campo ends in the south with the back of the Gothic **Palazzo Cavalli-Franchetti** and the long-secularized church **San Vidal**, which is the seat of the Interpreti Veneziani; about 200 concerts take place here annually.

Interpreti Veneziani, tel. 04 12 77 05 61; www.interpretiveneziani.com

North of Campo Santo Stefano lies the picturesque **Campo Sant'Angelo**, which owes its name to a church dedicated to the archangel Michael, which was torn down in the 19th century. All that remains is the small **Oratorio Annunziata**, which was donated by the Morosini family.

*Campo Sant'Angelo

The composer **Domenico Cimarosa** (1749–1801) spent the last years of his life in Palazzo Duodo (no. 3584) diagonally opposite in the north-east corner of the square. It is bordered by the Benedictine church of the same name and the Gothic **Palazzo Pesaro degli Orfei**, where the highly talented Mariano Fortuny lived until his death in 1949 (▶p. 287).

** Scuola Grande di San Rocco

——————————————————————— ✦ E 11

Location: Campo San Rocco
Quay: San Tomà
❶ daily 9.30am – 5.30pm, admission €10, **www.scuolagrandesanrocco.it**

The brotherhood, which was founded in the name of St Roch, patron of the victims of plague, was originally devoted to nursing the sick

The scuola came out of the flagellant order of the Battuti and it became one of the richest scuole in Venice (▶p.44). Its meeting house was begun under Bartolomeo Bon (1517); after his death, Antonio Scarpagnino brought the work to completion in 1549. Opposite the great façade of the church San Rocco ("below), in which the relics of the saint are kept, the Renaissance structure of the scuola seems almost modest. In 1564, **Tintoretto**, himself a member of the scuola,

Tintoretto pinacoteca

won the competition to decorate the building – instead of a sketch, he had submitted the finished painting. In the years to 1588, he created one of the most extensive **Biblical cycles in Italian painting**, including some of his greatest works.

Ground floor Tintoretto's ****cycle of paintings about the life of the Virgin** in the large columned hall on the ground floor – where the poor were once fed and the sick cared for – begins on the left wall with the **Annunciation**. The Counter-Reformation is the historical background to Tintoretto's style of painting, which emphasizes the mystical with his exciting effects of light and shade, emotional coloration and dramatic gestural language. Thus the archangel steps into the Virgin's chambers, which are rendered as ruins, in blinding light and shrouded in cloud. **The Adoration of the Magi** is a complicated diagonal composition, in which the Virgin and Christ sit on a kind of bridge arch, surrounded by light, and accept the tribute. **Rest during the Flight** is dimly lit, but nonetheless the scene with the most naturalistic composition of landscape and figures. **The Massacre of the Innocents**, whose details remain somewhat in the dark, is – again – a dramatic representation. The paintings of **Mary Magdalene and Mary from Egypt** reflect a melancholy, serious mood, emphasized by the landscape of wilderness around

Scuola Grande di San Rocco • Large Hall

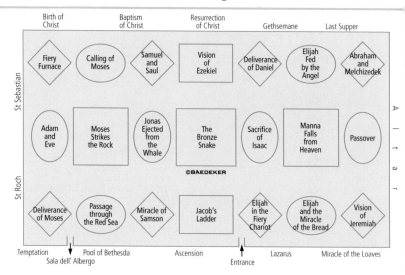

Birth of Christ / Baptism of Christ / Resurrection of Christ / Gethsemane / Last Supper

St Sebastian

Fiery Furnace / Calling of Moses / Samuel and Saul / Vision of Ezekiel / Deliverance of Daniel / Elijah Fed by the Angel / Abraham and Melchizedek

Adam and Eve / Moses Strikes the Rock / Jonas Ejected from the Whale / The Bronze Snake / Sacrifice of Isaac / Manna Falls from Heaven / Passover

©BAEDEKER

St Roch

Deliverance of Moses / Passage through the Red Sea / Miracle of Samson / Jacob's Ladder / Elijah in the Fiery Chariot / Elijah and the Miracle of the Bread / Vision of Jeremiah

Altar

Temptation / Pool of Bethesda / Ascension / Lazarus / Miracle of the Loaves

Sala dell' Albergo

Entrance

the two figures, who seem not to be of this world. The cycle ends with depictions of the **Circumcision of Jesus** and the **Assumption of the Virgin**.

A stairway with paintings of the plague raging in Venice leads to the 44 × 17 m (145 × 56 ft) meeting hall in the upper floor. The **wall paintings** show **scenes from the New Testament**, from the birth of Christ, then the baptism of Christ, the resurrection, the Mount of Olives and the Last Supper scene. On the other side, the cycle on Christ's life continues with the miracle of the loaves. These are followed by the resurrection of Lazarus, the ascension of Christ, the healing of the sick man at the pool of Bethesda and the temptations of Christ. The end wall of the hall is occupied by the San Rocco altar, framed by statues of St Sebastian and John the Baptist by Girolamo Campagna. A graceful annunciation scene (c. 1526) by Titian and the *Meeting of Mary and Elizabeth* (1588), a late work by Tintoretto are displayed on easels. Two paintings by Tiepolo from 1732, *Hagar in the Desert Comforted by an Angel*, as well as *Abraham and the Angels*, came to the scuola in 1789. The wooden figures below the paintings were carved by Francesco Pianta in the 17th century. The male figure with the palette and brush (at the altar) is intended to represent Tintoretto.

** Upper storey Great Hall

Insider Tip

Great hall in the Scuola di San Roco

Ceiling paintings	The 21 ceiling paintings, which all give an underside view, show **scenes from the Old Testament** (there are hand mirrors for more convenient viewing). They refer partly to the wall paintings, and partly to the charitable tasks of the brotherhood – such as feeding the poor and caring for the sick. The central field of the ceiling describes the miracle of the bronze snake with Moses as saviour. In the scene in which Moses strikes water from the rock, he appears related to the figure of Christ and points out the spring of life as a source of salvation. Jacob's Ladder, which Tintoretto painted in an extremely tall format as a stairway to heaven with light swirling around it, has a fascinating perspective.
*Sala dell'Albergo	In the small meeting room for the leadership of the brotherhood, what is probably Tintoretto's most moving work, the *Crucifixion*, catches the eye. Christ, illuminated in glory, announces his victory over death and the salvation of humanity. On the entrance wall, there are scenes from the passion of Christ: Christ before Pilate, the misericordia domini and the bearing of the cross. The ceiling paintings are part of Tintoretto's first commissioned work; at that time, he won the competition with *St Roch in Glory*. The easel painting of Christ bearing the cross is ascribed to Titian or Giorgione.
San Rocco	The choir of the church, which was dedicated in 1508, on the opposite side houses two noteworthy paintings by Tintoretto; both were painted around 1550. One depicts St Roch in a dungeon in Montpellier, the other shows him caring for people stricken with the plague.

* Scuola di San Giorgio degli Schiavoni

✦ J 12

Location: Calle dei Furlani/Ponte dei Greci
Quay: San Zaccaria
🕐 Mon 2.45pm – 6pm, Tue – Sat 9.15am – 1pm, 2.45pm – 6pm, Sun 9.15am – 1pm, admission €5

In the Scuola of the Dalmatians are some of the most beautiful paintings of the Renaissance painter Vittore Carpaccio.

The brotherhood building of the Schiavoni, the Dalmatian (or Slavic) merchants, which lies slightly hidden at Rio di S. Agostin, is a very plain 16th-century building, which **Vittore Carpaccio** decorated with a wonderful cycle of paintings in 1502 and 1508. The scenes from the lives of the saints George, Tryphon and Jerome – the three patron saints of the brotherhood that was founded in the 14th cent. – are the most significant work by this exceptionally gifted Renaissance painter, who achieved a perfect combination of realistic detail with a sense for decoration. The scenes on the left wall show the *Battle of St George and the Dragon* and *St George Brings the Dragon into the City*. To the left and right of the altar are *St George Baptizes a Heathen King and Queen* and *St Triphon Drives Out a Demon from the Emperor's Daughter*; on the right wall: *Christ's Prayer in the Garden of Gethsemane*, *The Calling of St Matthew*, *St Jerome Leads the Tame Lion into the Monastery*, *The Burial of St Jerome* and *The Vision of St Augustine*.

AROUND SCUOLA DI SAN GIORGIO

The so-called Greek quarter with popular trattorias and bars, beneath the crooked bell tower of the orthodox church **San Giorgio dei Gre-**

Riva degli Schiavoni: much coming and going

ci, which was built in 1539, is evidence of the once important Greek community in Venice. In the Scuola di San Nicolò in Palazzo Flangini (17th century, B. Longhena) immediately next to the church, a collection of valuable Byzantine icons can be seen (open: Mon–Sat 9am–noon, 2–4.30pm, Sun 10am–5pm).

Museo Dipinti Sacri Bizantini: daily 9am – 12.30pm, 1pm – 4.30pm, Sun 10am – 5pm, admission €4

San Giovanni in Bragora The church, which is located east of Rio della Pietà, was built in late Gothic style between 1475 and 1494. The interior with wooden roof trusses has three highlights of early Renaissance Venetian painting: in the choir apse, the *Baptism of Christ* by Cima da Conegliano (1494), who chose an atmospheric Veneto landscape as his background; in the left choir chapel, a triptych with the *Virgin, St John the Baptist and St Andrew* (1748) by Bartolomeo Vivarini. In the first side chapel on the left beside the entrance, a *Resurrection* (1498) by Alvise Vivarini; above the entrance there is a notable work by Palma the Younger, *Christ before Caiaphas* (1600). The choir walls are decorated with *Washing of the Feet* and *The Last Supper* by Titian's pupil Paris Bordone (1500–1571). The composer Antonio Vivaldi was baptized in the font in the left aisle; a copy of his baptismal certificate is displayed.

> **!** *Pearls* **Insider Tip**
>
> **MARCO POLO TIP**
>
> Outstanding craft products, guaranteed to be made locally, as well as real Venetian pearls, are available in the little store Il Coccio di Marina, Salizzada dei Greci, Castello 3446 (Mon–Sat 10am–12.30pm and 3.30–7.30pm).

❶ Campo Bandiera e Moro, Mon – Sat 9am – 11pm, 3.30pm – 5.30pm

Campiello del Piovan To the south, on Campiello del Piovan, stand three of the typically Venetian well heads (vere da pozzo).

*Riva degli Schiavoni Riva degli Schiavoni, the quay of the Dalmatians, extends from the Ponte della Paglia (▶Palazzo Ducale) almost to the ▶Arsenale. Where small passenger ships dock today and hawkers try to sell their wares to the tourists, the ships of the Dalmatian merchants once docked.

La Pietà The late Baroque church called Santa Maria della Visitazione or della Pietà, which you pass on the way to St Mark's Square, is also simply called **Vivaldi's church**. The composer Antonio Vivaldi ("Famous People) was violin teacher in the adjacent girls' orphanage Ospedale della Pietà for many years. Regular concerts take place here even today. A small museum tells the story of the hospice and its most famous musician. The hospice also has simple, reasonably priced rooms (www.pietavenezia.org).

Insider Tip

Teatro La Fenice

✦ F 12

Location: Campo San Fantin
Quay: Santa Maria del Giglio
❶ Programme info: www.teatrolafenice.it; here and at tel.
0 41 78 66 72 also information on viewing times, admission: €9 with
audioguide

Venice's opera house, along with Mialn's Scala and the San Carlo in Naples, is one of the most famous opera houses in the world.

»The fabulous Teatro La Fenice is returned to Italy and the world«, said Venice's mayor Paolo Costa when, on 13 December 2003 after eight years of rebuilding, the curtain was first raised again in Venice's famous opera house, which had burned down completely in 1996. The project by the architect **Aldo Rossi** cost €55 million or more. It should have been completed in 1999, but spent years stuck in a morass of objections and disputes. Since then, however, La Fenice radiates its former glory: 174 theatre boxes have been re-created in their original form, including gold leaf. Even the new chandeliers are exactly the same as the old ones. And the Graces dance on the turquoise ceiling as before. The opera now holds an audience of about 1,000 – approximately 150 more than before. The theatre can be viewed (changing times, infor at Hellovenezia).

Risen from the ashes

Venice's **opera house**, which faces water on two sides at a place where three canals meet, is among the most famous opera houses in the world, together with Milan's Scala and San Carlo in Naples. The luxurious house was built between 1790 and 1792 as a replacement for a predecessor which had burned down in 1773, the popular opera house San Benedetto. At that time, it received the symbolic name La Fenice, »the phoenix arisen from the ashes«. On 16 May 1792, the theatre was opened with Giovanni Paisello's *I Giochi di Agrigento*. In 1836, a major fire destroyed this opera house as well, but one year later, it had already been rebuilt, a faithful copy of the original in the neo-classical style. The magnificent theatre probably owed its burgeoning reputation as the »queen of the opera world« in the 19th century to its well-considered statutes and the rich Venetian musical tradition. At its foundation the showing of two new operas annually was specified. Rossini, Bellini, Donizetti and Verdi composed major works especially for this opera house. In 1873, visitors to La Fenice saw Wagner's *Rienzi*, in 1881 *Lohengrin*, and shortly after the death of the celebrated composer, the Ring cycle was shown at La Fenice for the first time in Italy. In the 20th century, Igor Stravinsky conducted

Some history

the first performance of his opera parody *The Rake's Progress* at La Fenice (1951). Later, Benjamin Britten's *The Turn of the Screw*, Sergei Prokofiev's *Fiery Angel* and Bruno Maderna's *Hyperion* premiered here. In 1960, Luigi Nono's *Intolleranza* triggered a staged scandal, and in 1985, Pina Bausch enjoyed an ecstatic reception at La Fenice for her idiosyncratic choreographies. The special atmosphere of the theatre is probably the reason why singers from Caruso to Pavarotti, conductors such as Leonard Bernstein and directors from Giorgio Strehler to Luca Ronconi were delighted to work here.

Palazzo Contarini del Bovolo

Palazzo Contarini del Bovolo to the north-west is probably the only palace in Venice whose inner courtyard is more interesting than the canal façade, which faces Rio dei Barcaroli. The inner courtyard contains the wonderful spiral staircase, the »bovolo«, which was built onto the palazzo in 1500 by the Lombard architect Giovanni Candi (others think Giorgio Spavento; *bovolo* is the Venetian word for *chiocciola*, snail). The stair tower links the five loggias of the palace, and its round-arch arcades are reminiscent of the Leaning Tower of Pisa. The spiral staircase is accessible and offers a beautiful view.

Spiral staircase: quay: Rialto, www. scalabovolo.org, currently closed for renovations; the easiest way to get to it is from Campo Manin: next to the monument for the freedom fighter Daniele Manin (1848) follow Calle della Vida to the palace.

> **! MARCO POLO TIP**
>
> *Fortuny* **Insider Tip**
>
> Fortuny also has a showroom on Giudecca; the legendary Fortuny fabrics are on sale at Trois (San Marco, Campo San Maurizio 2666, tel. 04 15 55 29 05). Venetia Studium sells fabrics inspired by Fortuny as well as hand-painted lamps to Fortuny designs and other items (Calle Larga XXII Marzo 2403, tel. 04 15 22 92 81, Mercerie S. Zulian 723, tel. 04 15 22 98 59 and at Marco Polo Airport; www. venetiastudium.it).

Museo Fortuny

At the pretty Campo San Benedetto, the eye falls on the Gothic palace **Palazzo Pesaro degli Orfei** with two rows of eight pointed arches. From 1899 to his death in 1949, the Granada-born painter, sculptor, theatre-set maker and designer Mariano Fortuny y Madrazo, **known as Fortuny**, lived here. He became famous for his precious pleated fabrics and filigree silk lamps. Inspired by Greek tunics, Fortuny designed a dress in tiny pleats of silk satin in 1907. This design brought him world fame. The fabric was hand-pleated and dyed in various steps, so that it shone in different shades depending on the light. The cut itself was simple, flattered the figure, and transformed its wearer into a cross between an ancient goddess and an oriental princess. His clothes struck a chord in the early 20th century; his clients included stage stars like Sarah Bernhardt, Isadora Duncan and Eleonore Duse. In 1919, Fortuny even patented his process for permanently fixing pleats. On the island of Giudecca, fabrics are still manufactured to his designs today (Giudecca 805, open for visitors, info at www.fortuny. com). The piano nobile of his palazzo houses a small museum, which tells of his life and accomplishments, and shows unusual designs by this all-round genius. The Benedictine church also located on the square has a painting of St Francis by **Tiepolo**.

Palazzo Pesaro degli Orfei: Campo San Benetto, quay: San Zaccaria, Vallaresso San Marco; the palace is only open for exhibitions, fortuny. visitmuve.it

✳ **Torcello**

────────────────────────────── ✦ **Excursion**

Population: 30
Location: North lagoon (get there via Burano; change boats to go to Torcello)

Torcello, the island of the »little tower«, was once the first and for centuries the most powerful settlement on the lagoon.

It once had its own bishop, many churches and palaces, a large port and shipyards, its own laws and more than 20,000 residents. The unstoppable rise of Venice and the hazard of malaria in the increasingly swampy surrounding land were probably the reasons why the population gradually moved away from the early 16th century. Today, reminders of a great past can be found in the ✳**Basilica S. Maria Assunta**, the oldest building in the lagoon, and a handful of houses scattered across the island.

According to an inscription to the left of the high altar, the basilica was built in 639 in the Venetian-Byzantine style. In the 9th century,

✳**Santa Maria Assunta**

it received a crypt, a narthex and the two side apses. In the early 11th century, the naves were raised and the bell tower (accessible) completed. In front of the church, the foundation walls of the 17th-century baptistery are still identifiable. The floor tiles of the basilica date from the 11th century, while the mosaic of the subfloor is even from the 9th century.

The oldest mosaics are found in the cross-vault of the right apse. The an-

> **!** *Al Ponte del Diavolo*   **Insider Tip**
>
> MARCO ⊕ POLO TIP
>
> The osteria on the way to the basilica, which is named after its location near the »devil's bridge«, is a good (and inexpensive) alternative to its better known neighbour Cipriani, not just because of its shady terrace (Al Ponte del Diavolo, daily except Wed, tel. 0 41 73 04 01).

gels bearing a medallion with the lamb of God (apse vault) are very similar to Byzantine examples and reminiscent of the famous mosaics in Ravenna. The latter are from the 6th century, and it is thought that mosaic artists from Ravenna participated in the work on Torcello. The main apse with a stepped seat for priests is graced by 12th-century mosaic decorations: the Virgin with the apostles. The enthroned Christ with archangels in the right apse dates from the 12th and 13th centuries. The opposite wall is occupied by a large Last Judgment mosaic from the 12th/13th centuries. The six scenes on the wall should be read from the top to the bottom.

Next to the basilica stands the small church Santa Fosca, a significant 11th-century building with a central plan, surrounded by a 12th-century arcade. The square interior space – analogous to tombs from antiquity – with its rectangular choir serves as a place of remembrance for St Fosca, a martyr from Ravenna, and has an unusually harmonious spatial effect. The marble block in the form of a seat in the courtyard is said to be the 5th-century throne of Attila the Hun.

Santa Fosca

Exhibits in the adjacent museum document the long history of the island: capitals, fragments of mosaics, ceramics, icons and paintings from former churches are presented here, as well as writings, seals and everyday objects.

Museo di Torcello

❶ Tue – Sun March – Oct 10.30am – 5.30pm, otherwise 10am – 5pm, admission €3

In Santa Maria Assunta the usual iconostasis of a Greek Orthodox church is a rood screen that separates the altar area from the nave

PRACTICAL INFORMATION

How do you get to Venice? How do you say »I need a room« in Italian? Which ferry goes to the lagoon? Find out here – ideally before yor trip!

Arrival · Before the Journey

GETTING THERE

By car Except for the Lido cars are not allowed in Venice. Anyone coming by car crosses the 4km/2.4mi long Freedom Bridge (Ponte della Libertà) into the city on the lagoon. For day-trippers the somewhat expensive and often overfilled parking garages around Piazzale Roma (opposite the railway station) and on Tronchetto Island (www.venice parking.it; 3 €/hr., 21 €/day) are recommended. The People Mover has been running between the two since 2010; it is a 900m/3000ft-long rail line on 7m/24ft high stilts (one-way trip: €1.30). From Piazzale Roma continue by taxi and ferry (vaporetti) into the centre. Parking on the mainland in Fusina is definitely cheaper (€15/day; ferry return trip €13); for longer stays in Mestre (at the railway station), Treporti, Punta Sabbioni or the parking lot »Marco Polo 2002« near the airport, continue by train, bus or boat into the city.

> **Note**
> Service numbers with charges are marked with an asterisk: *0180

For those who do take their car to Italy (the distance from London to Venice is 1,515km/940mi), the city is easily accessible via the Italian autostrada system: from the north from Switzerland through the St Bernard tunnel or from Austria across the Brenner pass, from the west on the European E70 route through the Mont Blanc tunnel at Chamonix and then eastwards via Turin, Milan and Verona. Use of most stretches of autostrada in Italy is subject to tolls (information is available from automobile clubs, at border crossings and gas stations; the **autostrada tolls** are paid in cash, by credit card or with the Viacard, which is available from automobile clubs, at main toll stations and service stations).

By rail The train journey from London to Venice via Paris takes about 17 hours. There are also good direct connections to Venice from Germany, Austria and Switzerland (travel time from Munich, Zurich and Vienna approx. 7 to 8 hours). The railway terminal Stazione Santa Lucia lies at the north end of the Grand Canal, where it is possible to switch to a vaporetto or water taxi. Information is available from the railway station and travel agencies. **Temporary storage for luggage** (Deposito bagagli) upon arrival or until depar-

> ! **MARCO POLO TIP**
>
> *Waiting times* **Insider Tip**
>
> The railway terminal buffet of Stazione Ferrovia Santa Lucia in Venice is a good place to while away waiting times. In Italy, it is customary to pay for the drinks at the cash desk and then take the scontrino (receipt) to the bar. Open: daily 6.05am-9.55pm.

ture: at platform 1. Luggage transport to or from hotels is handled, at set prices, by the **luggage carrier service** (Cooperativa Trasbagli; Piazzale Roma, www.trasbagagli.it, Tel. 0 41 71 37 19).

PARKING
Isola del Tronchetto
Tel. 04 15 20 75 55
www.veniceparking.it

Piazzale Roma
San Marco: tel. 04 15 23 22 13
Toderini: tel. 04 15 20 79 79
Communale: tel. 04 12 72 73 01
Sant'Andrea: tel. 04 12 72 73 04
www.asmvenezia.it

Mainland
Fusina: tel. 04 15 47 01 60
www.terminalfusina.it
S. Giuliano: tel. 04 15 32 26 32
www.asmvenezia.it
Marco Polo 2002: Tel. 04 15 41 53 74
www.marcopolo2002.com

RAILWAY TRAVEL
In London
Rail Europe Travel Centre 178 Piccadilly
London W1V 0BA
Tel. 0870 8 37 13 71
www.raileurope.co.uk

In Italy
Trenitalia (FS): tel. *89 20 21
From abroad: 06 68 475 475
www.trenitalia.com
Railway station (Stazione Ferroviaria)
Venezia Santa Lucia tel. 0 41 78 56 70

AIRPORTS
Aeroporto Marco Polo
Viale G. Galilei 30/1
30173 Tessera-Venezia
Information: tel. 04 12 60 92 40
www.veniceairport.it

Aeroporto di Treviso Canova
Via Noalese 63/E, 31100 Treviso
Tel. 04 22 31 51 11
www.trevisoairport.it

AIRLINES IN ITALY
Air Canada
Tel. 06 650 11 462
www.aircanada.com

Alitalia
Call centre Italien
Tel. 06 22 22
Marco Polo Airport
Tel. 8 48 86 56 41/2/3
www.alitalia.com

American Airlines
Tel. 06 660 53 169
www.aa.com

British Airways
Tel. 199 71 22 66
www.britishairways.com

Delta Air Lines
Tel. 800 47 79 99
www.delta.com

easyjet
Tel. 848 88 77 66
www.easyjet.com

Qantas
Tel. 06 524 82 725
www.qantas.com

Ryanair
Tel. 899 67 89 10
www.ryanair.com

By air Venice's international **Marco Polo Airport** is 13km/8mi north-east in Tessera. **Blue ATVO busses** (www.atvo.it) and yellow ACTV busses (www. actv.it) run from here to Piazzale Roma for €6 (travel time about 30 min.; airport – city 7.50am until 10.20pm, city – airport 5am – 8.50pm), by taxi (travel time about 30 min.) it costs about €40. As of 2015 a tram is supposed to run between the airport, Piazzale Roma and the cruise ship terminal Stazione Marittima. Express busses also run to Treviso, Padua and the railway station in Mestre, from where trains run to Venice Santa Lucia. Travel between the airport and the inner city (Piazza San Marco) is also possible by **water taxi** (motoscafi, €100, about 30 min. trip; the 800m/2700ft from the airport terminal to the pier is covered by a shuttle car; more info ▶p. 314) and **ferry** (vaporetti, (www.ali laguna.it), €13 one way); the total time to Piazza San Marco is 60 minutes. Some budget airlines, such as Ryanair, use **Canova Airport** west of Treviso (about 20km/12mi north of Mestre, www.trevisoairport.it), from where ATVO bus service runs to Piazzale Roma (about 1 hr. 10 min. trip, one way €10, tickets in the terminal, www.atvo.it)..

By ship Those who come on their own boat can head for the harbours of S. Elena or S. Giorgio. Venice, which is accessible by ship from all major Adriatic ports, is also a popular stop for cruises; the mooring is Stazione Marittima (Tronchetto; info: www.vtp.it).

IMMIGRATION AND CUSTOMS REGULATIONS

Personal documents Even as an EU citizen, do not travel to Italy without an identity card or passport. Since 2012 children under the age of 16 years must have a children's identity card or their own passports.

Loss of documents If your travel documents are stolen or lost, the consulate of your country will help. However, the first place to go is the police, as nothing will proceed without a copy of the theft report. It is much easier to obtain replacement documents if you can show copies or access them from an electronic mailbox.

Vehicle papers What to bring: driving licence, the motor vehicle registration certificate and the International Green Insurance Card. Motor vehicles must bear the oval nationality identification sign unless they have a Euro licence plate. As usual, it is a good idea to photocopy all documents and keep them separate from the originals.

Pets Persons wishing to bring pets (dogs, cats) to Italy require an EU pet ID issued by a veterinarian (with a rabies certification). Bring a muzzle and leash.

The European Union member states (including Italy) form a common economic area, within which the movement of goods for private purposes is largely duty-free. There are merely certain maximum quantities which apply (for example 800 cigarettes, 10 litres of spirits and 90 litres of wine per person). During random inspections customs officers must be convinced that the goods are actually intended for private use.

Customs regulations for EU citizens

For travellers from outside the EU, the following duty-free quantities apply: 200 cigarettes or 100 cigarillos or 50 cigars or 250g of tobacco; also 2 litres of wine and 2 litres of sparkling wine or 1 litre of spirits with an alcohol content of more than 22% vol.; 500g of coffee or 200g of coffee extracts, 100g of tea or 40g of tea extract, 50ml of perfume or 0.25 litres of eau de toilette. Gifts up to a value of €175 are also duty-free.

Customs regulations for non-EU citizens

Citizens of EU countries are entitled to treatment in Italy under the local regulations in case of illness on production of their European health insurance card (EHIC, Ital. TEAM, Tessera europea di assistenza malattie). Even with this card, in most cases some of the

Health insurance

Torcello with an Alpine backdrop

costs for medical care and prescribed medication must be paid by the patient. Upon presentation of receipts the health insurance at home covers the costs – but not for all treatments. Citizens of non-EU countries must pay for medical treatment and medicine themselves and should take out private health insurance.

Private travel insurance

Since some of the costs for medical treatment and medication typically have to be covered by the patient, and the costs for return transportation may not be covered by the normal health insurance, additional travel insurance is recommended.

Electricity

The power network carries 220-volt alternating current. For three-pin plugs, an adapter (riduzione) is required, as the standard European 2-pin plugs are used in Italy.

Emergency

The emergency call numbers are on the first page of the telephone books (elenco telefonico) under the key word »Avantielenco«.

EMERGENCY CALL NUMBERS
Emergency
Tel. 112 (carabinieri)
Europe-wide free number

Breakdown help
Tel. 116
(soccorso stradale, ACI)

Fire department
Tel. 115 (vigili fuoco)

Accident, ambulance
Tel. 118 (emergenza sanitaria)

City hospital
City hospital SS. Giovanni e Paolo
Tel. 04 15 29 41 11

Etiquette and Customs

What is acceptable in Italy?

Bella figura, a beautiful appearance, is a deep-seated need for most Italians. Everyone who goes out in public likes to dress up, even for a trip to the post office or market, following Coco Chanel's motto: always be dressed to meet the love of your life. When there is a choice, money is always spent on fashion (and good food) rather than furniture or a coat of paint for the façade. Unfashionable tourists who stroll into cathedrals with flip-flops on their feet, wear shorts to visit the art gallery, sit in a restaurant in sandals or even dare to stroll through the old city with a naked chest – something not even the tifosi, soccer fans from Juventus Turin, Lazio Roma or Sampdoria Genoa, would consider – are looked down upon with amusement or a complete lack of comprehension.

Bella figura can also be admired in the baristi, who truly play the leading role in the hundreds of thousands of bars up and down the country: at their hissing espresso machines they usually wear smart waiter's jackets and snappy little caps; they are the sovereign rulers of the public standing before them, who hand out cappuccini with artistic foam, freshly-baked cornetti and of course glasses of fresh water with matchless elegance. Compared to this performance, a sit-down breakfast in other countries is boring. Break out of the hotel routine for a change, and treat yourself to a *colazione all'italiana*. And leave a few coins as a tip for the boys behind the counter – service professions are often low-paid.

Colazione all'italiana

Venice is not Naples, where every photograph becomes a public event. On the contrary many Venetians are irritated by cameras – many shop windows have large signs: No photos! In a place like this it is important to be diplomatic when photographing: chose the quiet times of the day to take pictures, always ask first or start a conversation before photographing a Venetian, and make sure not to block traffic when taking pictures in narrow streets.

Taking pictures

Italians are also spontaneous behind the wheel. Although the government of Silvio Berlusconi decided to introduce a points system for traffic offences in 2004, southern Italians in particular constantly prove their mastery of the art of living, airily attempting to overtake on the wrong side or parking their Fiats three deep – how nice it is when the chaos then unsnarls and as many people as possible join in with all the gestures at their command. Then the street becomes a living piazza, the machine-like routine of day-to-day life is interrupted. The purpose of all this is to communicate, and only rarely to be proved right, a fact proven by the Italians' courtesy towards pedestrians, which is a pleasing contrast to other Mediterranean countries.

Italians at the wheel

To enjoy life in Italy, approach people and let them know through a smile or a gesture just how much you appreciate and enjoy dealing with such a competent and winning counterpart. Do not hesitate to ask for the waiter's first name, and call out a »bravo«, »grande« or »bello« too many rather than one too few. And if things are not working out, bring the ancient Italian art of »arrangiarsi« into play. With

Contact

Venetians, Romans and Milanese, a sympathetic compliment is usually more effective than a threatening attitude, which – you guessed it – are detrimental to the bella figura. This is a nation which prefers to be adored than to be told what to do.

Health

CITY HOSPITAL
Santi Giovanni e Paolo
Tel. 04 15 29 45 16

EMERGENCY DOCTOR
Tel. 118

PHARMACIES
Pharmacies (farmacia) are open Mon – Fri 9am – 12.30pm and 4pm – 7.30pm. They close on alternating Wednesdays and Saturdays. A list of all emergency service pharmacies (farmacie di turno) is on display at all pharmacies.

Information

ITALIAN NATIONAL
TOURIST OFFICE
ENIT (Ente Nazionale Italiano per il Turismo)
www.italiantourism.com

IN AUSTRALIA
Italian Government Tourist Office
Level 4, 46 Market Street
NSW 2000 SIDNEY
Tel. 02 92 621 666

IN CANADA
Italian Government Tourist Office
175 Bloor Street E, Suite 907
Toronto M4W 3R8
Tel. 416 925 48 82

IN UK
Italian State Tourist Board
1 Princes Street, London W1B 2AY
Tel. 207 408 12 54

IN USA
Italian State Tourist Board
630 Fifth Avenue, Suite 1565
10111 New York
Tel. 212 245 48 22

IN VENICE
Venice
Azienda di Promozione Turistica
di Venezia (APT):, Castello 5050
I-30122 Venezia
For written inquiries and complaints:
Tel. 04 15 29 87 11
(Mon – Fri 8.30am – 2.30pm)
www.turismovenezia.it

Uffici informazioni
(information offices) in Venice:
Tel. 04 15 29 87 11
Piazza San Marco
S. Marco 71/f (daily 9am–3.30pm)
Venice Pavilion, Giardini Reali
(daily 12am–6pm)
Stazione Santa Lucia (railway terminal)
daily 8am–6.30pm)
Piazzale Roma, Garage ASM
(daily 9.30am–3.30pm)
Aeroporto Marco Polo (airport, daily
9.30am–8pm)

Lido di Venezia
Gran Viale 6, Tel. 04 15 29 87 11
(June – Sept. 9am – 12pm, 3pm – 6pm)

Chioggia e Sottomarina
Lungomare Adriatico 101
30019 Sottomarina Lido Venezia
Tel. 041 40 10 68
www.chioggiatourism.it

Lido di Jesolo
Piazza Brescia 13
30016 Lido di Jesolo
Tel. 04 21 37 06 01
www.jesolo.it

Hello Venezia
www.hellovenezia.com
Tel. 041 24 24
The place to get tickets for public transportation, the Venice Card as well as
tickets for many events. Hellovenezia
also runs the internet reservation system
VeniceConnected ("Prices and discounts). Website in English and French.

CONSULATES
Australian Consulate
Nearest consulate is in Milan
Via Borgogna 2, Milano

Tel. 02 7770 42 27
www.italy.embassy.gov.au

British Consulate
Piazzale Donatori die Sangue 2
Mestre
Tel. 041 505 59 90
www.britishembassy.gov.uk

Canadian Consulate
Nearest consulate is in Padua
Riviera Ruzzante 25, Padua
Tel. 049 876 48 33,
www.canada.it

Irish Consulate
Nearest consulate is in Milan
Piazza S. Pietro in Gessate 2
20122 Milano
Tel. 02 5518 88 48
www.ambasciata-irlanda.it

New Zealand Consulate
Nearest consulate is in Milan
Via Guido d'Arezzo 6, 20145 Milano
Tel. 02 499 02 01
www.nzembassy.com

United States Consulate
Nearest consulate is in Milan
Via Principe Amadeo 2/10, Milano
Tel. 02 29 03 51
www.usis.it

LOST PROPERTY OFFICES ·
UFFICI OGGETTI SMARRITI
City Lost Property Office
San Marco, Ca' Farsetti 4136
Tel. 04 12 74 82 25-8107

City transport operators
Piazzale Roma
Tel. 04 12 72 21 79
(ACTV, Vaporetti)

Stazione Santa Lucia
Railway terminal, tel. 0 41 78 56 70

Aeroporto Marco Polo
Airport, tel. 04 12 60 64 36

INTERNET ADDRESSES
www.turismovenezia.it
Website of the Venetian tourism office
in English with current themes and a lot
of information

www.actv.it
Useful information, fares and vaporetti
schedules of the Venetian transport
company ACTV

www.hellovenezia.it
Useful information in Italian and English

www.venicecard.it
Info about the Venice Card

www.veniceconnected.com
Website of the reservation system Venice
Connected ("Prices and discounts).

www.venicewiki.org
Internet encyclopaedia with many articles written by Venetians

www.bacari.it
The latest news about culinary Venice.

www.meetingvenice.it
Tourism portal with a calendar of events
and a lot of other information.

www.veneziasi.it
450 hotels online, lots of good general
and current information

veniceexplorer.net
A great deal of useful information, including hotels, restaurants, shops,
schedules

www.gondolavenezia.it
History and technology of and stories
about the gondola

www.venicebanana.com
www.veneziadavivere.it
Event information and other tips for
young visitors to Venice

www.promovetro.com
About glass art on Murano, from history
to tours

www.venessia.com
Authentic info instead of ad banners.
English-Venetian lexicon.

www.marcatreviso.it
Info for excursions around Venice (also
in English).

Language

Italian   Italian developed from Latin and is the closest to it of all the Romance
languages. Due to the earlier political division of the country, among
other reasons, numerous dialects developed, of which the Tuscan dialect prevailed and is the official written language to this day. Venetian
is regarded as the softest dialect in Italy; the words themselves are
changed, e.g. frari instead of frati (brothers), ca' instead of casa
(house), anzelo instead of angelo (angel), pesse instead of pesce (fish).

LEARN ITALIAN IN VENICE
Italian Courses Istituto Venezia
Dorsoduro 311/a
Campo S. Margherita
Tel. 04 15 22 43 31
www.istitutovenezia.com

Venice Italian School
San Polo 2504, Venice
Tel. 340 75 10 863
www.veniceitalianschool.com
A range of 1-week language courses,
but also courses on Venetian culture

? Odd weights

MARCO POLO INSIGHT

Don't be surprised to hear strange weights named while you are shopping. The term »pound« is completely unknown in Italy (454 g), instead they talk about »mezzo chilo« (a half kilo). And with smaller quantities, do not ask for 100g but un etto, and for 200g, 300g etc. due etti, tre etti, etc. For lengths and other measurements Italy, like the rest of Europe, uses the metric system.

Italian Phrases

At a glance

Sì/No	Yes/No
Per favore/Grazie	Please/Thank you
Non c'è di che	You're welcome
Scusi!/Scusa!	Excuse me!
Come dice?	Excuse me?
Non La/ti capisco	I cannot understand you
Parlo solo un po' di ...	I only speak a little ...
Mi può aiutare, per favore?	Can you please help me?
Vorrei ...	I would like ...
(Non) mi piace	I (do not) like that
Ha ...?	Do you have ...?
Quanto costa?	How much does it cost?
Che ore sono?/Che ora è?	What time is it?
Come sta?/Come stai?	How are you?
Bene, grazie. E Lei/tu?	Fine, thank you. And you?

Getting around

a sinistra	left
a destra	right
diritto	straight ahead
vicino/lontano	close/far
Quanti chilometri sono?	How far is that?
Vorrei noleggiare ...	I would like to rent ...
... una macchina	... a car
... una bicicletta	... a bicycle

... una barca	... a boat
Scusi, dov'è ...?	Excuse me, where is ...?
la stazione centrale	the central railway station
la metro(politana)	the metro/subway
l'aeroporto	the airport
all'albergo	to the hotel
Ho un guasto.	I have broken down.
Mi potrebbe mandare un carro-attrezzi?	Can you please send a tow truck?
Scusi, c'è un'officina qui?	Is there a garage nearby?
Dov'è la prossima stazione di servizio?	Where is the next gas station?
benzina normale	regular gasoline
super/gasolio	super/diesel
Deviazione	detour
Senso unico	one-way street
sbarrato	closed
rallentare	drive slowly
tutte le direzioni	all directions
tenere la destra	drive on the right
Zone di silenzio	honking forbidden
Zona tutelata inizio	start of the no-parking zone
Aiuto!	Help!
Attenzione!	Attention!

Chiami subito ...	Quickly, call ...
... un'autoambulanza	... an ambulance
... la polizia	... the police

Going out

Scusi, mi potrebbe indicare ...?	Where can I find ...?
... un buon ristorante?	... a good restaurant?
... un locale tipico?	... an typical restaurant?
C'è una gelateria qui vicino?	Is there an ice cream parlour nearby?
Può riservarci per stasera un tavolo per quattro persone?	Can I reserve a table for four, for this evening?
Alla Sua salute!	Good health!
Il conto, per favore.	The bill, please.
Andava bene?	How was everything?
Il mangiare era eccellente.	The meal was excellent.
Ha un programma delle manifestazioni?	Do you have an events diary?

Shopping

Dov'è si può trovare ...?	Where can I find ...?
... una farmacia	... a pharmacy
... un panificio	... a bakery
... un negozio di articoli fotografici	... a photo shop
... un grande magazzino	... a department store
... un negozio di generi alimentari	... a grocery store
... il mercato	... the market
... il supermercato	... the supermarket
... il tabaccaio	... the tobacconist
... il giornalaio	... the newsagent

Accommodation

Scusi, potrebbe consigliarmi ...?	Can you please recommend ...?
... un albergo	... a hotel
... una pensione	... a bed and breakfast
Ho prenotato una camera.	I have a room reservation.
È libera ...?	Do you have ...?
... una singola	... a single room
... una doppia	... a double room
... con doccia/bagno	... with shower/bath
... per una notte	... for one night
... per una settimana	... for one week
... con vista sul mare	... with a view of the sea

Quanto costa la camera ...?	What is the cost of the room ...?
... con la prima colazione?	... with breakfast?
... a mezza pensione?	... with half-board?

Doctor and pharmacy

Mi può consigliare un buon medico?	Can you recommend a good doctor?
Mi puo dare una medicina per ...	Please give me medication for ...
Soffro di diarrea.	I have diarrhoea.
Ho mal di pancia.	I have a stomach ache.
... mal di testa	... headache
... mal di gola	... sore throat
... mal di denti	... toothache
... influenza	... influenza
... tosse	... a cough
... la febbre	... fever
... scottatura solare	... sunburn
... costipazione	... constipation

Numbers

zero	0	diciannove	19
uno	1	venti	20
due	2	ventuno	21
tre	3	trenta	30
quattro	4	quaranta	40
cinque	5	cinquanta	50
sei	6	sessanta	60
sette	7	settanta	70
otto	8	ottanta	80
nove	9	novanta	90
dieci	10	cento	100
undici	11	centouno	101
dodici	12	duecento	200
tredici	13	mille	1000
quattordici	14	duemila	2000
quindici	15	diecimila	10000
sedici	16		
diciassette	17	un quarto	1/4
diciotto	18	un mezzo	1/2

Menu

Prima colazione	breakfast

caffè, espresso	small coffee, no milk
caffè macchiato	small coffee with a little milk
caffè latte	coffee with milk
cappuccino	coffee with foamed milk
tè al latte/al limone	tea with milk/lemon
cioccolata	hot chocolate
frittata	omelette/pancake
pane/panino/pane tostato	bread/roll/toast
burro	butter
salame	sausage
prosciutto	ham
miele	honey
marmellata	marmelade/jam
iogurt	yogurt
Antipasti	Appetizers and soup
affettato misto	mixed cold cuts
anguilla affumicata	smoked eel
melone e prosciutto	melon with ham
minestrone	thick vegetable soup
pastina in brodo	broth with fine pasta
vitello tonnato	cold roast veal with tuna mayonnaise
zuppa di pesce	fish soup
Primi piatti	Pasta and rice
pasta	pasta
fettuccine/tagliatelle	ribbon noodles
gnocchi	small potato dumplings
polenta (alla valdostana)	corn porridge (with cheese)
agnolotti/ravioli/tortellini	filled pasta
vermicelli	vermicelli
Carni e Pesce	Meat and fish
agnello	lamb
ai ferri/alla griglia	grilled
aragosta	crayfish
brasato	roast
coniglio	rabbit
cozze/vongole	mussels/small mussels
fegato	liver
fritto di pesce	baked fish
gambero, granchio	lobster, crab
maiale	pork
manzo/bue	beef
pesce spada	swordfish

platessa	plaice
pollo	chicken
rognoni	kidneys
salmone	salmon
scampi fritti	small fried shrimp
sogliola	sole
tonno	tuna
trota	trout
vitello	veal
Verdura	Vegetables
asparagi	asparagus
carciofi	artichokes
carote	carrots
cavolfiore	cauliflower
cavolo	cabbage
cicoria belga	chicory
cipolle	onions
fagioli	white beans
fagiolini	green beans
finocchi	fennel
funghi	mushrooms
insalata mista/verde	mixed/green salad
lenticchie	lentils
melanzane	aubergine
patate	potatoes
patatine fritte	french fries
peperoni	paprika
pomodori	tomatoes
spinaci	spinach
zucca	pumpkin
Formaggi	Cheese
parmigiano	parmesan
pecorino	sheep´s milk cheese
ricotta	ricotta cheese
Dolci e frutta	Dessert and fruit
cassata	ice cream with candied fruit
coppa assortita	assorted ice cream
coppa con panna	ice cream with cream
tirami su	dessert with mascarpone cream
zabaione	whipped egg cream
zuppa inglese	cake soaked in liqueur with custard

Bevande	Drinks
acqua minerale	mineral water
aranciata	orangeade
bibita	refreshing drink
bicchiere	glass
birra scura/chiara	dark/light beer
birra alla spina	beer on tap
birra senza alcool	alcohol-free beer
bottiglia	bottle
con ghiaccio	with ice
digestivo	digestive
gassata/con gas	sparkling, carbonated
liscia/senza gas	not carbonated
secco	dry
spumante	sparkling wine
succo	fruit juice
vino bianco/rosato/rosso	white/rose/red wine
vino della casa	house wine

Literature

Venice must be one of the most described and photographed cities in the world. The following provides a small selection of recommended reading.

Paolo Barbaro: *Venice Revealed: An Intimate Portrait.* Souvenir Press, 2002. A poetic description by a gifted writer with a profound knowledge of the city.

History and culture

Christopher Hibbert: *Venice – Biography of a City.* Norton, 1989. Well-written and informative chronicle by the biographer of Florence, Rome and London.

Jan Morris: *Venice.* Faber & Faber, 1993. Classic portrait of the city by one of the best British travel writers of recent times.

Giovanna Scire Nepi and Alberto Prandi: *Treasures of Venetian Painting: The Gallerie Dell'Accademia.* Arsenale, 2006. A sumptuous volume showing the development of Venetian painting through works in the main art gallery of the city.

John Julius Norwich: *A History of Venice.* Penguin Books, 2003. A highly readable account of the history of the Venetian republic.

Philip Rylands and Robert Krens: *Peggy Guggenheim Collection.* Guggenheim Museum, 2004. An informative guide to 20th-century art in the Palazzo Venier dei Leoni.

Peter Ackroyd: *Venice: Pure City.* Vintage Books, 2010. The sea power from a British perspective.

Photo books **Luca Campigotto:** *Venice – The City by Night.* Thames and Hudson, 2006. Atmospheric black-and-white images of the canals and city.

Tudy Sammartini: *The Decorative Floors of Venice.* Merrell, 2000. Numerous detailed photographs of the often overlooked stone floors of 59 Venetian buildings.

Tudy Sammartini, Daniele Resini: *Venice from the Bell-Towers.* Merrell, 2002. The photographer climbed the church towers and took dizzyingly beautiful photographs.

Novels **E. M. Forster:** *Where Angels Fear to Tread.* Penguin Books, 2001. A young English widow shocks her conservative family by marrying an Italian.

Ernest Hemingway: *Across the River and into the Trees.* Scribner Classic, 1998. First published in 1950, the novel tells the story of the last days of a retired American army officer, who hunts duck in the lagoon and seduces a beautiful young contessa.

Henry James: *Aspern Papers.* Oxford Classics, 1994, a darkly ironic tale, first published in 1888, by a master of the psychological novel, and *The Wings of the Dove* (Penguin Books, 2001), in which Venice is the setting for the attempts of a penniless man to secure the fortune of an heiress.

Donna Leon: The incorruptible Commissario Guido Brunetti battles against a corrupt, avaricious society which – behind the mask of Venice – will stop at nothing to defend its privileges. The successful American author has made Venice her home and the backdrop for a series of thrillers including *The Anonymous Venetian* and *Death at Le Fenice.*

Thomas Mann: *Death in Venice*, Vintage 2001 (▶MARCO POLO Insight, p.62)

Ian McEwan: *The Comfort of Strangers*, Picador 1982 (▶MARCO POLO Insight, p.62)

William Shakespeare: *Merchant of Venice*, Oxford 1998. Shakespeare's classic tragic comedy – or comic tragedy, if you prefer – is set in the Venice of the Middle Ages. While the story doesn't say much about Venice itself, it shows that human nature hasn't changed much, and that certain topics – racism, love, friendship and female ingenuity – never become irrelevant.

Media

English-language newspapers and magazines are sold at the bus and railway stations and at news stands all over the city. The most important Italian dailies are Corriere della Sera, La Stampa and La Republica. Local newspapers include La Nuova Venezia and Gazzettino di Venezia. Both always include useful telephone numbers and addresses as well as information about ▶Festivals, Holidays and Events.

Newspapers

Money

The euro is the official currency in Italy. Citizens from EU member countries are allowed to import and export any amount of EU currency.

Euro

The usual opening hours of banks are Mon–Fri 8.30am–1pm, afternoons approx. 2.30pm–3.30pm. Banks close at 11.20am on days preceding holidays.

Banks

Travellers **cheques** can be cashed at banks. However, some Italian financial institutions charge high fees for cashing them! The numerous **cash machines** (ATMs; in Italian: bancomat) provide problem-free access to money with credit cards (PIN) and/or bank cards around the clock.

MARCO⊕POLO INSIGHT

Exchange rates

€1 = US$1.28
US$1 = €0.79
£1 = € 1.27
€1 = £0.78

Detailed rates ▶
www.oanda.com

The common international **credit cards** are accepted almost everywhere. Usually a credit card is required to rent valuable items such as a car, or a deposit has to be made.

In the event of lost bank or credit cards contact the following offices in Italy or the number given by the bank in your home country (Visa: tel. 8 00 81 90 14, Mastercard: 8 00 87 08 66). Have the bank sort code, account number and card number as well as the expiry date ready.

Lost card

Receipts   In Italy, purchasers are obliged to ask for and keep the **cash register receipts** (ricevuta fiscale or scontrino). You may be asked to show the receipt after leaving a shop – this is intended to make tax fraud more difficult.

Opening Hours

Retailers   Most stores are open 9am–12.30pm and 4pm–7pm. Nearly all are closed on Saturday afternoons and Sundays, some also on Monday mornings.

Chorus   Viewing times of the 15 Chorus churches (▶p.314): Mon–Sat 10am–
churches   5pm; special opening times apply for I Frari, Mon–Sat 9am–6pm, Sun from 1pm and for San Giobbe (Mon – Sat 10am – 1.30pm). The churches are closed on Sundays in July and August with the exception of the Frari church (www.chorusvenezia.org).

Further   Pharmacies ▶Health; Banks ▶Money; Post offices ▶Post and Com-
information   munications

Post and Communications

Mail   There are abput a dozen post offices (poste italiane) in Venice at Piazzale Roma and Rialto, among other places. They only handle mail and postal banking services (Mon–Fri 8.30am–1.30pm and Sat to 12 noon). **Stamps** (francobolli) are also available in tobacco shops,

COUNTRY CODES
From Italy
to other countries: 00 followed by the country code, e.g.
to UK: 0044
to USA: 001

From other countries to Italy:
+39

CITY AREA CODES
The local area codes are part of the Italian telephone numbers. Both in local calls and when calling from foreign countries, the area code including the 0 must also be dialled.

TELEPHONE DIRECTORY INQUIRIES
In Italy tel. 12,
Abroad tel. 4176

FEES
Lower fees are charged daily from 10pm to 8am and on weekends.

which are identified with a »T« sign (tabacchi). **Postage** for post-cards and letters (up to 20g/7oz) within Italy and to European foreign countries is €0.85 (posta prioritaria).

International direct dialling is possible from public long-distance telephones with an orange telephone receiver symbol. They operate with **telephone cards** (carta/scheda telefonica), which are available in bars, at news stands or in tobacco shops for 5 or 10 euros. Note: there are different systems, so make sure to get information before buying! Remove the marked corner before using for the first time. The use of **mobile telephones** (telefonino, cellulare) from other European countries is normally trouble-free in Italy. *Telephoning*

Prices and Discounts

The Venice Card, which is available for 2 age groups (under/over 30 years, €39.90 or €29.90), allows you to save money. The card includes public transportation (incl. airport transfer by bus) and the use of public toilets. Walk right by the long queues when visiting the Doge's Palace, ten state museums and 15 churches and use the card to gain admission free of charge as well as other collections at a reduced rate. *Venice Card*
Buy the Venice Card at the sales points for **Hello Venezia**, Venezia Si and ATVO as well as at the APT/IAT offices at Piazzale Roma, railway station, Tronchetto, Accademia, Rialto, San Zaccaria Danieli, Punta Sabbioni, Marco Polo Airport and Canova Airport in Treviso. More information at www.hellovenezia.com (▶p. 301), tel. 0 41 24 24. The Venice Card is available online at www.veniceunica.it.

The online portal Venice Connected offers discounts for various public services and facilities (transportation, parking garages, museums etc.) – but only when reserving it seven days in advance at **www.veniceconnected.com**. Payable with a credit card. The reservation number (PNR) is then sent by e-mail; it is then used to pick up the card on the first day of validity at one of the sales points (Venice Connected Points): *Venice Connected*
Railway station (vaporetto station to the left of the railway station, 7am – 9pm)
Isola Nova del Tronchetto (Hellovenezia office near the vaporetto stop, 7am – 8pm)
Marco Polo Airport (Hellovenezia office, 8.30am – 10pm)
Santa Chiara (2nd vaporetto stop after Ponte della Costituzione, Piazzale Roma, 7am – 9pm)
Venice Pavilion (Giardinetti Reali, 10am – 5.30pm).

Rolling Venice
Young people between 14 and 29 years old can get other discounts with the Rolling Venice card for €4 (info/sales: www.venicecard.it).

Museum Pass
For anyone who only wants to visit museums the Museum Pass is the bets value (€24,50; it is valid for sic months for the museums at St Mark's Square (Palazzo Ducale, Museo Correr, Museo Archeologico), Ca' Rezzonico, Palazzo Mocenigo, Casa Goldoni and the museums on Murano and Burano Islands (Info: www.venice-connected.com).

Many churches charge admission; the income is then used to maintain the property. »Chorus« is an association of 16 churches, which can all be viewed with one combined ticket (€12); it is available in the churches and the APT offices. More info at www.chorusvenezia.org.

? *What does it cost?*

MARCO POLO INSIGHT

- Simple double room: from €80
- Simple meal: from €12
- Espresso: from €1.50
- One way ticket on a vaporetto: €6.50
- Gondola tour (ca. 40 min.): about 100 €

Time

Italy uses Central European time (= GMT +1 h). From the end of March to the end of October, Central European Summer Time applies (= GMT +2 h).

Toilets

Most cafés and bars have toilets (bagno, gabinetto), which can be used. But it is expected that something is bought in return. There are also some public toilets, which are generally clean; they are open to the public daily 7am – 7/8pm (charge €1.50). The Venice Card includes »2 stops a day«; Venice Connected allows you to reserve in advance.

Transport

By water
The most practical means of transportation in Venice are the **vaporetti** of the public transportation system ACTV. They run on the Canal Grande and the main side canals. The larger two-tiered **motonavi** run on the longer routes, like to the airport, the Lido or the la-

Ferry boats connect Vencie and Burano

goon islands (between about 5am and 11.15pm). The smaller **moto-scafi** (water taxis) are quicker but more expensive. The **traghetti** (gondola ferries) are used to transport Venetians and tourists cheaply across the Canal Grande. The **Alilaguna** boats connect the airport, Piazza San Marco, Lido and the remaining islands, but they also offer various tours (www.alilaguna.it, www.venicelink.com, tel. 04 12 40 17 01). Use the **gondolas** to tour wider and narrower canals (▶p. 316) .

Route plans and timetables – for festivi (Sundays and holidays) and feriali (weekdays) – are available at the Hellovenezia sales points, ACTV offices at Piazzale Roma and at St Mark's Square (Ponte dei Fuseri) as well as online at www.actv.it, www.hellovenezia.it, www.alilaguna.it. A one way vaporetto ticket (1 hour, 1 piece of luggage) costs €7. The passes for one or more days (between 12 and 72 hrs up to 7-day tickets at €18 to €35 or €50), available at Hellovenezia ticket counters (▶p. 301), other ticket counters, ticket machines and in tabacchi (tobacco shops). The Venice Card (▶p. 313) is worthwhile when staying several days. Tickets must be validated at the machines at the boat stops.

Timetables, tickets

City centre, Canal Grande One of the most used vaporetto lines in the city centre is Line 1 from Piazzale Roma or the railway station through Canal Grande (stops at all stops) to the Lido and back. Line 2, the quickest on the Canal Grande, runs from Tronchetto via Piazzale Roma, railway station, Rialto, Vallaresso San Marco, San Zaccaria and back through the Giudecca Canal. Lines 4.1/5.1 run around the old city counter clockwise, 4.2/5.2 run clockwise (the former stops at Murano, the latter stops at the Lido).

> ! **Venice Card** *Insider Tip*
>
> MARCO POLO TIP
>
> So that vaporetto rides (one way €7) don't eat up the budget – and because it's much more convenient to ride with a day pass than always to have to buy tickets, the Venice Card is worthwhile (▶p. 305).

Linee Lagunari The »lagoon lines« run across the lagoon to Chioggia, Treporti and Punta Sabbioni on the Litorale del Cavallino. Line 17, a car ferry, runs between Tronchetto and Lido San Nicolò.

Vaporetto dell'Arte Recently an **extra vaporetto line** was added on the Canal Grande **for art lovers**. It runs daily between 9am and 7pm from S. Stae, Ca' d'Oro, S. Samuele, Accademia, Salute, Giardinetti to San Giorgio and stops at all art venues. You can get on and off as often as you want (stan-dard ticket: €24, cheaper with day or multi-day pass; information: ▶Hello Venezia p. 301).

Traghetti (gondola rides) Apart from the four pedestrian bridges there are cheap gondola ferries (per trip €2) to cross the Canal Grande: railway station – Fondamenta San Simeon, San Marcuola – Fondaco dei Turchi, Santa Sofia/ Ca' d'Oro – Pescheria, Riva del Carbon – Riva del Vin (Rialto), Ca' Garzoni – San Tomà, San Samuele – Ca' Rezzonico, San Maria del Giglio – Palazzo Genovese.

Gondolas The epitome of romance is a ride on one of the around 400 slender, black gondolas, Venice's most famous trademark (▶MARCO POLO Insight p. 262/264). The charges for gondola rides are fixed: minimum (40 min.) €80, each additional 20 min. €40. There are many gondola stands (▶Information).

Water taxis The water taxis (motoscafi) are expensive (from Marco Polo Airport into the city about €100; when booking online with Consorzio Venezia Taxi there is a 10% discount).
The (fixed) rates are posted at all taxi stands: including Marco Polo Airport, Santa Lucia railway station, at the Fondamenta Nuove, Lido Viale Santa Maria Elisabetta, Piazzale Roma, Rialto, San Marco and Tronchetto (www.motoscafivenezia.it, www.veneziataxi.it, tel. 04 15 22 23 03).

Venice is also connected to the mainland by bus: Line 5: Piazzale   Busses
Roma – Aeroporto Marco Polo; Lines 2, 4, 7, 12: Piazzale Roma –
Mestre; Line 6: Piazzale Roma – Marghera; Line 19: Piazzale Roma
– Favaro – Altinia.
On the Lido buses on Lines A and B (routes differ in places) connect
the dock Santa Maria Elisabetta with the end stations Alberoni and
San Nicolò. In the summer there are some circular routes as well as a
bus line from Santa Maria Elisabetta to Alberoni, Pellestrina and Chi-
oggia (Line 11).

There are no car taxis in the city. From Piazzale Roma taxis run to the   Taxis
mainland to Mestre, Marghera and the airport (tel. 04 15 95 20 80,
04 15 41 63 63). Taxis on the Lido: tel. 04 15 26 59 74 and 04 15 26 59 75.

On the Lido, in Marghera and in Mestre there is a city bike system for   City bike
Venetians and tourists (http://bicincitgta.tobike.it).

TRAFFIC REGULATIONS

In Italy tolls (pedaggio) are charged on most of the motorways (autostrada); allow for €5 – €10 per 100km/60mi. Tolls are paid in cash
or – most convenient – with a debit or credit card (in lanes marked
»Carte«). Viacard is too inconvenient for tourists.

Petrol stations are usually open 7am – 12noon, 2pm – 8pm; on the
motorway they are mostly open round the clock. Many petrol stations are closed on weekends; larger petrol stations have petrol
pumps that accept cash as well as credit and debit cards (but they do
not always work).

The following speed limits apply in Italy: cars, motorcycles and
campers up to 3.5 t: within city limits 50 km/h (30mph), outside city
limits 90 km/h (55mph), on 4-lane roads (2 lanes in each direction)
110 km/h (65mph), on motorways (autostrada) 130 km/h (78mph);
cars and campers over 3.5 t: outside city limits 80 km/h (50mph), on
4-lane roads 80 km/h (50mph) and on motorways 100 km/h
(60mph). Anyone caught speeding faces high fines.

Parking in Venice ▶Arrival • Before the Journey

Blood alcohol limit is **0.5 per mille**. **Low beam lights** must be on
outside of towns and cities during the **daytime**. In cities with good
street lights driving with parking lights is allowed. Helmets are required with motorcycles of more than 50 cm³. Telephoning while
driving is only allowed for the driver with a hands-free system.

Warning vests are required in Italy; only one vest needs to be in the car, but every person who leaves the car at a breakdown site must wear a vest. Private towing from the motorway is not allowed. In case of breakdown ►Emergencies. In case of an accident with injured persons the highway police must be notified. The **European Accident Statement** (available from insurance companies and automobile clubs) is very helpful for processing accident details since Italian insurance companies use the same form in Italian. If the car is a total loss the Italian customs offices must be informed; otherwise they might charge import duties for the wrecked car.

RENTAL CARS

For excursions to the mainland it is best to rent a car at Piazzale Roma, in Mestre or at the airport. Rental agencies are listed in the local telephone books under »Autonoleggio«. The minimum age for renting is 21 years; a national driver's license is necessary as well as one year of driving practice. Cars can be rented at home already from international rental companies.

When To Go

Best times for visiting:
April–June and September–October

Venice is worth a trip at any time, but the unpleasant weather holds from November to March with many foggy days (an average of 20 in December), rain and even snow. The weather improves from April. The downside: the feared Genoa low is particularly active in spring. It makes itself felt about every third to fourth day with showers and thunderstorms into June. High summer brings a lot of sun and sweaty temperatures. In July/August, the thermometer usually rises at least to 28 °C, while night-time temperatures drop to a balmy 18°C. And with hot southerly winds from Africa (sirocco), temperatures may even climb above 35 °C. Little wind and high air humidity make the summer muggy at times. Then the Lido offers a welcome chance to cool off with water temperatures around 24°C. September is also an excellent month for travelling. This is due to the more moderate daytime temperatures of 24 °C, the low number of rainy days (only 5, the lowest in the year) and the still-warm sea. The beautiful late-summer weather frequently lasts into the first week of October. Then autumn comes with lower temperatures, severe thunderstorms and sometimes torrential rainfall.

Index

List of Maps and Illustrations

Photo Credits

APT Venedig   2 right below, 102, 156, 159, 185, 285
Baedeker Archiv   211, 329 (2 x)
DuMont Bildarchiv   37, 60, 52, 57, 175, 202, 203, 204, 212, 248, 259, 270, 283; 10, 45, 122, 165 right below, c 4 below and 233 (R. Kiedrowski); c 2, 2 left above, 19 above and centre, 74, 96, 154, 315, 234, 251, 256, 267, 292 (S. Lubenow)
gettyimages   7 (J. Cobb); 223 (R. Gerometta); 3 right below, 275 (B. Holland)
Huber   164, 165 left above and below, 166; 101 (Dutton); 3 left below, 12, 146, 153, 273, 297 (Fantuz); 50 (Giovanni); 2 right above, 3 left above, 32, 237 (Gräfenhein); 5 right above (Renier); c 4, 54, 134 (Scattolin); 36 (Schmid); 31, 39, 104, 90, 167, 226, 254, 258, 290 (Simeone)
Lade   2 left below, 95
laif   18 below (hemis.fr/C. Guy); 1, 215, 243 left above and below (Galli); c 3 below, 35 above, 243 right above (Klein); 3 left centre, 19 below (Le Figaro Magazine/Martin); 18 above, 65, 171, 263, 304 (Zanettini)
Look-foto   98 (age fotostock); 6, 92, 261, 278 (S. Lubenow); 218 (Photononstop); 183 (H & D Zielske)
Maander, Hilke   5 left, 124
Mauritius   126 (age); 83, 106, 117, 199 (Cuboimages); 76 (D. Scott); 280 (Imagebroker/Dr. W. Bahnmüller); 176 (Imagebroker/C. Guy)
Mosler, Axel M.   230
picture-alliance   48, 63, 71, 181, c 8 (akg-images); 88 (Chromorange/ Tipsimages/C. Pefley); c 3 above, 23, 24, 25, 47, 66, 69, 70, 73, 196, 209, 243 right below, 244, 245 (dpa); 130 (allOver images); 228 (Lonely Planet Images/K. Dydynski)
Dr. Reincke, Madeleine   165 right above
Schliebitz, Anja   4 below, 9, 35 below, 79, 160, 178, 210, 238
stockfood   5 right below, 112 above (M. Brauner); 112 below (J. Cazals); 113 (K. Iden)
Wrba, Ernst   4 left
Wurth, Andrea   193

Cover photo:
Jacques Boulay/hemis.fr/laif

Publisher's Information

1st Edition 2015
Worldwide Distribution: Marco Polo
Travel Publishing Ltd
Pinewood, Chineham Business Park
Crockford Lane, Chineham
Basingstoke, Hampshire RG24 8AL,
United Kingdom.

Photos, illlustrations, maps::
144 photos, 30 maps and and illustra-
tions, one large city map
Text:
Dr. Evamarie Blattner, Rupert Koppold,
Michael Machatschek, Peter Peter,
Dr. Madeleine Reincke, Anja Schliebitz,
Reinhard Strüber, Wolfgang Veit
Editing:
Anja Schliebitz, John Sykes
Translation: John Sykes
Cartography:
Christoph Gallus, Hohberg; Franz Huber,
Munich; MAIRDUMONT Ostfildern (city
map)
3D illustrations:
jangled nerves, Stuttgart
Infographics:
Golden Section Graphics GmbH, Berlin
Design:
independent Medien-Design, Munich
Editor-in-chief:
Rainer Eisenschmid, Mairdumont
Ostfildern

© MAIRDUMONT GmbH & Co KG
All rights reserved. No part of this book
may be reproduced, stored in a retrieval
system or transcentred in any form or
by any means (electronic, mechanical,
photocopying, recording or otherwise)
without prior written permission from
the publisher.

Printed in China

Despite all of our authors' thorough
research, errors can creep in. The pub-
lishers do not accept any liability for thi
Whether you want to praise, alert us to
errors or give us a personal tip Please
contact us by email or post:

MARCO POLO Travel Publishing Ltd
Pinewood, Chineham Business Park
Crockford Lane, Chineham
Basingstoke, Hampshire RG24 8AL
United Kingdom
Email: sales@marcopolouk.com

FSC
www.fsc.org
MIX
Paper from
responsible sources
FSC® C011918

MARCO 🌐 POLO

HANDBOOKS

MARCO 🌐 POLO
TRAVEL HANDBOOK
ANDALUCÍA
INFOGRAPHICS · 3D ILLUSTRATIONS · PULL-OUT MAP
Insider Tips
NEW

MARCO 🌐 POLO
TRAVEL HANDBOOK
BARCELONA
INFOGRAPHICS · 3D ILLUSTRATIONS · PULL-OUT MAP
Insider Tips
NEW

MARCO 🌐 POLO
TRAVEL HANDBOOK
BERLIN
INFOGRAPHICS · 3D ILLUSTRATIONS · PULL-OUT MAP
Insider Tips
NEW

MARCO 🌐 POLO
TRAVEL HANDBOOK
DRESDEN
INFOGRAPHICS · 3D ILLUSTRATIONS · PULL-OUT MAP
Insider Tips
NEW

MARCO 🌐 POLO
TRAVEL HANDBOOK
FLORIDA
INFOGRAPHICS · 3D ILLUSTRATIONS · PULL-OUT MAP
Insider Tips
NEW

MARCO 🌐 POLO
TRAVEL HANDBOOK
GRAN CANARIA
INFOGRAPHICS · 3D ILLUSTRATIONS · PULL-OUT MAP
Insider Tips
NEW

MARCO 🌐 POLO
TRAVEL HANDBOOK
ICELAND
INFOGRAPHICS · 3D ILLUSTRATIONS · PULL-OUT MAP
Insider Tips
NEW

MARCO 🌐 POLO
TRAVEL HANDBOOK
LONDON
INFOGRAPHICS · 3D ILLUSTRATIONS · PULL-OUT MAP
Insider Tips
NEW

MARCO 🌐 POLO
TRAVEL HANDBOOK
NEW YORK
INFOGRAPHICS · 3D ILLUSTRATIONS · PULL-OUT MAP
Insider Tips
NEW

MARCO 🌐 POLO
TRAVEL HANDBOOK
PARIS
INFOGRAPHICS · 3D ILLUSTRATIONS · PULL-OUT MAP
Insider Tips
NEW

MARCO 🌐 POLO
TRAVEL HANDBOOK
ROME
INFOGRAPHICS · 3D ILLUSTRATIONS · PULL-OUT MAP
Insider Tips
NEW

MARCO 🌐 POLO
TRAVEL HANDBOOK
VENICE
INFOGRAPHICS · 3D ILLUSTRATIONS · PULL-OUT MAP
Insider Tips
NEW

www.marco-polo.com

Venice Curious Facts

Eight months of carnival, an art collector who lent a hand out of respect for the church, noble beggars – Venice has a few curiosities to offer.

▶**Eight months of carnival**
During the Settecento (18th cent.) the Venetian carnival lasted eight months. Masked people would meet in convents to flirt, used gondolas with cabins for dates and squandered their wealth in casinos. Today many of the most beautiful masked couples that tourists encounter are hired by the office of tourism – a welcome additional income for actors.

▶**Pious provocation**
On high religious holidays Peggy Guggenheim would personally unscrew the phallus from the Marino Marini statue in front of her palazzo on the Canal Grande.

▶**Cucina povera**
During the 19th cent. Venice was dirt poor. Authentic Bacari wine rooms still serve unpopular delicacies like rumegal (gullet), nerveti (gristle with onions) and spienza (spleen).

▶**Loden coat and hat**
In the winter months Venice is overrun by fashion-conscious »Austriacanti« who stand out with their Austrian-Alpine outfits from the mass of tourists and other Italians. A real Venetian can be recognized by his loden coat.

▶**Schèi and strudel**
From 1797 to 1805 and 1816 to 1866 Venice was part of Austria. Austrian expressions like strudel and krapfen, spritz and schèi – short for schellini, or shilling.

▶**Gondola rebels**
The German woman Alexandra Hai showed how: she was the first woman in 1000 years to try to gain admission to the noble guild of gondoliers. After failing the test in front of male testers several times a court allowed her to work as »gondola navigator« for a hotel. In 2010 Giorgia Boscolo passed all of the tests and is now officially the first female gondolier.

▶**Noble beggars**
Impoverished, ragged descendants of doges who beg for alms from travellers – in the 18th and 19th cent. This was one of the »attractions« that Venice had to offer. As members of the nobility, the »Barnabotti« were not allowed to work and lived in subsidised housing near the church S. Barnaba.

▶**Boring for ragazzi**
Venice has more residents who are over 80 years old than ones who are under 18 years old. Actually that is not funny at all!